WOMEN AND SEX

LEAH CAHAN SCHAEFER

WOMEN AND SEX

*Sexual Experiences and Reactions
of a Group of Thirty Women as
Told to a Female Psychotherapist*

PANTHEON BOOKS

A DIVISION OF RANDOM HOUSE, NEW YORK

Library of Congress Cataloging in Publication Data

Schaefer, Leah Cahan, 1920–
Women and Sex: sexual experiences and reactions of a group of
thirty women as told to a female psychotherapist
Based on the author's thesis, Columbia University, 1964.
    Bibliography: pp. 263–69
    1. Sex (Psychology)   2. Woman—Psychology.
I. Title. [DNLM: 1. Sex behavior.   2. Women.
HQ 21 S294w   1973]
BF692.S24   155.3'4   72–12388
ISBN 0–394–47914–9

Manufactured in the United States of America by Haddon Crafts-
men, Scranton, Pennsylvania

9 8 7 6 5 4 3 2

FIRST EDITION

For Thomas
and
Katie and Hal
and
Miriam and Boas

ACKNOWLEDGMENTS

THIS BOOK represents specific research over a period of ten years, but the thoughts in it represent the energy and influences of a lifetime. For those influences I am thankful to many.

My father and mother, Rabbi Boas Cahan and Miriam Cahan, I thank for instilling in me a belief that the mysteries of life are worth the unraveling, and for their love of knowledge and their respect for its pursuit. I am the recipient of this rich heritage.

I wish to express my everlasting gratitude to my dear friend and teacher the late Ernest G. Osborne, who gave me permission to do a study about sex under the hallowed aegis of Columbia University Teachers College, back in the "Dark Ages" of 1962. He was my advisor, and the illustrious Margaret Mead my consultant. One couldn't hope for two more original and stimulating thinkers as guides.

Many colleagues generously gave me their time and knowledge, through suggestions, example, and inspiration, most particularly Drs. Russell Dennis, Mark Flapan, David Fox, Harold Greenwald, Arthur T. Jersild, Otto Klineberg, Gerald Leslie, Arlene Otto, Bertram Pollens, Richard Robertiello, Betty L. Thompson, Paul Vahanian, Alexander Wolf, and the Society for the Scientific Study of Sex, with particular mention of Wardell Pomeroy, Robert Sherwin, and the late Henry Guze.

A special thanks to Thomas Kline, who at all times shares with me his singular viewpoint and his outrageous wisdom.

I feel unbounded admiration for the superb editing of Verne Moberg and Jane Clark Seitz. Any praise for this book is willingly shared with them, but all errors are my own. The technical help of Maura Davis, Helen Salinger, and Susan Schoch deserves thanks beyond the words I know how to put on this page.

To my dearest family, natural as well as chosen, and especially to my brothers, Sidney, Haskell, and Nissen, and to Hal Schaefer and my most treasured daughter, Katherine Schaefer, I express my love and gratitude for their support, understanding, and *almost* limitless patience.

And most, most especially, to the thirty courageous, generous, and thoughtful women, my everlasting thanks for joining with me in this unique experience.

—L.C.S.

New York City, 1972

CONTENTS

FOREWORD

Regrettably, women seem to understand too little about themselves not only sexually but generally. By tradition women have suppressed representation of self in order to concentrate on fulfilling a culturally assigned role. This study finds sufficient justification in this fact alone, since it requires rethinking of woman's sexual role in the interest of her effectiveness as a person.

There is another reason to applaud the intent of this book by a woman with Dr. Schaefer's professional commitment. A review of available scientific and pseudo-scientific literature pertaining to women and sex reveals the unfortunate truth that in most instances men have been defining and interpreting woman's sexuality and women have not only allowed but obviously abetted this inappropriate exclusivity.

There apparently has been little choice in the matter in view of the unevenness of cultural transition. A recollection of the fates of Marie Stopes, Kate Chopin, and others who tried to depict women as they feel and think seems to affirm this. There is an even better example revealed by study of the masculine attitudes and stances assumed by professional women who were accredited as behavorial scientists during this same era. What they may have believed privately most of us will never know. Their contributions, however, remarkable as some of them were, reflected varying degrees of distortion of female emotions, attitudes, and physical responses. Their writings include one which supports the contention that women have no significant sexual feelings. By this and similar stands these women forfeited a unique opportunity to make a contribution of objective insight into the nature of their own sex. They filtered their observations and subjectivity through the demands of double standard values. This seems to have been the price exacted from women for being allowed a place in the professions. Leah Schaefer has availed herself of the opportunity to be both representatively female *and* professional.

Until men and women can understand one another better through experientially achieved objectivity and compassion and through scientific investigation—until baseline differences and similarities of maleness and femaleness are sorted carefully by unbiased minds making use of the existing facts—men should assume the primary responsibility of defining, interpreting, and representing men. But women should fulfill the same commitment for women. Let us trust that the two halves of understanding can be united to produce a representative whole.

During the "sex is sin" era, woman in her inescapable, traditional role of teacher or learning model has tended either to conceal or belie her own sexual learning process. Too rarely have her experiences been put into perspective so that other women might assume more easily their birthright of sexual identity. Beyond calling attention to the need for this kind of learning and teaching, a book such as this can serve two purposes. It can be used as a mirror for women who wish to explore their own sexual attitudes and feelings, or it can be used effectively as source material for other studies.

While the premise and dedication of the study are praiseworthy, development of new information is sparse, as would be expected from the restricted number of women interrogated, and the fact that the interviews were conducted approxiamately ten years ago. However, this limited windfall of new material is important and should be marked in part by the following.

In Dr. Schaefer's population, culturally induced feelings of guilt and anxiety relating to masturbation were not modified by time or learning, nor do the histories reflect realistic sex information received at any age from any reliable source. There is specific evidence that the women in this population experience a high level of anxiety in confrontation with the subject of parental sexual function, and even more important, evidence equally high levels of anxiety as parents when considering the sexual attitudes and activities of their children.

The fact that all thirty of the women interviewed were orgasmic with intercourse is an unusually high statistic, just as a positive history of lesbian activity in only two of these sexually sophisticated women is somewhat lower than expected.

While most of the women in this study are shown to be very much involved with feelings of affection, closeness, and other emotional elements in their relationships with men, direct representation of these feelings in their sexual experiences is not evident. This study may very well reflect a microcosm representing many women whose sexual identities and sexual expectations are formed by social environments which negate or dissemble female sexuality. As these women experience sexual responsiveness under such circumstances, there is little opportunity for them to conceptualize orgasm as a natural product, attained spontaneously through a blend of physical and emotional expression of sexual identity and feelings. For them, this dichotomy established between the psychological and the physical structures must be reckoned with on any given occasion.

This suggests that the relationship between the female orgasm and the learning process as conceptualized by the author is subject to question. Certainly there could be no disagreement with the concept that individual values and preferences which become a part of the sexually stimulative process come about through a learning process, but I cannot accept the author's concept that female orgasmic attainment is a learned experience. In light of present-day knowledge, drawn in part from the perceptions and experiences shared by women who have had an opportunity to develop real objectivity about themselves, another premise should be given consideration. It may be more reasonable to conclude that the ability of the female to achieve orgasm develops as a spontaneous expression of a natural function which has reached a required level of physical and social maturation. Learning, then, would concern attitudes and pertinent aspects of social interaction and emotional environment in which sexual response to orgasm can occur naturally as a birthright.

In presenting the results of her study in this book, Dr. Schaefer demonstrates an attribute somewhat rare in women, as well as in men, who work in scientific and professional areas related to sexuality: that is, sufficient objectivity and scientific concern to invite exploration of some aspects of woman's sexual nature without burdening the material with prejudice. She does not use publication as a medium in which to savor or propound personal sexual conflicts, discomforts, or joys.

Her contribution is real and conclusions in her study appropriately provocative.

—Virginia E. Johnson

January, 1973

WOMEN AND SEX

CHAPTER ONE

INTRODUCTION

Sex is a human response which can be delayed indefinitely, or even obviated. We have confused a natural physiologic process and lifted it out of context. We need to return this natural process from its distraction. Instead of questions like "when, where, and how much," regarding sex, we should really ask *why*.
—William Masters at a meeting of the Society for the Scientific Study of Sex, November 3, 1967

Why this paradox? That the origin of life is a thing to be denied and put down?
—Artemis

Sex is everything (as Freud says): You either know this or you don't. If you don't, you don't. It's not what can be taught.
—e.e. cummings

SEX CAN BE the most intimate, most public, most obscene, most sacred of activities, women can be the most desired, most abused, most repressed, most seductive, most vicious, most loving of creatures.

Sex can be used in countless ways to achieve countless ends, and the infinite variety of ways in which a woman expresses herself sexually have an infinite variety of meanings—gross and exquisite. Sex is used by women—as well as men—for self-enhancement or for degradation, to draw close to or to alienate another person, to build and enrich family life or to demolish it. Sex can be used as a gambit in an interpersonal power struggle, or for the most profound physical expression of human love and understanding.

This is a book about sex and thirty women.

While it is a study of female sexuality based on actual facts of women's lives, it is mainly concerned with the feelings, attitudes, thoughts, desires, and fears that permeate and surround women's sexual lives. This is a study of how women *feel* about sex, how sex causes them to feel, and how their feelings and individual experiences influence the expression of their sexuality.

The general material in this book was drawn from my experience over a number of years as a practicing psychotherapist; its specific content—its soul—was derived from a series of face-to-face depth interviews I conducted with thirty white, middle-class, married women between the ages of twenty-five and forty, each of whom had married at least once and had at some time experienced psychotherapy (fifteen of them with the author).[1] The women were asked to discuss their feelings about sex and sexuality—not only as adults, but since earliest childhood. They attempted to recollect and examine their first vague sexual sensations from infancy; all that they had learned about sex and the various ways in which they learned it; their experiences with menstruation and adolescent sex play; their premarital, marital, extramarital, and postmarital sexual experiences; and, always, their feelings and thoughts as a result of remembering. As the women looked into their sexual histories and described their feelings about these experiences, they traced—and frequently discovered—the complex, hidden sources of personal values and attitudes.

My original intention in designing this study was to investigate the phenomena of female orgasm. In spite of the prevailing attitude that everyone responds to sex in the same way, I found, through both professional and personal conversations, that women experience a great variety of sexual responses. Some women seemed to experience orgasm easily, some with difficulty, and some not at all. Some seemed to care a great deal whether they had this experience, and some seemed not to care at all. It soon became clear to me that it would be impossible to understand orgasm without understanding the stages of stimulation or interest that lead up to it. And, in order to understand how or why a woman involves herself in these stages of stimulation, I would have to learn a great deal about her development. I realized that I would have to trace a sexual life history of each woman, with particular emphasis on feelings and attitudes. To do this, I developed an interview guide whose questions explore the development of self-concept and motivation, particularly in relation to sexuality.

Sex is best understood in the light of, and as the result of,

[1]The basic material was gathered in a scientific research study for a doctoral degree in education, begun in 1961 and completed in 1964. See Leah Cahan Schaefer, "Sexual Experiences and Reactions of a Group of 30 Women as Told to a Female Psychotherapist," Report of an Ed.D. Doctoral Project, Teachers College, Columbia University, 1964.

a total life. Not as a particular area, genital sex, isolated from the rest of the organism, but as a unique and crucial aspect of it. By studying people's sexual relationships, one can learn about their relationships in general. Sexual responses correspond, in a symbolic way, with responses in most other areas of life.

Studying sex and sexuality is obviously not the only way to explore a personality, but it is unique in two respects. Because this area is taboo and comes so early in the learning process, it influences all subsequent behavior; and because sexual responses so directly express thoughts and emotions, it is very difficult to deceive oneself about their meaning.

Although sex is clearly a natural function, sexual behavior, like all other behavior, is learned, and its expression is invariably molded from the moment of birth. How we feel about our gender and sexuality can determine the patterns of our lives, because gender is the primary factor of a person's identity. What is the first question asked about any infant when it is thrust into the world? "Is it a boy or a girl?" Since no one is born with any notion about what is male or female, the fact of being one or the other affects the sense of self from that very first moment of life. How does the great world of society feel about females and males? And how does the small world of family feel? How does the parent of the same sex feel about his or her sexuality and gender?

How we feel about our own sex and about the opposite sex is determined early by environmental experiences and by the example set by our parent gender models. How we are treated, how we are reflected back to ourselves by important authority symbols (father, mother, siblings, or surrogates for these), and what we learn through attitudes, feelings, etc. are all woven into the background of our unique gifts and potentials to form a self-image. Do we subsequently feel lovable or unlovable? Competent to love and be loved? That self-image, which motivates, guides, and molds our behavior, is rooted in the emotional ambiance of our gender and sexuality.

One of the thirty women described her reactions to participating in this study:

> This experience gave me a feeling of an evolutionary development that took on such a very specific quality . . . almost like extrapolating from a great mass of material the very *essence* of it. . . . I feel I have added another kind of dimension to my experiences . . . being confronted with the vision of my own sexual history, a history that is so emotionally charged, evoked certain aspects of the original experience which never came to mind before.

What initially was intended to be a study of female orgasm—a specific moment in the human sexual experience—evolved into a special method of studying one's self.

Relatively little empirical research has been done in the field of human sexual behavior. Much of what has been written about this multifaceted human activity has contained misinformation, contradiction, and outright fabrication. As of this writing, there are not many more than a hundred studies in the field of sex research that fulfill the scientific standards of statistical accuracy, replicability, and theoretical and pragmatic importance.

While the amount of adequate scientific research on human sexual behavior in general is small, scientific research on *female* sexual behavior is almost negligible, and research on female *feelings* and *attitudes* regarding their sex and sexuality is infinitesimal. The empirical studies that have been done in the United States (Katherine Davis, Dickinson and Beam, Ford and Beach, Kinsey *et al.,* and Masters and Johnson are the principal ones) have focused on female sexual behavior patterns per se, neglecting for the most part the underlying emotions and motivations that form an integral part of any human behavior.

Until very recently, with the advent of the Women's Liberation movement, women themselves have been reluctant to investigate and report their sexual experiences and feelings. As of 1964, when the original research for this book was completed, there were, to the best of my knowledge, only two totally personal published accounts of female sexual response and feeling. The first appeared in 1950 in a now extinct publication, *The International Journal of Sexology.*[2] In two letters to the editor Mrs. Hilda O'Hare, an Englishwoman, described her sexual responses, the various types of stimuli that induced climax, and what she felt was the difference in experience and sensation between clitorally stimulated climax and that stimulated through genital penetration.

Nothing further of such a personal nature was published until 1960, when *The Housewife's Handbook of Selective Promiscuity: A Psychosexual Document,* by Rey Anthony, appeared. In this book, Mrs. Anthony describes her thoughts, feelings, and reactions before, during, and after she engaged in sexual relations. She relates conversations between herself and partners, makes observations about sex language, obscenity, abortion, and what she considers sexually normal behavior, and offers suggestions for the improvement of sexual relations. On the basis of her experiences, Mrs. Anthony questions the alleged superiority of simultaneous climax, deflates the myth of the "vaginal" orgasm, and emphasizes the importance of focusing on sexual imagery. The book was immediately impounded by the United States Postal Authorities on the grounds that the material was of dubious value.

Today we tend to take for granted the quantity and quality of material available about female sexual experience. Yet, a mere ten years ago, only two personal accounts were available. Even now almost all of the thousands of popular as well as scientific books about women and sex have been authored by men. These men have written mainly about what women *should* feel, or what they *think* women feel, without any con-

---

[2]Hilda O'Hare, "Letter to the Editor," *International Journal of Sexology* 4 (May, 1950): 117–18; (November, 1951): 243–44.

ception that women's experiences and responses are different from their own.

Almost all the scientific researchers in the area of female sexuality have been men—Kinsey, Pomeroy, Hamilton, Terman, Dickinson, and Masters, to name a few. Laura Beam and Virginia Johnson have been associated with outstanding female sex research studies—but in collaboration with men. In twentieth-century America, there exists only one significant scientific study of female sexuality conducted entirely by a woman: Katherine Davis's *Factors in the Sex Life of Twenty-Two Hundred Women,* published in 1929.

In making this point I wish neither to antagonize nor to deprecate men. In fact, practically all the scientific knowledge we have about sex has come from research by men. Rather, I want to emphasize the importance of what Clara Thompson, a noted psychoanalyst, once said: "A man cannot know how a woman feels."[3] Not only in the realm of subtle, elusive feelings, but also in the area of concrete, physiological fact, the female's sexual experience is basically different from the male's. It appears to be *so* different, in fact, that when women have reported their experiences, men have simply refused to believe them.

For instance, psychiatrist Edmund Bergler, upon hearing reports that women experienced multiple orgasms, responded with flat disbelief. Such accounts, he wrote, were either the "exaggerations of nymphomaniacs whose perpetual state of unrelieved sexual tension was mistakenly described as multiple orgasm," or the result of "semantic misunderstanding."[4] To these explanations, he added a third possibility, that the women were outright liars! Clearly, Bergler was deceived—not by the women reporting multiple orgasms (a capacity verified by Masters and Johnson scientifically and conclusively), but by his own inability to recognize that women are

[3]Clara Thompson, *Psychoanalysis: Evolution and Development,* p. 18.
[4]Edmund Bergler and W. S. Kroger, *Kinsey's Myth of Female Sexuality,* p. 152.

profoundly different sexually from men.

Bergler exemplifies those professionals—physicians, psychotherapists, social workers, etc.—who serve as forceful antagonists of the scientific study of sex. Ironically, it is they who stand to gain the most from the results of such studies. But professionals, like everyone else, fear the unknown and resist change.

The prevalent Western theory of female sexuality originated with one man: Sigmund Freud.

Freud's original observations about female sexuality were based on his female patients, who lived in the puritanical elegance of Vienna, with its tacit strict sexual double standard. Freud interpreted his observations through a male bias, tending to deprecate females in explaining their sexual symptoms.

The Freudian orgasm controversy involves an evaluation of "clitoral" and "vaginal" orgasms. Freud stated that women who find sexual pleasure primarily through clitoral stimulation are immature and neurotic, in contrast to women whose sexual pleasure is experienced through intercourse and inner vaginal stimulation. Until quite recently, most other authorities upheld and promulgated this theory. Thanks largely to Masters and Johnson, it is now losing some of its validity, but today women of all ages still contend with its effects. A thirty-seven-year-old woman who participated in this study remarked:

> I have real feelings of inferiority about that controversy because I consider myself a real clitoral type, and I feel that that somehow reflects very badly on me. Intellectually, I *know* it's nonsense, and yet what I read and hear does affect my feelings about myself.

Recently I asked a young woman, aged twenty-three, who came to me for counseling, why she felt she needed psychotherapy at this time. She spoke of several painful emotional conflicts, then added quietly and nervously, "and I *think* I also have a sex problem."

"What do you *think* is your sex problem?" I asked.

"Well, you see, I don't think I come[5] correctly."

I thought about this for a moment, and then commented, "How can you come *in*correctly?"

Such feelings of inferiority result from *male* conjecture about female sexuality.

The fictitious, seriously scientific, and pseudoscientific sex literature with which American publishers have inundated the market has covered in photographic and written detail all the "erogenous zones." All, that is, except two, the most erogenous of all—the human heart and head. They have been either misinterpreted or utterly neglected in attempts to advance our understanding of human sexuality. Obviously the researched statistics and tabulations are important contributions to human knowledge, but one omnipresent variable has not yet been isolated: the *why*—the emotions, the feelings that motivate actions. At no time does a woman, or a man, feel less like a statistic than when sexually aroused or frustrated, elated or heartbroken.

Since Freud stunned the world with his description of infantile sexuality, much important and useful information has been gathered about the behavioral *when, where,* and *how often* (Kinsey *et al.*) and the physiological *what* and *how* (Masters and Johnson) of sexual activity. This study attempts to begin to understand the psychological *why,* by illuminating the motivations underlying the sexual behavior of thirty women.

[5] "Come" is a slang expression for orgasm.

STUDY DESIGN

Method

The research method used here was of necessity descriptive and formulative. Because relatively little research in the area of woman and sex has elicited information directly from women themselves, because no comprehensive study has employed depth interviews and open-ended questions, and because, as a practicing psychotherapist, I have experience in depth interviewing, the focused interview schedule seemed to me to be the best tool for this investigation.

Since the purpose of the study was to gain insight into women's feelings about their sexual attitudes and experiences, it seemed wiser to study thirty women in depth than a larger group less thoroughly.

For the depth interviews I developed an interview guide with primarily open-ended questions, in order to probe for material dealing with sexual experiences, feelings, attitudes, patterns, and habits throughout the subjects' lives, from their earliest memories to the time of the interview. The questions were based on my own ideas, as well as on the thinking of Katherine Davis in her study of college women[6] and the questionnaire schedule of G. V. Hamilton in his early study, *A Research in Marriage.*

The majority of the questions in the interview guide were aimed specifically at obtaining information about sexual experiences and feelings of all kinds. Other questions were included to get a rounded picture of the woman's family environment as a child and adult, and a sense of her life style. Some of these questions were about perceived resemblances or differences between subject and parent(s); relations with siblings; social popularity; economic status of parents and spouse; career and work satisfaction outside the home; and general attitudes held by parents and subject concerning male

[6]Katherine B. Davis, *Factors in the Sex Life of Twenty-Two Hundred Women.*

and female differentiation. (The complete interview guide appears in Appendix A.)

As the investigation was to be of a personal and historical nature, the following chronological sequence was established to structure the interviews:

I. Early Childhood through Prepuberty
II. Puberty and Early Adolescence
III. Late Adolescence and Premarital Period
IV. Marital and Adult Period
V. General Personal Reactions and Concluding Questions

Because of the scope of the data reported for the four age periods, I selected for analysis one specific area in each that I felt was the developmental and/or sexual cornerstone of that stage of life. From Early Childhood through Prepuberty (I), the area selected for analysis was early sexual memories; from Puberty and Early Adolescence (II), the area was menstruation; from Premarital and Marital (III and IV), the areas were initial intercourse—expectations and experiences—and experiences concerning orgasm.

The areas selected for analysis, in addition to providing a chronological sequence, were reasonably rich in information and seemed to be areas in which an original contribution might be made.

Procedure

I approached potential subjects in person, informing them as fully as possible of the nature and purpose of this research project and of the method to be used.

All interviews took place in my private office, in an atmosphere created to suggest acceptance, warmth, and privacy—conditions that, it was hoped, would make the subject feel at ease. We sat in soft, comfortable chairs separated by a small round table on which were a microphone to the tape recorder, a softly lit lamp, ash trays, cigarettes, and coffee or tea.

Each interview was recorded on tape, with the explicit permission of the woman, and each tape was subsequently transcribed verbatim. All subjects were assured of the absolute confidentiality of the material and of their identities.

Each complete interview took approximately twelve hours, consisting of at least three sessions of three to four hours each. Every effort was made to schedule the sessions within a two to four week period, for both freshness and continuity.

In the first session I tried to cover the categories of early and late childhood; in the second session, early adolescence leading up to late adolescence (or approximately eighteen to twenty years of age); and in the third, and if necessary fourth, sessions, the remaining period.

At the end of each session, the subject was asked to make notes of her reactions to the session, or of any additional memories that may have occurred to her later, to be reported at the beginning of the next session.

The first session began with an explanation of the research project, its purpose and method, and of the sequence of the interview guide. At this time, it was made clear to the interviewee that there were no "right" or "wrong" answers to the questions and that there was no objection to any type or amount of sexual behavior. The purpose of the study, I explained, was not to prove that women did or did not do something in particular but rather to find out how sexual attitudes developed, to learn what experiences some women had and how they felt about these experiences, and ultimately to compare the experiences and attitudes of these thirty women with generally held opinions about female sexual behavior. I asked each woman to tell me if discussion of any area caused too much anxiety, emphasizing that, for the purposes of the study, it would be far more important to learn this than to receive noncommittal or untrue answers.

As for the credibility of the answers, a long and intensive interview by an experienced interviewer has its own system of checks and validations. Also, it is my belief that no one would give this much time to a project without a desire to be as honest as possible at all times. As Pomeroy points out, "Persons who volunteer to gives their histories will be more cooperative than persons who are preselected and then asked to give histories."[7] All the women approached for this study were very interested in the subject matter, and all expressed a wish to contribute something valuable to human sex research. They knew that honesty would serve this aim and that evasion would destroy it.

Subjects

Since the sampling was small, subjects with some homogenous characteristics were selected: these included economic or social background (all were middle-class); education (all had completed high school); age (all were between twenty-five and forty); race (all were white); place of residence (all were living in or around metropolitan New York); and all were married. (While marriage is undoubtedly not essential for sexual experience, it confers a special social status which adds a significant dimension to an individual's life experience.) These factors provided the homogeneity of the sample required for acceptable scientific research.[8]

Potential subjects were selected from among women in my private practice and friends and acquaintances who fitted the category limitations, who had been or were still in psychotherapy, and who volunteered to participate in the study. Because of the taboos and restrictions regarding sex in our culture, most women find it difficult to speak freely about sexual matters. I thought that those experienced with psychotherapy might be more comfortable in this particular situation. This

[7]Wardell Pomeroy, "Human Sexual Behavior." In Norman Faberow, ed., *Taboo Topics,* p. 23.
[8]It is important to note that because the subjects in this study were born between 1920 and 1936 they have made an important contribution to sex history. They are in one of the last generations of women to experience the necessity of virginity for marriage, with all its attendant ramifications (pregnancy fears, etc.).

also added one more common factor to the sample.

Here I wish to mention something well known to experienced psychotherapists: people who seek psychotherapy
are not necessarily those members of the population who have
the greatest degree of psychopathology. Often the choice is
determined by objective circumstances, such as the individual's ability to pay and the geographic proximity of psychotherapy facilities, as well as personal and social attitudes
toward psychotherapy. Also, it is my strong belief that it is
often a matter of motivation for personal happiness—that
those who seek therapy have a greater desire to live more
satisfying lives.

All subjects finally selected for the study were married at
the time of their interviews (2 were subsequently divorced).
The duration of the marriages was from approximately six
months to twenty years and the average was about six years.
Thirteen of the subjects were previously married, 8 with one
previous marriage and 5 with two previous marriages. Fourteen had from one to three children.

Of the 30 subjects, 29 worked outside the home at a variety
of professions, in a variety of fields. More specifically, 7 were
in the theater, 6 were writers, 9 were psychoanalysts or psychologists or attending a university in preparation for these
professions, 2 were fashion models, and the remaining 6 were
in social work, teaching, architecture, business, interior deco-
ration, and costume design.

The husbands of the subjects represented a wide variety of
professions: 6 writers, 5 actors, 3 artists, 1 lawyer, 3 psychia-
trists and psychologists, 4 musicians, 5 businessmen, 1 high-
school teacher, and 2 physicians.

Twelve of the subjects had completed or were completing
graduate work, 8 had completed undergraduate work and
received degrees, and the remaining 10 had completed two or
more years of undergraduate work or had taken courses on the
college level.

The incomes of the subjects (combined with those of their
spouses) ranged from under $5,000 to over $20,000 with 13

earning less than $10,000, 21 earning less than $20,000 and 9 over $20,000 a year.

Eight of the subjects came from homes in which divorce had occurred, 7 when the subject was under fifteen and 1 when the subject was an adult. Of the 7, only 1 remained with her father. In 8 of the 22 remaining cases one parent had died (five fathers and three mothers) when the subject was still under thirteen.

HIGHLIGHTS OF FINDINGS

At this point I would like to note briefly some general highlights in the findings of this study in order to prepare the reader for the chapters that follow:

—The variety and range of first memories to which the subjects attributed sexual connotations were great, and the age span for these was from infancy (less than one year) to eight years of age.

—The cultural attitude of guilt and anxiety attached to female masturbation seems to have remained unchanged, despite general increased sexual activity and freedom.

—No women reported realistic sex instruction from any single source at any developmental stage.

—It was easier to nullify early negative teachings that associated intercourse with pain than associations of intercourse with "dirt."

—There was almost total negative reaction to the concept of parental intercourse, whether observed, overheard, or fantasied. (For some subjects the feeling of revulsion and disbelief carried over even into adult life.)

—Motivations and feelings surrounding virginity revealed a change in cultural pressures.

—The ability to experience orgasm through heterosexual sex does not necessarily ensure an ability to achieve warm and satisfying heterosexual relationships, and vice versa.

—How the human female experiences orgasm seems to be a learned rather than automatic experience; although physiologically identical for all women, orgasm was experienced in various subjective ways.

—The experience of orgasm, in and of itself, is *not* always an integral part of sexual contentment.

The data suggested three other major conclusions: 1) sexual behavior in civilized humans is a drive, or a capacity, with a potential for pleasure which may or may not be fulfilled by any given individual; 2) an important aspect of sexual gratification, which characterized all the women in the sample, is a strong life drive (i.e., strong wishes for happiness and achievement and a strong need to defy early negative influences); and 3) there is a need for change in sex education, stressing the development of specialists in the field, who would require training in this unique subject matter, as well as in teaching and administrative methods.

The findings of this study are in agreement with the research of Davis, Hamilton, Dickinson, Kinsey *et al.,* and Masters and Johnson, and in general accord with the conceptual orientations of Margaret Mead and Clara Thompson (shared by Kinsey *et al.* and Ford and Beach), which emphasize cultural determination and social conditioning of human behavior. The findings are in general disagreement, however, with Freudian theories of female sexuality—his concepts of penis envy, "masculinized" women, clitoral versus vaginal orgasm and psychosexual maturity, the menarche trauma, and the cessation of sexual activity during the so-called latency period of childhood.

Some of the specific findings of the present study that tend to contradict Freud's theoretical views on female sexuality are the following:

—Nearly 75 percent of the women in this study recalled no wish to either possess a penis or be a boy in spite of the fact that every woman was, or had been, in psychoanalysis or psychotherapy, during which such material, if present either consciously or unconsciously, is usually revealed and interpreted.

—One hundred percent of the women were "masculinized"

according to Freud's definition, by virtue of the high level of their educational and professional pursuits; yet none were in conflict about their professional status and, moreover, all got a great deal of satisfaction from their work.

—Over 75 percent of the women experienced no feelings of displeasure or trauma at their menarche. Only 37 percent recalled fears of physical harm associated with the initial menstruation, but of these, 36 percent had *no knowledge* of the phenomenon before the menarche and could therefore be expected to experience fear at seeing their first menstrual flow.

—The period from seven to twelve years of age (the so-called latency period) was replete with sexual activities and memories for one hundred percent of the women.

One interesting note perhaps reflects more the psychoanalytic sophistication of the sample than a basic agreement or disagreement with Freud's theory of the "clitoral-immature" versus "vaginal-mature" orgasm. Several women did report feelings of sexual incompetence because of the way in which they preferred to experience orgasm, but they based their conceptions of inferiority and sexual inadequacy exclusively on their readings of Freudian psychoanalytic theory.

Had Freud lived long enough to be exposed to the findings of later scientists, especially the cultural anthropologists, it is certainly possible that his theories on female sexuality would have been substantially altered. Essentially, Freud was a scientist; he never ceased searching for more comprehensive answers to questions involving human behavior, and was constantly revising his theories to conform to new evidence. Toward the end of his life, Freud acknowledged that scientific understanding of woman's sexual nature was "admittedly incomplete, fragmentary," adding, "If you want to know more about femininity, you must interrogate your own experience, or turn to the poets, or else wait until science can give you more profound and coherent information."[9]

[9]Sigmund Freud, *Three Essays on the Theory of Sexuality.*

The inevitable limitation of any study of sexuality is the researcher's own bias. In no other field of the social sciences, and in no other branch of knowledge, is the attitude of the researcher so influential or the instrument of investigation so intimately related to the personality of the investigator. Whether I intend them to or not, my own biases and prejudices will manifest themselves throughout this book. In the words of the noted historian G. Rattray Taylor, one of the tenets on which my judgments have been based is to "regard health—physical and mental—as better than disease; and . . . to regard love and kindness as better than cruelty and hate."[10] I suppose one special bias should be noted here. I am prejudiced against forcing human beings into conduct without their consent, and I am prejudiced against prejudices concerning the expression of sexuality.

The views I hold were arrived at through life experience. I cannot say that everyone will agree with them, or that they should. Because sex can be every kind of experience imaginable, anyone who claims it should be one thing or another deprives us of the freedom to discover our own potential and capacities, to realize our own individuality and sexual uniqueness. People should have the freedom to fulfill the capacities they are born with, even the freedom to waste them.

We are often too willing, it seems to me, to accept the philosophies and psychologies imposed upon us by others. But only by courageously assuming the personal responsibility for one's life is it possible to enjoy its privileges. By not permitting others to give us the answers, we assume the privilege of asking our own questions. What do *I* feel about sex? Am I pleased with how I feel? Is sex beautiful or ugly? Delightful or disgusting? Is it everything? Or is it nothing?

Change is possible. Knowledge can be a tool for change. In order to change the patterns of life, which are not mere coincidences, one must first discover what those patterns are. I have

[10]G. Rattray Taylor, "Foreword," *Sex in History,* p. xiv.

attempted in this study of thirty women to suggest a way to relearn the story of one's life, and possibly to learn new patterns that will be more satisfying in profound, personal ways.

If sharing the experiences of these thirty women causes the reader to say at least once, "I felt like that, too!"—to lose, even momentarily, the feeling of isolation and perversity—then this study will have accomplished some of its purpose.

If this book inspires each reader to change one petrified thought, or elicits even one compelling feeling of identification with these women—one more second of connectedness to life and to another person—then it will have accomplished still more of its purpose.

If the findings in this study approach some truth about humanity and sex, or provide a stepping stone toward humanizing the study of sex, their contribution is of value. More truth should make human beings freer—to make better choices, to develop more satisfying and perhaps more loving relationships, as well as more profound and meaningful personal lives.

For several years, I counseled a withdrawn, borderline schizophrenic boy in his late teens. Although early in his therapy he could barely speak except when spoken to, as he began to develop confidence, he manifested high intelligence and artistic ability laced with an especially subtle sense of humor. During one of his sessions, he asked about all the books and papers spread across my desk.

"That's material for my doctoral thesis," I explained.

"What are you doing your thesis on?" he inquired softly.

"I'm doing a dissertation on women and sex."

"Oh," murmured the boy, still softly. He sat for several seconds thinking about the answer, then blushed somewhat and with a quiet, small smile commented, "That sounds like a good combination."

I hope that readers of the following chapters will arrive at the same conclusion.

CHAPTER TWO

EARLY SEX MEMORIES

There are substitute gratifications for things a child gives up as he is weaned and toilet trained: solid foods are found to be tasteful and pleasant; parents reward one for cleaning one's plate; being dry and clean have their virtues. But for sex, there are no substitutes until the time of adolescence. This leaves mothers with no possibility of guidance through substitute rewards; they can only *inhibit* sexual behavior.
　　　　　—Sears, Maccoby, and Lewin, *Psychology*

It seems a truth to me that when you discover something, or come upon something which is being kept a secret, you immediately think it has something to do with sex—even if it does not.
　　　　　　　　　　　　　—Rosemary

The more society obscures . . . relationships, muffles the human body in clothes, surrounds elimination with prudery, shrouds copulation in shame and mystery, camouflages pregnancy, banishes men and children from childbirth, and hides breast feeding, the more individual and bizarre will be the child's attempts to understand, to piece together a very imperfect knowledge of the life-cycle of the two sexes and an understanding of the particular state of maturity of his or her own body.
　　　　　—Margaret Mead, *Male and Female*

EARLY SEX MEMORIES was the area of analysis selected as most representative of the age group designated in the interview guide as Early Childhood through Prepuberty.

Sexuality during childhood is much more pervasive and less specific than it is in later years.

Although most researchers in the field of psychosexual development recognize the importance of early childhood experiences, no study has sought out all significant memories of a sexual nature of any and every type whatsoever and the recollected feelings accompanying them. Some investigators have collected data on the remembrance of specific early sexual events. Kinsey and his associates cited the first sexual experience and the age at which it occurred; however, they did not specify the type of activity that qualified as a "first experience" in the pre-adolescent stage of development, or note the feelings associated with the memory.[1] Katherine Davis reported the number of early sex memories and the subject's age at the initial one.[2] Eustace Chesser discussed the correspondence between early impressions of sex and the subject's image of the parental relationship, and correlated these early impressions with the subject's marital happiness.[3]

One objective of my study was to discover how the events and feelings recollected from childhood might influence a woman's adult sexual responses. Through the kinds of questions asked and the examples suggested each woman was urged to recall as many significant events of a sexual nature or connotation as came to mind.

[1]A. C. Kinsey *et al., Sexual Behavior in the Human Female.*
[2]Katherine B. Davis, *Factors in the Sex Life of Twenty-Two Hundred Women.*
[3]Eustace Chesser, *Women.*

The areas I investigated included initial memory (the first "sexual" memory that came to mind), associations between learned eliminative functions and sexual pleasure, incidents of real or fantasied sexual activity between parents or others and feelings about these events, childhood dreams and daydreams, first knowledge of the nature of intercourse and its relation to birth and feelings about these in relation to self, parents, and others, incestuous wishes or experiences with siblings, incidents of seeing the sexual organs of self and others, autoeroticism, and early childhood homosexual experiences. (Although homosexuality was discussed throughout the interviews, only 2 women had homosexual experiences as adults—not enough to warrant a special area of analysis in this book.)

VALIDITY OF MEMORIES

It is a truism that the validity of early sex memories reported by any subject can be questioned on various grounds. Freud learned (to his astonishment and our theoretical enrichment) that much of what his patients remembered was sexual fantasy (sometimes even an obfuscating screen to occlude additional memories of other, more real and/or disturbing wishes and events). To understand the significance of reported memories, one must consider both the psychological nature of the subject reporting them and the circumstances under which they are reported.

All the women who participated in this study were volunteers. It is my conviction that as volunteers they had no need to consciously fabricate or distort, but rather were motivated to contribute positively to the investigation for their own benefit as well as for the benefit of others. They gave of their time, their fears, their privacy to this investigation, and I believe that the memories presented here are forthright reports of what each woman remembered. Kinsey and his colleagues, in their celebrated study, stated as follows:

It has been asked how it is possible for an interviewer to know whether people are telling the truth, when they are boasting, when they are covering up, or when they are otherwise distorting the record. As well ask a horse trader how he knows when to close a bargain! The experienced interviewer knows when he has established a sufficient rapport to obtain an honest record, in the same way that the subject knows that he can give that honest record to the interviewer. Learning to recognize these indicators, intangible as they may be, is the most important thing in controlling the accuracy of an interview. Beyond that there are . . . checks among the questions, inconsistencies to watch for, questions which demand proof, and other devices for testing the validity of the data.[4]

All thirty women who participated in this study were at the time, or had been, in some kind of psychotherapy treatment —fifteen with me and fifteen with other psychotherapists—for periods ranging from one to nine years. The sophistication gleaned from the experience of psychoanalysis may have sparked the kinds of initial remembrances reported. It is possible that because of their awareness of psychoanalytic theories and ideas, these women may have attributed sexual significance to certain childhood experiences in which individuals without therapy experience might have found no such connotations.

The material reported in this area was most striking for its variety, inconsistency, and yet a certain similarity. Each woman in this study, as women everywhere, had a different life situation and, consequently, a different quality and type of memory; even similar experiences are perceived in an individual's own terms. However, pervading the multifarious situations reported, notwithstanding their variety and the levels of feeling attached to them, was a degree of similarity. This similarity was in the expressions of a need for secrecy, the feelings of wrongness, and the fear of discovery and punish-

[4]Kinsey *et al., Sexual Behavior in the Human Female,* p. 43.

ment which colored most of the recollections. Guilt was the *predominant* feeling associated with the early experiences recalled by the majority of women. Yet surely there were innumerable other events from childhood with which guilt and punishment were also associated. What caused these memories to be remembered vividly was their sexual content, with the associations of wrong, bad, sinful, secretive.

The taboo overtones of childhood sexual experiences give them a unique status in our life histories. The prohibited and dangerous quality of these experiences is perhaps what imbues childhood sexual memories with the vividness with which they are experienced and recalled. The degree of intensity with which they are repressed and the resulting conflicts may in part cause childhood sexual memories to influence so importantly our adult personalities, attitudes, and behavior over and above other guilt-ridden childhood memories of a nonsexual nature. These memories retain their shine almost as though they have been fixed in amber below the level of our conscious mind, eternally influencing our lives in the most profound and subtle ways.

INITIAL MEMORY

The first question asked of each woman was: "To the best of your knowledge, what seems to you to be your very earliest recollection of any kind whatsoever having some sexual significance? It might have been an actual experience, something you oversaw or overheard, a fantasy, a dream, a daydream, or a memory of any nature that seems to you to have a sexual connotation, significance, or overtone."

The first experiences that these subjects reported remembering spanned a period from infancy (less than one year) to over eight years of age and a variety of events and sensations. Twelve women reported memories involving sensual feelings arising from visual stimuli, body contact, bathing experiences, mutual exploration, mutual exposure, physical attraction to others, and self-exposure. The emotions associated with the initial memories ranged from pleasure and interest (11 instances) to fear of discovery, secretiveness, shame, confusion, revulsion, and guilt (19 instances).

What follow are verbatim accounts of the initial sexual memories of some of the women in the study. The variety and individuality of each woman's experience is illuminating. Norma's first memory is:

> Me and two other little girls who lived next door were under a blanket. I was four, maybe going on five. One little girl had wanted to explore and so we were under this blanket, and we all had our pants down and a little boy looked into this hole in the blanket, which was right by my head, as I recall. Then he ran off to tell my mother, or his mother—actually, I'm not sure *whose* mother he told. My mother eventually knew it by evening, and it seems that even before this incident my mother was aware of this investigatory curiosity of the other two girls. And it seems to me she had warned me about this before, because I seem to recall going under that blanket with some mild—maybe not protest, but some kind of expiation of her warning, saying, "You know, we aren't suppose to do this," and the girls saying, "Come on, come ahead, do it anyway." We were right outside the kitchen windows. And that's the first thing I recall.

Louise's first memory:

> I don't know how old I was—five, six, seven, maybe. A boy I liked and I were examining each other and our mothers walked in. It was horrible! I was punished for it . . . I don't remember how, but we were too scared to continue after that.

Several other women remember their first sexual awareness or experiences as having occurred while bathing with their brothers.

Frances traced her first memory to playing with friends at age five:

It was sort of a traumatic experience. I was about five years old and playing in the sandbox in the backyard with two little boys. I think what we had done was pull down our pants or take them off—I don't know which—and played bare-bottomed in the sand. When I put my pants on and went home, my mother saw that I had sand on my bottom—oh, she was very angry and very upset, and grabbed me by the hand and took me down to this little boy's house and made me apologize for having been bad, for what I did. This was very easy to remember because it was such an emotional experience. It gave such meaning to something which had actually been a very simple thing.

Several women related first sexual memories involving their parents. Roxanne recalled:

I don't see why I should remember this in answer to your question [about initial memory], but what comes to mind is when I was five (my parents were already separated) my mother's boy friend, whom she later married, brought her a present—a pair of bedroom mules. I remember, when I saw the present, I thought, who is he? And why did he bring her those? Then later that night, they went out and left me and my younger brother all alone. I felt horrible because they had left me alone, and I cried and cried.

Carol's first memory concerns her father.

Well, the first thing that comes to my head is when I was really very little, I always used to talk to my father or say that I was wishing my father would take me out on a date. Especially me—that was going to be a big thing—on New Year's Eve or some special night. My mother—I don't know what was going to happen to my mother—she'd be too old. That was the first time I thought I would like to be with a man.

Barbara remembers

being attracted to little boys in kindergarten, so I guess I must have been about five. The feelings were bewildering: they were wrong, I just *felt* it, but still they were pleasurable—very exciting—like I desired something, but I can't really tell you what it was.

Karen's first memory involves masturbation:

It's very vivid. I would have to be under four, because we moved when I was four, and I'm absolutely positive about the way the room looked. I was still in a crib—they kept me in a crib until very late. I think I was 21 *(laughter)*. I remember masturbating or at least touching myself. When I was in this crib, I used to tell my mother to put blankets over the side because the light bothered me. But it wasn't that. It didn't occur to me then that anybody could look over the edge, but actually I didn't want them to know what I was doing there. It was a very definite and very strong sexual feeling. My analyst suggested that perhaps I didn't want to look out because the crib was in their bedroom. But I don't know. I have no recollection of witnessing any scene with them or anything. But I was very aware of my own genitals and how pleasurable the sensation was.

In several women's recollections of sensations or events that occurred at very early ages, there is a notable quality of pleasure without guilt. Cathleen, for example, remembers a very intense relationship with her mother from birth to eight months of age, although her mother subsequently neglected and abused her.

I have feelings of my mother being warm and seductive to me while nursing. She was said not to have too much energy after giving birth to me, so she just stayed in bed and slept and nursed me. I have memories of her not having any clothes on, because it was summer, and me dressed in diapers.

Rachel thought at first that her earliest memory was of self-exploration. But during the interview,

> suddenly a feeling just popped into my mind—a sensation of bathing in a warm bathtub with my younger brother. There is no feeling that he and I were involved in any kind of play . . . just the feeling of the warm water and the look of that old white tub . . . and my little brother there . . . it's a very sweet feeling. Strange that that memory, that image, has never appeared to me before.

Sarah remembered her earliest sexual feelings at about age two, as "something very vague—simply the warmth of my mother's body."

And Zoe recalled

> being rocked . . . as in a cradle . . . and I associated it with sex because it was pleasant, and with my father. I was told much later in my life that we never had a cradle . . . I have a feeling now that perhaps my father would rock me and play with me when he came home from work.

This is the only memory she has of her father, who was separated from her mother when Zoe was less than one year old.

The unusual absence of feelings of guilt from these recollections suggests that sexual taboos and prohibitions had not yet been thoroughly communicated to, or assimilated by, the subjects.

OTHER MEMORIES

In this study I sought to record not only the initial memory, but also every other childhood memory of a sexual or sensual nature that the women could recall, spontaneously or with the encouragement of the interview. The majority of these fell naturally into several categories: memories about nudity of other children and adults, genital comparisons, seductive encounters with adults, penis envy, childhood sex games, long-term childhood relationships of a sexual nature, genital exhibitionism, fantasies and daydreams, and self-stimulation.

Nudity

Twenty-four women (80 percent) of the 30 in the study recalled incidents in which as children they saw adults nude. Twenty-one recalled incidents involving their parents: 12 saw their fathers, 9 saw their mothers, and 2 recalled observing both parents nude. Eight women remembered seeing nonfamily adult males nude; 1 recalled having seen a nonfamily adult female. For such a supposedly natural occurrence, the large number of recollections and the importance attached to them is striking. The subjects' traumatic associations seem to be due to the confusion, anxiety, and even anger with which adults often responded to being observed.

Eve, who had no brothers, remembered that at age nine she had seen her father's penis when his pajamas gaped open. "It distressed me greatly, and frightened me . . . and I felt afraid of ever seeing a man's penis . . . that of a grown man, that is . . . and I never saw another until about age nineteen."

Erin, at age six, peeked through the keyhole of her parents' bedroom door and saw her father sleeping naked. "I saw his genitals and it was very exciting, but I felt that I was very naughty to be doing this." The incident was filled with "mysteriousness" for her, and she felt "terrified that he should ever find out I had done this."

Helen recalled walking into the bathroom at age six and seeing her father on the toilet. "I remembered there was a big commotion, I had done this horrible thing—that there was something awful about walking into the bathroom when *he* was in there and that I should never do it again."

Rosemary, whose initial memory at age four was of "being afraid of what was between my brother's legs," remembered that a year later she had walked into her father's room where he was undressing and not wearing any underwear. She was startled and frightened. Her first sexual experience with an adult male, she said, was shocking "because he took his pants off in front of me, and I saw this thing which I think is so ugly!"

At age six, Irene remembered

> seeing my father naked. He had either cut himself or something and came rushing out of the bedroom. And I made some kind of remark about him because I had never seen an adult male naked, and the feeling I remembered from what happened then was a kind of response of horror—my parents were horrified at my reaction. I think it struck me funny for some kind of connection that I made, a certain kind of discovery, like an *amused* kind of discovery about it, but they were very upset with me.

At seven, Karen remembers walking into the bathroom while her mother was douching. When Karen asked her what she was doing, her mother replied: "Once a month I get a boil and it breaks and I have to wash it out."

Watching her mother bathing, Rebecca had asked her about her genitals. Her mother responded that "one's sexual parts were something you didn't show and you didn't pay too much attention to." This information was imparted, Rebecca felt, in a "giggly" way which conveyed to her that it was "all right to have a vagina, but socially one doesn't have too much to do with it. It's all right in the bathtub, though, for cleanliness purposes." (Much later in her interview, Rebecca stated that she "didn't have anything to do with sex personally" until she was engaged.)

Eight women reported memories of seeing nonfamily adult males nude.

Roxanne had some amnesia about things she "ought to" remember in her childhood, but she clearly recalled, at age six, sitting in a parked car and noticing a man urinating in the street.

I saw this man, who I'm sure was a nut, start to go to the john in the street, and my shock was something that I can still recall today.

Although Cathleen slept in her parents' room until she was three, she was eleven when she first saw an adult male nude, a workman repairing a road.

His overalls were very stiff. They apparently were new and would bucket out in the front when he bent over. His fly was open, and he wasn't wearing any shorts. I remember seeing this great mass of black hair—I don't remember actually seeing his penis—and thinking there was this sort of big wig there. I think I was frightened, because I had *forgotten* what my father's looked like. I must have known, but I had forgotten.

Zoe reported two different incidents:

. . . looking through my brother's things when he was at work. I loved to see all the things he had and just touch them. I found these funny little pornographic books that I thought were comic books. and I looked at them. I was absolutely fascinated but felt kind of sick with excitement. Afterwards, I kept remembering the look of those great big cocks and wondering if men could *really* be that big. [About age eight]

. . . walking home from school and seeing this man parked by the curb with the car door open and he was masturbating. His penis looked huge and purple and gave me a terrible scare, but I was still able to keep on walking, pretending I didn't even see it. [Age ten]

Virginia remembered seeing a young friend's father nude on his bed, and feeling

it was wrong of me to see a man undressed because I had never seen my parents naked, and bedroom and bathroom doors were always shut in our house. So somehow I just *knew* I wasn't supposed to see a man naked. [Age four]

Artemis was the only woman who could recall seeing a nonfamily adult female nude. Her parents had divorced when she was four, and she visited her father on weekends. One weekend she chanced upon her father's mistress urinating outside the house. "I was shocked that she wore no panties, that she seemed to urinate standing up, and that there was something about blood in it." Because Artemis had not yet learned about menstruation, she felt concern that the woman was ill.

Genital Comparisons

Eight women recalled discovering differences in genitals and other sexual characteristics between themselves and others. They remembered these experiences as being accompanied by varying degrees of puzzlement, surprise, disgust, or distress—admixed with fascination.

Bizarre distortions in the perception of sexual structure and function generally originate in early childhood with misinformation from adults.

Nancy, whose voluptuous mother was very affectionate and seductive toward her, had an undefined but strong feeling about breasts: "I remember about age ten going through fashion magazines and drawing breasts with half-moon nipples on the models—but with a light pencil so they wouldn't show." When her stepfather discovered this he accused her of being "dirty and filthy," which made her feel very guilty. Once, at about the same age, she was in the bathroom with her mother, who was sitting on the edge of the bathtub. Nancy was startled

> that she had a big clitoris. I thought, my God! It looks like a big penis! I think I must have felt inferior because I didn't have one like that.

Victoria recalled that at the time of her menarche she and a girl cousin, aged nine, had examined and compared each other's genitals: "I felt different from her. I don't know how to explain it, but it was as though her genitals didn't show—

didn't protrude at all. And then I remember feeling there was something wrong with *me*. It was an awful feeling."

Reactions to adult male genitals and male children's genitals were often very different. Eight women had been so impressed with the difference between men and boys that they didn't realize that they were seeing the same organs at different stages of growth.

"My father looked monstrous to me," reported Celeste, "gross—huge. He appeared tremendous . . . and I felt scared when I would look at him." But with her five-year-old male friend, what she felt was curiosity. She and her sisters marveled over him, "because of the way he could pee all over the tub . . . but the feelings about this little boy had to do with a kind of pleasure, as over a toy . . . rather than something to do with sexual excitement." This reaction was typical among those who had early occasion to make this comparison.

Virginia never connected the sight of her friend's naked father when she was four with the boy cousin with whom she "played at intercourse when we were age six . . . it didn't seem to be the same thing at all. One was shocking, one was—well, I just didn't *think* of my little cousin's genitals at all!—I just thought of what we were *doing*." In realizing that she had made a distinction between adult and child genitals as a child, Virginia commented, "Men seemed so big and impressive while boys weren't so astonishing at all."

Role Preference: Penis Envy or the Wish To Be a Boy

Twenty of the women (66.7 percent) could recall no childhood wish to have been born a boy or to have been like a boy. However, 10 women (33.3 percent) did recall such wishes. They were based on a variety of conceptions about the relative worth of males and females. Both parents played important roles in conveying these values to the child.

The 10 women gave several reasons for having wanted to be male: 5 perceived males as aesthetically and/or physically superior to females; 2 observed their mothers' preference for the male power role; 3 thought their fathers controlled the affection in the family.

Helen, whose first sexual memory was of walking around with her dress picked up over head in order to "show the boys I had something too," recalled:

> . . . I must have been about three or four and I was standing in front of a mirror without any clothes on, trying to find something. But it was just a plain old body.

At age four or five, Victoria realized that she "wanted a penis . . . because I knew that my mother seemed to favor males. I took some oranges once and filled my panties with them, and pretended I was a boy."

Celeste stated that

> I surely did used to want to be a boy. There were all girls in my family, and I felt that my father would have liked to have a son and I wanted to be it. I wanted to be very much like my father, and I tried to emulate his intellectual accomplishments.

Jane, who considered her mother very unfeminine, aggressive, and unsexual, and thought she rejected both her and her father, remembers

> feeling that I would like to be a boy. I was very physically active and good at sports just like my father, and we used to share these activities together. I got more approval from my father than my mother in every way. I was a boy, I said to myself, because I never played with little girls, and I never made any differentiation between the boys and myself . . . Boys were the only human beings—little girls were dull, you know.

Carol felt accepted by and close to her father and painfully aware of her mother's denial of her own as well as her daughter's femininity and sexuality. She remembered:

... I was around six when I think I tried once to look at my vagina in the mirror. I couldn't see much there so I tried to look inside and really didn't like what I saw. I thought it was very ugly and still do. But I think a man's penis is the most beautiful thing in the world.

Eve, who remembered "trying to urinate through a funnel while standing over a toilet bowl," attributes her wish to be a boy to the confusing role reversals she sensed in her parents' relationship. She felt her mother was "the male in the family ... and I don't think I *really* wanted to find out which parent had the penis." The real advantages of being a male, she thought, were in the power one derived from working, earning money, and assuming importance through work. "The *female* female was never important, and the power in our household seemed to sit with the one who brought in the most money—in this case, it was my mother."

Modifying Freud's views of the inevitability of female penis envy and castration complex, Ernest Jones wrote, "The sight of the boy's penis is not the sole traumatic event that changes a young girl's life; it is only the last link in a long chain."[5] And Margaret Mead locates "penis envy"

in a society that has so over-rewarded male positions that an envy for the role which is played by the father can coalesce with an experience of the little brother's or a boy companion's more conspicuous anatomical equipment.

Envy of the male role can come as much from an under-evaluation of the role of the wife and mother as from an over-evaluation of public aspects of achievement that have been reserved for men. When all achievement is outside the house, women of enterprise and initiative hate to be told they must confine themselves there.[6]

The 20 women who were relatively satisfied with their gender, and recalled no explicit feelings of preference for the male

[5]Quoted in Helene Deutsch, *The Psychology of Women,* vol. i, p. 266.
[6]Margaret Mead, *Male and Female,* pp. 85, 92.

role over that of the female, expressed this through an absence of conflict in their replies to questions in this area. Since their statements were undramatic compared to those of the women who preferred the male role, I chose not to include quotations from them here.

"Penis envy" as Freud saw it—a universal conflict in women, especially acute in women who, through education and career choice, have been "masculinized"—does not appear to be in fact universal or inevitable. Where it does exist, it seems to be determined at least as much by social as by biological factors, and is usually a symptom of more fundamental psychosocial problems.

Childhood Sex Play

Twenty-five of the 30 women reported incidents of sex play and games, which demonstrate the compelling force of sexuality and sensuality in childhood. The games, including mutual exploration and/or exposure of the genitals, were played with those who were most accessible—siblings and relatives.

Most of the reported incidents occurred only once or sporadically until the activity was either discovered by an adult or discontinued because of guilt feelings.

When I was seven, my thirteen-year-old brother decided to give me a bath and was very insistent that he wash me between my legs. I remember that it felt very good when he did it, and I kept hoping he would bathe me again, but he didn't. Only that one time. Maybe he got frightened of his own feelings, I don't know. But that was about the first sexy, pleasant thing I can remember with *another* person. [Rachel]

I think I was about seven and visiting my eight-year-old boy cousin that summer. We went out to pick blackberries, started playing around with each other, and either he or I said that he should put his penis in me, although I didn't know any words or terms like that then. I know both of us were completely oblivious that this was the sexual act. We were just fooling around with each other. And I remember thinking—this is clear as a bell—we were trying to decide whether he should "let go" or not, and I remember I had no idea that there would be anything *in* him. I knew this was what he urinated with, and I think that's all he thought it was for. And I remember saying, "Well, now, let's see. You had beans for lunch and I don't like beans, so don't do it." I can remember that just as clearly! This, I guess, is the part where the sex comes in. His oldest sister saw us and ran off and told his mother. We didn't know she had seen us and we walked into the house perfectly innocent, and his mother told him that we were not to do that any more and that's when I found out there was something wrong about it. [Virginia]

When she was four, Cathleen approached her two-year-old sister in an attempt to imitate her parents whom she had witnessed having intercourse.

I wanted to lay on her, but I didn't know what it meant exactly. She didn't object to what I was doing. I can remember feeling very excited just feeling her foot running up and down my stomach and touching my vagina. That's my first recollection of sex with someone else.

Several subjects played sexual discovery games with neighboring children. Roxanne associated strong guilt feelings with memories of sexual exploration and mutual stimulation with two neighborhood girls. They would "stick weeds into each other, down there." She also recalled "feeling around with a boy and a girl in Sunday school" and being discovered. The guilt was compounded by the fact that "it was Sunday school."

Notable exceptions to the prevalent pattern of single or occasional experiences were some long-term, well-established relationships of immature sexual activity. These were accompanied by varying degrees of pleasure, confusion, fear, and guilt.

Karen told of a friendship with a boy her own age.

> Davey and I played little sex games from the time we were five until we were ten. We would play at "show me" and rubbing together. It wasn't really intercourse, but we definitely imitated the act, no question about it.

Were you ever afraid that someone would find out?

> Continually, continually. And then a fascinating thing happened. One day when I wasn't with him, Davey tripped and fell on some loose wire in a construction area. One of the wires went into his groin. He was in bed for about three weeks. It was really a terrible accident. And I remember him saying that God had punished him because of our games and that he was never going to play them again. And I remember thinking to myself that I didn't like the idea that he felt this was a punishment, and I thought to myself in a very crafty although ladylike fashion (maybe we were eight), "I'll wait till it gets better; he'll play them again." Because I wasn't about to give them up, and apparently I wasn't interested in finding another friend for those kinds of games.

She described their sexual games:

> He licked me, and I did that to him. Neither of us could have read about this anywhere; I don't know how we even stumbled on it, but it was very fancy, really, and it was so natural. I think we were like little animals—like puppies, you see, the way they lick and sniff and touch, and it was just that natural.

Upon learning at age ten "how babies are made," Karen became

> frightened to death of pregnancy. I kept asking questions for reassurance, like, I didn't menstruate yet, could I get

pregnant? I would ask my girl friend things like, "How do you know? Do you promise I won't get pregnant? " I wanted to make sure she had the right information . . . I wanted to be reassured that Davey couldn't make me pregnant. Then I guess I got scared and figured I was going to stop with Davey while I was ahead. I was also afraid that I would talk in my sleep and tell about our games, just scared to death of that.

Frances had a durational childhood sexual relationship between the ages of nine and twelve with a male relative five years her senior who lived in her home.

The sexual experiences I had with George were not connected in any way in my mind with having babies. It was just a way of having some pleasurable feelings that I knew were wrong, because it was always very secret. I guess I didn't really undersand *why* it was wrong, but I did know it was wrong.

She described how during the night he would come into the bedroom she shared with her sister:

I was sound asleep and I would slowly awaken to these pleasurable sensations, but even as I was coming awake, I would act as if I was still asleep for a long time, and he would be feeling around my legs and around the clitoris and vagina and that whole area. It was a very pleasant sensation. At some point I remember wondering to myself, how could he take such chances because here I'm in bed with my sister and he risked waking my parents on the way to my room. And I also wondered, how did he know that I wasn't going to shriek when he woke me in my sleep like that.

This went on for some time, and then one night he knew I was awake, and he wanted me to touch his penis, and I couldn't and I wouldn't and I was scared to death. It was as if I was petrified. I didn't know what a penis looked like or felt like, and yet I didn't even want to touch it. It was so wrong to touch it that I couldn't; I knew it was wrong.

He pulled my hand to him and put it on his penis. Just even having him touch my hand and hold it was a very traumatic experience. Then one time we were in the house alone, and he wanted me to undress—said he would too, and we'd get into bed, but I didn't want to do that. Maybe I just took off my panties or something like that, but I can remember feeling terrified. And then there were times when—again I marvel at his taking such chances!—there were times when we would be sitting in the dining room playing cards, and he would reach under the table and start feeling me, and I would wonder to myself, what if somebody walks in? But no one ever walked in.

Describing the termination of the relationship, Frances continued:

It ended very abruptly one evening when I was sitting and reading, and George walked up behind me and started feeling my breasts, and my mother walked in.

Frances felt compelled to lie to her mother about the duration and extent of the sexual play:

I just felt there was something secret about it. I suppose the fact that he came in at night and mostly only did it at night made it seem that it was something secret and something that couldn't be done in the open. And there was some vague feeling on my part that *even though* it was enjoyable, it wasn't the thing to do. But I couldn't—or didn't really want to—put a stop to it.

Fear of discovery is a recurrent theme throughout these memories of childhood sex play. Each woman knew as a child, that certain kinds of play were socially acceptable, while others—sexual—were not; none was able to trace the exact source of this knowledge. Fourteen women mentioned this fear explicitly, and the other 16 recalled feelings that reflected the apprehension attached to any type of childhood sexual activity or thought.

Twelve women reported being punished, directly or indirectly, upon being discovered in some sort of sexual activity. Seven were discovered by an adult more than once; even though they had been previously punished, they continued doing what they knew would displease their parents and was sure to elicit a punitive or negative response. Apparently the stimulation and pleasure inherent in this mysterious and forbidden pastime were more compelling than the possible punishment.

Genital Exhibitionism

Eight women recalled episodes in which they exposed or wished to expose their genitals to others. Among the recollections:

> I remember when I was about seven showing myself to my brothers. We were in the playroom and I asked them if they wanted to look. I wanted to show myself to them. They didn't really say yes we want to see, but they didn't say no either—they sort of led me on so that I *had* to do it. The reason why I remember it is that my younger brother told my mother about it, and I expected her to be angry with me, but she sort of ignored the whole thing. Not that it was all right to have done it or that it was natural, but that it was something that children do, you just don't talk about it. I remember that my feeling about wanting to show them was that I knew they *wanted* to see, but they wouldn't admit it, so that left all the responsibility on me. [Gloria]

Sarah recalled that, at age four, she and another girl friend were playing in a backyard with several neighborhood boys and "leaning on the steps, sort of on our knees and elbows, with our pants down and the boys looking at our asses."

> Never to my knowedge did they look at the front, only at the backside. And it was the boys looking at the girls and not the girls looking at the boys. I don't think I felt fear —just a kind of excitement. But I hoped that this boy's

father wouldn't notice what we were doing and make a big fuss over it because his father's fuss would be crude.

Celeste, aged seven, and her two girl cousins sat on the window sill of a ground floor apartment and "all pulled down our pants and revealed ourselves to people passing—then we ran away from the window, squealing with excitement."

When she was about ten, Nancy recalled an incident at the window of a friend's apartment: "I remember so clearly pulling the shade down halfway, so no one could see my face, and exposing my vagina in the open window. It gave me a thrill. I felt I was terribly daring to expose my sexual parts."

Many of the memories of exhibitionism occurred during the so-called latency period of late childhood, which are not to be underestimated in the development of sexuality. All of the women in the study recalled overt sexual activities between the ages of seven and twelve. Hence, their accounts do not verify Freud's concept of a universal latency period.

Fantasies and Dreams

Only 7 women remembered sexual fantasies from their early lives,[7] but some of these were rich in emotional content.

Louise daydreamed about sex when she was a child, and the figures in her fantasies were "always the 'dirty' boys in my school." This differentiation was firm: there were no sexual associations attached to the "nice, 'clean' boys . . . only with the 'dirty' boys, and the 'dirty' ones I could fantasize myself with." Her fantasies at age seven or eight were limited to "boys touching me—since I didn't understand anything beyond this. It was at this time I really started to associate sex with being 'dirty.' It was always some kind of repulsive thing."

[7]Fantasy is not dealt with at any length in this book, primarily because little material was reported in this area. Most people tend to think that what constitues a fantasy is of a bizarre or illicit nature, with no relation to the experience of the moment. I believe this is why many women were unable to report any fantasies.

Several women reported fantasies about romance, kissing, movie heroes, etc. Amelia's fantasies, for example, went "only to the point of the asterisks. I never knew what happened after that."

Norma recalled:

> I used to go to the movies a lot when I was a kid and was always dreaming about being in the same situations that I would see portrayed in the movies. Once I saw this movie where some prisoners were making a prison break, and one guy held a guard in front of him and ran a knife up the guard's rear. This so impressed me that I imagined trying it on myself, which I did when I went home. I had a rubber knife and tried to do it with that. In the movie it had looked like it would be sexually stimulating, but I found it wasn't. I never did it again, but I used to think about it a lot anyway.

Frances's daydreams centered on the princes and princesses she had read about. She imagined herself to be an active character in whatever story she was currently reading—"but no kissing or anything because that was wrong and not nice."

Other women had fantasies that were somewhat more sophisticated. At age eight or nine, Amelia fantasied a "man lying on top of me, and I would experience a terrific amount of pleasure from this." And Virginia, at age ten, reported fantasies that included intercourse.

> . . . but in my sugary daydreams, I had to see myself married. I was quite sanctimonious about the whole deal. In fantasying being married, I would have the justification to say to this dream-husband, "Give me the life-giving fluid," or some such awful holy thing. Lord, how embarrassing!

Carol reports

> getting crushes on boys that were impossible for me to get near. I'd pick the greatest athlete or baseball player. I used to just get pleasure reading about them, their marvelous

athletic builds and where they lived and all. I knew all these very personal statistics about them. I used to save every bit of money I could get to go to baseball games about three times a week. I'd like to watch them walking around the park and thought they had such neat-looking asses, and such broad shoulders and they looked so handsome. I mean I was really living vicariously with all those men—all of them—in my fantasies.

Irene, the only woman in this study who experienced orgasm through fantasy, recalled:

The fantasies I had would take place in Turkish harems where I would see myself as being part of the harem and sort of at the disposal of a man who would come in and take all the responsibility. They weren't rape fantasies, but the man was in complete control and was very strong and I was sort of being taken. It wasn't the idea of my being taken and *forced* to do something I didn't want to do; it seemed to be something pleasurable for me. But I would never make any kind of move. [About age ten]

Then when I was older I would literally make up a figure out of a pillow and bedclothes and have a fantasy with this pretend person. But it was absolutely impossible for me to touch myself. For so long I didn't want myself, I wanted a man.

CONCLUSIONS

"From the time it is born, and probably before it is born," wrote Kinsey, "the infant comes into contact with some of the elements that enter into its later sexual experience."[8] Certainly the patterns that emerge from even this limited sample of thirty women demonstrate that sexual reactions and attitudes are not instinctive, by any means, but are rather the result of learned experiences. The kind of experiences a child has are

[8]Kinsey *et al., Sexual Behavior in the Human Female,* p. 644.

dependent upon a great variety of factors of environment and coincidence. Children accumulate information and attitudes through far more channels than the *spoken* word, and they learn of the ways of the world—certainly of *their* world—from myriad sources. Memories of early childhood that are associated with sexual feelings or knowledge are riddled with the words "frightening," "dirty," "dangerous," "mustn't," "don't," and "guilt." Guilt! Guilt! Guilt! Over and over again, these women were told that they "mustn't," that they "shouldn't," and that if they did, they were "bad."

But the human spirit is not easily broken. In the face of traumatic events in their childhoods, or unfortunate encounters in later adolescence, these women manifested an intense determination and drive for sexual survival.

CHAPTER THREE

EARLY SEX "EDUCATION"

The destruction of periods of sexual expression
before they come to full development diverts the
sexual cycle into solitude and opposition. In
states of opposition, excitement exists but it is
against the partner, not with him.
—Robert L. Dickenson, A *Thousand Marriages*

I don't ever remember not knowing about sex.
. . . I felt that I had *always* known. And yet I felt
I was the only one in the world who knew, and
I mustn't let anyone know about it.
—Erin

Children ask about sex in more ways than with
words.
—Dorothy Baruch, *New Ways in Sex Education*

> They are playing a game. They are playing at not
> playing a game. If I show them I see they are, I shall
> break the rules and they will punish me. I must play
> their game, of not seeing I see the game.
>
> —R.D. Laing, *Knots*

A PARTICULARLY STRIKING finding that emerged in the foregoing analysis of early sex memories was a violation of trust in the communication between parent and child. I call this "The Big Lie."

There seems to be an astonishing assumption in our culture that there are not two genders, but three: male, female, and parent. Upon having children, adults change suddenly from mortal human beings into parents—a superior species invested with every ideal characteristic: patience, altruism, sagacity, psychological sophistication, spiritual and philosophical wisdom. Some human beings believe complacently that they acquire these virtues simply by becoming parents; others, more modest, think that there must be something radically wrong with them because they do not possess these traits even though they are parents.

In either case, parents feel they must protect their special position and keep from their children the secret of their fallibility and mortality. By so doing, they create a primary distortion in their relationship to their children.

The communication system between parent and child is complex, operating on two levels. The conscious level, usually but not always expressed through words, is what the parents feel, or what they think they feel, and what they think they ought to be teaching their children. What the parents or other authorities actually feel often remains on the unconscious level. Sometimes what they feel and what they say are consonant, but often they are not.

What adults fail to recognize is that children pick up both communications, spoken and unspoken. They are tuned into both levels, as if listening to a two-track tape recorder. When there is a discrepancy between what parents feel and what they say about what they feel, the inarticulate but very real code of trust between them and their offspring is violated. Children assume that their parents are telling or showing their true feelings, and when this assumption is proved wrong, they are deeply disillusioned.

Especially in the area of sex, parents who have been no more wise or naïve than other adults suddenly feel that they must have the answer to every question about sex and sexuality. Although they are confused, perplexed, and probably as guilt-ridden, as anyone else, they feel that they must not let their dependent infants and children know.

Children, however, observe many contradictions in their parents' attitudes toward sex. Adults generally prohibit sexual talk and behavior, implying that it is dirty or sinful; yet they themselves engage in sex. A parent will say that sex is for grownups: "after marriage" or when you're "in love," it's beautiful and wonderful. Yet children hear fighting and sexual power struggles and expressions of distaste, and sense that perhaps after marriage it is not always beautiful and wonderful. This appears to be the zenith of the Big Lie and may account for the totally negative reaction of every woman in this study to the thought of their own parents' involvement in the act of sex.

Throughout the phenomenon described above is the rather pathetic need of parents to appear omniscient and omnipotent in order to obfuscate their own devastating feelings of anxiety and uncertainty. The pathos lies in the very human need to be needed (the child is dependent on the all-powerful parent) and, even more, in the human desire for immortality through one's children.

Children grow up and become parents, and relive the myth of the "third gender," on which they saw their parents act. Adults, who as children learned guilt and inhibition about sex, unless re-educated, will transmit these attitudes to their children. This complex process of countertransference—in which adults perpetuate the confusing and contradictory teachings that they inherited from their parents—is exacerbated by the widely accepted but mistaken idea that guilt and confusion learned in childhood will magically disappear in the experience of adult sexual relations.

KNOWING WITHOUT KNOWING

Seven women in the study felt they had acquired sexual knowledge and guilt prior to any specific experience of learning about sex. None of them could recall the exact source of this knowledge, nor could they link their guilt with a particular event. Nevertheless, this sense of implicit foreknowledge was strong, and feelings of what was and was not taboo emerged throughout the interviews.

Karen stated, "I had a feeling that I had lots of information, but I don't know where it ever came from. It's almost as though I had another life."

Both Gloria and Susan felt that they "already knew" how babies were born before they were told anything specific about procreation.

Carol was about nine when

> I was putting something away in my father's drawer and I saw some prophylactics. I didn't know what they were but I saw this box which didn't say what was in it, just said Trojan or something. And I knew—Ah ha! What is this box doing in here with all his socks? I didn't *dare* open it . . . but I really wanted to know what was in that box. I stopped in my tracks and thought . . . This has got something to do with *something,* but it's so dangerous, I won't even touch it.
>
> And then one time I was making their bed and I found a wet towel. And I thought—What in the hell is this wet towel doing in this bed in the morning? And I knew that I didn't even want to *touch* that towel. I didn't know

anything about ejaculations or anything, but I knew I didn't want to touch that towel. So I picked it up by the corner and threw it in the washer.

THE NEED FOR INNER CONTROLS—SEXUAL AND EMOTIONAL

Like adults, children often feel guilty not only about actions but also about *feelings*. Findings of this study suggest that feelings of sexuality can seem overwhelming to a young girl. Great inner strength is required to handle these emotions in what she perceives to be an acceptable way. When her parents —or other significant figures in her environment—do not teach her by their own example how to develop a sense of self and self-control, she must either develop it by herself or depend on the strength of others.

Seven women reported experiences in which they expressed, consciously and voluntarily, an intense need to control their own or others' sexual feelings. This need manifested itself in a repression of all sexual feelings from consciousness, or in a deliberate solicitation of parental control, with its implied threat of punishment, disapproval, or abandonment.

Marion recalled playing with several little boys outdoors. They had dug a hole in the ground and placed boards over the top of it.

> The boys then suggested that I take off my panties and allow them to look at me. I refused and the boys pushed me into the hole and would not allow me to get out. There was no air. It was dark and I felt as if the whole thing was going to cave in on me.

Marion felt that the boys' request was insulting to her. She added, however, that although she felt *compelled* to refuse them, she would have *liked* to comply. But she could not allow herself to risk taking responsibility for such an action. (As an adult, Marion has severe fears of suffocating which she relates directly to her experience with these boys: "When I get very anxious, I can't catch my breath.")

Feelings of *responsibility* often accompanied feelings of guilt. Three women realized that they had felt somehow at fault, even though they had not initiated, provoked, or even participated actively in a sexual incident. In psychoanalytic terms, these unheralded incidents represented, at the unconscious level, the prophetic fulfillment of sexual fantasies or wishes and were, therefore, experienced as a fearful manifestation of infantile omnipotence.

At age four, Erin happened to see her friend's father naked on his bed. She had a strong, persistent feeling that it was wrong for her to have seen this, stemming, she explained, from "not ever remembering seeing my own parents naked." The doors were always shut in her own home, "so somehow I felt I wasn't supposed to see a man naked."

In his comments, Rachel's father subtly disapproved of the physical "overdevelopment" of her ten-year-old friend. To Rachel's recall, these were the only sexual allusions he ever made. Yet she feared that her father might also disapprove of her own adolescent development, and therefore she chose to wear clothing that would in no way reveal her figure.

In connection with the following encounter, Rosemary experienced a feeling of shame, which she either learned or taught herself, in an effort to control her unacceptable feelings.

> When I was about eleven, something really awful happened! I had to go somewhere on a train with this man who was a friend of the family. I had a nightmare while asleep in bed on the train and woke up to find this man on top of me, rubbing himself around on me. I was shocked and he knew it, but he pretended that it hadn't really happened and said that I must have been having a bad dream. I couldn't bring myself to tell him that I *knew* what he was doing. I was ashamed to admit that I knew about things like that. And it is a shameful thing unless you are married.

When I asked her why she felt guilty about something she hadn't done, Rosemary responded,

> Even if you are raped, *you* are the one who feels ashamed. *You* are the one who has lost your virtue through your own fault. It seems we're taught this from early childhood.

It is significant that when authority figures in their environment did not exercise sufficient control, these girls developed their own inner controls.

Others reported excessively stimulating sexual contacts to some adult, who was then forced to exercise control. Before she was twelve, Victoria and her aunt's husband would go to the basement together, and he would rub himself against her. This continued for quite a long time before Victoria decided she didn't like it. "I finally told my mother. . . . I felt I couldn't control my own feelings. They were getting out of hand."

PARENTAL EVALUATIONS OF CHILDHOOD SEXUALITY—OVERESTIMATED AND UNDERESTIMATED

Adults both overestimate and underestimate what children know and feel about sex. Parents frequently assume that if children are not yet at the "talking" stage they have no awareness of personal, bodily, sexual experiences. Yet they also overestimate children's sexual awareness by assuming that all childhood sexuality has an adult goal.

Adults who underestimate the level of development of a child's sexuality may believe that until they have *told* their child about sex he will be sexually "innocent." Though they may be aware of having experienced sexual feelings in their *own* childhoods, some parents forget or ignore the fact that their children are also experiencing sexual feelings. For example, when Frances, the mother of two girls aged seven and eight, was asked to describe the sex education she had planned for them, she replied:

Oh, they've already *had* it. We started out almost from the very beginning with kittens. We had a male and a female kitten in the house, and we've had hamsters and white mice and all that sort of thing . . . The mice were having babies and the girls know all about this. How babies are born and what the male does and what the female does and the sperm and the vagina and the penis and all that sort of thing. *That's* already done. And they already know about menstruation. I think probably *later on, when they begin to have some of their own sexual feelings,* I will have to talk to them about that. [Italics mine]

Even after recalling her own sexual feelings and memories from the age of five, the first of which involved being discovered *and* punished by her mother, Frances still believed that her seven- and eight-year-old daughters had not yet experienced any of "their own sexual feelings." This mother, like many others, conscientiously taught her children factual sexual information but seriously underestimated all the other ways in which they had learned and were learning about sex and human beings.

On the other hand, some parents tend to *overestimate* the extent of their child's sexual curiosity. Many assume that once the child has an awareness of sexual matters, he or she will desire adult sexual experiences: they project onto the child the feelings that *they* would have in a similar situation. Instead, the child desires the love-sex feelings commensurate with his or her development, expressed in closeness, fondling, "being special," etc.

Fathers, for example, may feel appalled or frightened when they become aware of sexual feelings toward their daughters. Such sexual feelings seem to be quite natural, but some fathers feel so frightened that they will have to act on them if they admit them that they force themselves to suppress the feelings. If the father's fear or guilt is great enough, it may emerge as anger directed toward the child. The child, naturally, becomes confused and crushed by this expression of parental rejection.

A little girl who crawls onto her father's lap to be cuddled is expressing a sensual desire and need; usually this need is satisfied by her father's physical warmth and acceptance of her little-girl sexuality. If the father becomes frightened and angrily pushes the child away, she may learn a grim and unforgettable lesson about men and women and sex. To the frightened and misunderstanding father, the child's sexual desire has one and *only* one meaning and means of satisfaction: the adult meaning and means—sexual intercourse. Therefore, the child's action seems to the parent precocious and unacceptable.

Carol's father, because of the guilt his strong attraction to his daughter caused him, forbade her to wear lipstick, tight trousers, or anything that would be sexually arousing to him.

Other parents, however, respond to their children's sexuality not with fear and repression but with their own (adult) sexual responses. Several women in the study recalled feeling that their fathers were extremely seductive toward them as little girls. Nancy did not label her father's actions as a seduction attempt, but she recounted an episode in connection with her father bathing her at about age three. As he washed her genitals, he said playfully to her, "Whose is that? Is it Daddy's? It belongs to Daddy, doesn't it?" She remembered answering uneasily, "Yes." As she talked about this incident, Nancy could not explain exactly what it was that disturbed her about her father's questions, but she knew that she always wondered why he asked in "that way."

Marion sensed that her father's relationship with her had certain seductive connotations. He was very affectionate, danced with her a great deal, and manifested more feelings of closeness to her than to her other sisters—even than to her mother. Marion perceived her mother's awareness and resentment of this closeness, which "always made me nervous."

And Irene recalls:

When I was about ten, I started to develop—physically, you know, breasts and all. My father—not my mother—always used to take me to the doctor. He would stay with me when I was examined . . . I objected to this strongly. Once the doctor had to come to the house for some reason, and I had to get undressed, and my father stayed in the room. I can remember him looking at the doctor and smiling, and I got a terrible feeling from it—a feeling of some kind of danger in the way they smiled at each other. And it seemed wrong. Not how I would expect a father to smile. It is very upsetting even now when I think of it. It really gave me a very bad feeling—I don't know, about men and the way they look at women. It seemed dirty, not even sexy. I just had the feeling there was something wrong.

Another parental anxiety has to do with feelings of responsibility for their children's sexual behavior: "I'm afraid to tell my daughter it's all right for her to masturbate because if I do, she'll do it all the time." This mother assumes that the child would exercise no self-control or judgment if her mother openly accepted her self-exploration. Conversely, she thinks that if she refrains, through her silence, from giving permission to her daughter, the child will *not* masturbate.

SOURCES OF SEX INFORMATION

Ten of the women in this study first learned about sex from their parents, 10 from other children, 4 from adults who were not their parents, 3 from observation (overseeing or overhearing), and 3 from books and pamphlets. Exactly what they learned, and how they fitted this new knowledge into their conceptions of themselves, along with all the other bits and pieces of information they had picked up from their families and environments throughout their early lives, is material for another book—or perhaps thirty books.

When Amelia was about four years old her parents took her to the zoo

> and they told me that the stork brought babies. I wanted a brother and the next year when we went to the zoo, I would have nothing to do with the stork because I was furious that he hadn't come through. Then when I was about eleven, my mother took me aside—I think she really wanted to tell me about menstruation, but she proceeded to give me the whole package and the package consisted of: When a man and a woman are married, they pray together and God plants the seed. This was idiotic. I had already learned from my girl friend or somebody else that they did something more than pray . . . In addition to which, my family were atheists!

Virginia recalled:

> When I was about ten, some little girl gave me one of these regular books they give children. She said, "My mother gave it to me to read, maybe your mother should give you one." I looked at it, and it was talking about insects, so I went home and told mother that Jean had a little book and I should have one, too. And my mother said, "Well, it takes nine months to have a baby"—and she left the room and that's the only conversation we ever had about it in my entire life.

Roxanne remembered:

> My best girl friend asked me one day when I was eleven if I knew what they called it when people have babies and when they get together and everything. I said no and she said, "It's called rape." So we went to the dictionary and it said "attack." And I thought, God, this is *something*, but I did not understand what intercourse *was*. I knew we were built differently and that a man must get inside a woman, but I couldn't see how because I didn't understand the idea of erections. I didn't know what it was, and I didn't find out for many years after that, when I was fifteen. I knew the sperm was there, and I said, what is it?

I used to think it was urine. That was all I could figure, so I said to myself, Well, that's that; I can't see doing *that*.

And Barbara made the connection between sex and having babies when she

read some books my mother had on child development, but I just couldn't figure out where the embryo came from. I know when I was thirteen a boy wanted to take me walking in the woods, and I wouldn't go because I was afraid I would come back pregnant.

When Helen was eight her sister told her that their

aunt had said that if you kiss a boy, you'll have a baby. Then sometime in my teens, my mother told me that marriage was the end of all lovemaking and I just couldn't believe her. I thought it *couldn't* be like that, there *had* to be more to it.

Such confusions and misconceptions were among the milder responses to the confusing and inadequate information these children received about sex. Many of the women, sensing the anxiety and fear inherent in their parents' attitudes about sex, found the idea of sexual intercourse to be "terrible" or "revolting," and every woman in the study found the idea of intercourse between her own parents distressing.

Carol's mother showed her a book on the birth process, and Carol was left with the feeling that

the whole thing was repulsive. She kept pointing out all these diagrams and all those things about how the egg was here and the sperm was there—all that shit! I finally must have asked about *how* they got together because she wasn't explaining that. I must have asked her that question and I think even have started to cry. She finally did tell me in that conversation what it was all about. You go to bed and take off your clothes and the man puts himself inside you and then out comes this sperm. Wow! I thought that was just terrible. I thought the whole thing was very dirty, and I thought nobody would ever catch me dead doing that, taking off my clothes and fooling around with all this. You know, here's where the man goes to the bathroom and here's where's where the lady goes to the bathroom and they both start rubbing around, and oh, it's filthy, you know! I thought: I can't think of a worse thing to do—the mess!

And then I think I tried to forget about it for a while. I did, I just tried to push the whole thing out of my head. I wouldn't even talk about it with my girl friend because I didn't want to remember how it happened.

Gloria's first knowledge also came from a book given to her by her mother.

There was no place in that book—or any other that I ever read, for that matter—that made any connection between babies and the sexual act and love. Later, when one of my girl friends told me about it, my mother turned to me, with a look of horror on her face and yelled, "Who told you about that!" Somehow I had hoped that she would react differently and tell me that sex was fun, or something nice like that. But all she did was confirm the horror by the way she handled it.

REACTIONS TO AWARENESS OF PARENTAL INTERCOURSE

One response is so consistently and intensely negative that its significance cannot be ignored—either as a symptomatic result of one particular kind of sexual indoctrination or as one cause of the distressing sexual responses so commonly reported by the women. Answers to the questions about overseeing or overhearing (in fantasy or fact) their parents in the act of sexual intercourse were *always* expressed in terms of shock, indignation, disgust, revulsion, anger, and disbelief. This reaction even took place when the woman recalled the incident where she first *learned* about the act of intercourse, and made an immediate association in fantasy to her parents' participation in such an act. In the interviews with these thirty women, there was not one exception to this reaction. (For many women, the feeling of revulsion or disbelief was as strong in adulthood as it had been in childhood.)

I believe that this reaction arose from the early learned guilt feeling that parental intercourse represented the acme of the "Big Lie": the forbidding parents were themselves discovered engaging in the most forbidden act.

Rachel learned about intercourse from

> a girl at school, when I was seven . . . she said that's what they did to get babies. I immediately realized that my mother and father must have *done* this several times—since they'd had several babies—and for weeks I simply could not even look at them. I felt horrified and disgusted and somehow as though they had been lying to me!

And after Rebecca was provided with information about intercourse and pregnancy by a nurse at camp, she began to notice when her parents' door was closed, and to think, "Parents weren't *supposed* to do that dirty thing." She then made an interesting slip of the tongue: "Parents were supposed to be a paradox [*sic*] of virtue and here they were doing something else."

Carol recalled:

> I used to overhear my parents in their bedroom—they often seemed like they were laughing and joking and having fun. Now I know that I *really* realized that they were doing something else—that they were having sex—but I could never admit that to myself. That thought was so shocking and disgusting to me that I would really cry when I did think of it.

Interestingly enough, Carol had no difficulties in attributing pleasant, romantic associations to the sexual relations of a favorite aunt and uncle:

With them I would think it was nice and marvelous, how they were having babies all the time, and in fact I could even experience a little jealousy because my uncle seemed so much in love with his wife.

Cathleen, who slept in her parents' bedroom until she was three, reported:

I have feelings of having seen them doing something at night which always looked violent to me. My mother's face always seemed to have in it a look of pain, and I recall wondering why my father was doing that to her? Why was he making her feel so terrible?

It is interesting to note that in almost all these responses the women not only expressed distress, but also mentioned that they identified mainly with their mothers. The young woman apparently always saw herself in the place of the mother and experienced the feelings that she imagined her mother felt, or that, perhaps, she thought her mother *should* feel.

Amelia was in her teens when

I was with a friend of my mother's whom I liked and could talk to. I kind of trusted her, and she talked rather decently about it. Sort of the way books say you should talk to a teen-ager. How when you're really very much in love, it's a very beautiful thing, and so on. She made it real and human, and she was willing to talk a little bit about how she felt, so this became something believable and pleasurable and brought it to a more normal level than anything I had ever heard.

CONCLUSIONS

Among the parents of the women in this study, were three professionals in fields with specific training and education for the communication of necessary factual biological information. They were a physician, a nurse, and a high-school health teacher. The societal trend has been to look to members of such professions to disseminate sexual instruction, supplementing or supplanting that provided (or omitted) by the parents. Yet Louise, whose father was a physician, was never given adequate sexual information: she was never told that sex might be pleasurable and felt dominated by the need to retain her virginity so as "not to lose respect." She was married for fifteen years before ever experiencing orgasm—from any source whatsoever.

In view of the fact that one of her parents is a specialist in the field of physical hygiene, Jane's knowledge and understanding was remarkably meager.

> When I found out about intercourse, I was tremendously shocked. I asked a girl friend, and she told me that the man put his thing into the woman's thing. It's not hard to talk about it now, just a little embarrassing. She wasn't a crude girl, so it was fairly childish and yet . . . I had never seen a kitten born or anything like that, and I didn't really know how babies pop out. My mother had said that they were in the stomach, and I remember trying to figure out where the hell they came out, and I just figured you cut open the stomach or something, and you brought it out. Never occurred to me where it *really* came from.

If parents who have had professional advantages and are looked to by society as sources of information can be thus delinquent, misguided, and misguiding in handling their own children's sexual education, what competence can be expected of their less advantaged contemporaries in the same emotionally charged atmosphere?

These early childhood and adolescent impressions of sexual relationships have profound and far-reaching effects. Dr. Eustace Chesser's study of women[1] found a distinct correlation between the degree of sexual satisfaction in marriage and early impressions of sex: among those women who found pleasure in intercourse, 67 percent had received the impression that sex

[1] Eustace Chesser, *Women,* p. 131.

was pleasant from their parents, while 32 percent got the impression that sex was unpleasant. Those whose parents had given them the impression that sex was unpleasant showed even more dissatisfaction with sex than those whose parents had not discussed sex at all—i.e., negative teaching seems to have been more harmful than none at all.

Poorly prepared emotionally and factually for their incipient womanhood, the thirty girls now enter adolescence and face their first menstrual experiences.

CHAPTER FOUR

ADOLESCENCE: THE MENARCHE AND RELATED EXPERIENCES

A girl who experiences this glandular process ... the menses ... is automatically an adolescent ... whether she has been well or badly informed about its nature.

—The French Institute of Public Opinion,
*Patterns of Sex and Love: A Study of
the French Woman and Her Morals*

My older sister had told me that this was "coming of age" and meant being a woman. When it happened I just *shrieked* with joy!

—Sarah

Nobody ever told me anything at all. It first happened while I was away at summer camp and when the period first began I thought I was bleeding to death.

—Irene

Conception and birth are as stubborn conditions as death itself. Coming to terms with the rhythms of women's lives means coming to terms with life itself.

—Margaret Mead, *Male And Female*

MENSTRUATION was selected as the area of experience most representative of the period designated in the interview guide as Puberty and Early Adolescence.

The time in a woman's life when she is capable of bearing children is bracketed by two distinct but related biological events, the menarche (the onset of menstruation) and the menopause.[1] Although there is often a considerable lag between the menarche and the development of a regular menstrual cycle, and sometimes between the menarche and the ability to conceive, the appearance of the first menses is generally considered to be the female's physiological introduction to adolescence or early womanhood. The menarche is such a well-defined physical signal of a female's sexual maturity that, for better or worse, it stands out clearly in her memory.

To date, no research into female sexuality has reported any information on individual women's feelings and attitudes about the menarche. The data usually reported are the age of onset and the source of information regarding menstruation prior to its onset. The psychological literature about menstruation and its subjective meaning to women is highly abstract, usually written from a narrow, Freudian perspective. Freud believed that the experience of the menarche is a "bloody trauma" that vividly and relentlessly reminds the female of her "castration" and "loss." Others who share this view, Therese Benedek and Helene Deutsch, have written:

> Before the onset of the menstrual flow, dreams and fantasies commonly express, consciously or unconsciously, that

[1]Menopause is not discussed here because none of the women interviewed had yet experienced it.

menstruation is identical with castration, that bleeding is the external evidence that woman has lost the penis. We find that this rebellion against femininity often expresses the fact that the mother has perpetuated this punishment.[2]

. . . the first genital bleeding mobilizes psychic reactions [in girls] so numerous and varied . . . [for] painful, bloody, cruel, and threatening are these manifestations of femininity in relation to her fantasy life. Psychoanalytic observations were the first to reveal the relation between the psychologic reactions to the first menstruation and the genital trauma [female castration complex].[3]

I would suggest that, on the contrary, a female's emotional reaction to the phenomenon of menstruation is a complex learned response—like other sexual responses–and that girls differ greatly in their expectations and behavior related to initial menstruation. In a sense, a girl's entire life up to this point has been a preparation for the menarche. She has learned attitudes and responses to her body and her mother (her gender model), as well as to her overall social status, which profoundly affect the initial menstrual experience and everything associated with it.

A strictly Freudian interpretation of the psychological significance of the menarche would yield a law of human female behavior that is neither valid nor universal. The subjective reactions of individual women to sexual identity in general, and to menstrual experiences in particular, are, in my opinion, better explained by an evaluation of the feelings and attitudes communicated to them by significant family members (especially the mother) and cultural values.

To test the validity of these observations, I asked each woman about the following: age at onset of menses; knowledge about menstruation prior to onset; source of prior knowledge; preparedness—expectations and feelings about the event;

[2]Therese Benedek, *Studies in Psychosomatic Medicine: Psychosexual Functions in Women*, p. 92.
[3]Helen Deutsch, *The Psychology of Women*, Vol. I, p. 50.

reactions to the event; explicit or implicit reactions of the mother and father; knowledge of the connection between menstruation and pregnancy at the time of the menarche; association of menstruation with physical injury. I asked what the menarche meant to each woman, what her subsequent attitudes were about femininity and sexuality in relation to menstruation, and what her preference was as an adult on engaging in sexual intercourse during the menstrual period.

As an example of the women's responses, one account of a menstrual experience is quoted here in full:

> I first learned about menstruation when my mother brought my sister *her* first box of Kotex. The box was wrapped in pretty paper and, since I and my sister had been asking my mother for a playsuit, I thought she had bought my sister one and not me. Everything was sort of mysterious because my mother wouldn't tell me what was in the box. I thought she was trying to spare my feelings because she couldn't afford to get us each one. I kept asking and asking her, and she finally told me in a very kind way that it wasn't a playsuit, but something that my sister needed now that I didn't. I don't remember how far she went into what menstruation was all about, but she did impress upon me that it was something physical that happened to girls when they got older. I must have been about eight at the time, and I very much wanted to "get older'" after she told me all this. My sister wasn't very close to me, and my mother no longer menstruated herself.
>
> I began menstruating at about eleven or twelve. I went to the bathroom one day at school and noticed some dark spots on my underpants. I thought at first that I hadn't cleaned myself well enough. When the spots reappeared even after I had changed underpants I realized that *this* was it—I was menstruating! It seemed to take me a day or so, I guess, to connect the spots on my clothing with what my mother had told me about "getting older," and then I was very happy and didn't feel any fear at all, just joy that I was menstruating—old enough at last. I told my mother, and she got me a belt and napkins. I can't remem-

ber any particular reaction on her part. She was cool about sex and nudity and all that. I didn't have any cramps, and I wasn't embarrassed about it at all. I was just glad that it hadn't happened to me the way it did to some girls I'd heard of who had their first period in school, and they were horribly embarrassed by it because it showed through their clothes. [Zoe]

The average age of the onset of menstruation for the 30 women in this study was 12.4 years; 28 reported their onset between twelve and thirteen years of age. The youngest age reported was eleven years [Rachel] and the oldest fifteen [Carol]. It may be significant that both of these women were "loners" throughout their childhood: they had little sexual *activity* during childhood but an intense romantic-fantasy life and reported highly satisfying sexual lives in their adulthood. One might conjecture that the effects on their personalities of their extreme ages at onset of menstruation might have been a factor in isolating them from their peers; also, as a result of their status they were not affected by the social standards maintained by their peer groups. Consequently, they may have had fewer of the same attitudes and ideas, negative or positive.

It is interesting to note that Rachel, who began menstruating at the earliest age, responded positively while Carol, who started at the latest age, reacted negatively. Rachel, who learned from the girls at school, recounted:

Menstruating to me was an event of a thrilling and unique nature because, you see, I realize now that it was perhaps the first time in my life that I really had the feeling of being just like other girls, and especially girls of my own age. Up to then, I had felt different in every possible way—nothing about me seemed to belong—I didn't dress like other girls, my background was different, my upbringing was different, my school experiences were different, but here finally in this one way I could be, and was, like all the other girls, and it was thrilling to feel that I "belonged."

Carol, who had prior information about menstruation, reported highly negative feelings about the onset, which corresponded closely to her general attitude about being a female.

> Mother gave me the information once, and that was all. When it happened, I was disgusted and thought, I was getting by without it this long, and now I'm stuck with it for the next many years.

REACTIONS TO ONSET: PRIOR KNOWLEDGE AND QUALITY OF PREPARATION

According to their own reports, 13 women were pleased by the menarche and 11 were displeased. Six expressed no specific feelings of either pleasure or displeasure.

Among the responses to the experience that women considered to be positive were feelings of belonging, pride, or outright delight at the onset of this variously, and often inadequately, heralded event.

> [I] . . . felt like a million dollars . . . [Nancy]

> The *first* feeling of . . . being glad I was a girl . . . I was so proud. [Victoria]

> I felt great—like one of the girls. And I was entranced by the physical change in myself and very vain and self-centered about it all. [Della]

Responses evaluated as negative included the following:

> All I knew was that I was bleeding and it was something that was emotional and disastrous, and I don't know, I also got the feeling that this, too, was my *fault*. [Frances]

> The whole thing was miserable for me . . . [my mother] made it seem so ugly and messy and dirty. [Marion]

Of the 13 women who expressed positive feelings at the onset of their menses, all had received previous information about this phenomenon. Of those expressing negative feelings, seven had prior knowledge and four did not. All 6 with no strong feelings of any specific kind had previous knowledge. Some preparation or education is clearly better than none at all, but the quality and source of that preparation appear to be extremely significant.

Some typical reactions of the women who had previous knowledge and responded positively were:

> I sent away to the Kotex company when I noticed my breasts beginning to develop . . . I thought I'd probably have my period soon . . . When I began to menstruate, I was actually very excited and there was nothing bothersome or scary about it, either physically or emotionally. [Barbara]

> I learned about it from girls at school, and while I didn't have the least idea *what* it all meant, it did seem something to look forward to . . . I felt it was going to make me kind of grown-up and like all the other girls. No one told me that it would be painful or anything like that—and it wasn't. [Roxanne]

Of the 11 women who responded negatively to the onset of their menses, some comments of the 7 who had previous knowledge were:

> On the day it happened, I phoned Mother, and she said matter-of-factly, "Well, you know what to do about it." I felt guilt and embarrassment about it happening because I thought it was connected somehow with my masturbating. I wouldn't tell anybody else about it for almost a year, I just didn't claim it. [Norma]

> I learned about menstruation when I was at camp through some lectures from the counselor. When I first menstruated, I felt worried and anxious for many months. I kept wondering, "Will the boys know about it, will it show through my dress, was it right or wrong?" . . . The only thing I feel now is that whatever feelings I had about menstruation, it connected up in my mind with sex and

naughtiness and hiding and feelings of worry and concern
. . . and maybe even shame. [Rebecca]

As one might anticipate, girls with no prior information
about menstruation were frightened by the mysterious and
uncontrollable flow of what appeared to be their blood, with
its connotations of intimacy and vitality. Some comments by
the four women who had no previous knowledge were:

It was just terrible—I thought I was having an appendici-
tis attack! [Donna]

No one had told me *anything!* My girl friend helped me
out with pads and a belt and told me not to be scared, but
I couldn't help it. For a long time after it began, it seemed
like my period, my blood, was somehow connected with
wounds and being terribly sick. I didn't even tell my
mother that I had started until months and months later.
I was afraid that she'd be angry with me because I'd done
something wrong again. [Irene]

I didn't know a thing about it until my mother one day
said accusingly, "There's blood on your panties!" Then
she proceeded to tell me I was menstruating and what that
was. The whole thing was miserable for me—she didn't
use pads, but made her own with pieces of cloth that had
to be washed and used again and again. She made it seem
so ugly and messy and dirty. [Marion]

It was a shock to me when it happened! I went home from
school and told my mother and grandmother and there
was a tremendous flurrying and scurrying around the
house, and finally Mother pulled out this old sanitary belt
that she had in a drawer and gave it to me. Somehow, in
the midst of all this uproar, she informed me that it would
happen every month. That's all. That's *all* she said! She
never told me what it was or why it was happening; all I
knew was that I was bleeding and it was something that
was emotional and disastrous, although exciting in a scary
way—and certainly my fault! [Frances]

SOURCES OF INITIAL KNOWLEDGE

Although 26 (nearly 87 percent) of the women received information about menstruation at some time prior to their first menstrual period, it was often neither accurate nor complete. The other 4 women had no clue that something extraordinary was about to happen.

Knowledge about the menarche came from the following sources (singly or in combination): 13 women learned of menstruation from their mothers or step-mothers; 4 from other female family members; 7 from girl friends; 3 from books; and the remaining 2 from miscellaneous sources, such as camp counselors, physicians, and other adults.

In the following comments the sources of information have been italicized.

> My *mother* gave me the information about menstruation once and tried to be very matter-of-fact about it when it finally happened. I told her about it . . . and she got me pads and a belt, but everything was always whisked away quickly like it was a big secret or maybe should be denied somehow. [Carol]

> My *mother* told me about it in her martyr-like way, saying, "You feel like the bottom is dropping out of you, but it's all right." Still, I was very excited about it and looking forward to it, I remember. [Susan]

> My *mother* had had a great scare with *her* first period, and therefore she explained the process carefully so that I felt that there should be no fears, that there was nothing scary here. [Karen]

> I learned about menstruation from the *girls* that I played with. Everything about sex in our house was sort of undercover. [Sarah]

> My *aunt* was the one who told me about menstruation. She told me that she wanted me to know about it before it happened so I wouldn't be as frightened as she had been

when it happened to her. She told me that she hadn't know anything about it, and one day was terrified to see blood running down her legs. It was really good of her to want to protect *me* from having *her* bad experiences. [Virginia]

The first I heard about it was at camp. They had a *woman doctor* there, and I asked her why my face was breaking out so much. She told me that perhaps it was because the "period was imminent." I think I also heard *other girls* talking about "the bleeding," but I never really knew what they were talking about. [Grace]

The only way I ever learned anything about menstruation was through *books* I got out of the library and *Parents' Magazine.* Mother never gave me any information, and I would have been scared to ask her about anything like that. Everything I read kept saying that menstruation was normal, normal—I remember wondering why, if it was so normal, they had to keep saying it over and over again. And another thing the books said was that to have cramps was normal, too. Well, I never had any cramps, and I used to wonder if I was normal since I didn't. [Cathleen]

In only two cases was there a positive correlation between the *source* of the original knowledge and the pleasant or unpleasant experience that resulted. All 3 women who got their information through *books* had pleasant associations with the onset of menses. A possible relationship between source and reaction is the communication of either anxiety or acceptance. Since most books with information on menstruation are largely factual, the anxiety communicated in a person-to-person contact may be absent.

The majority of the 13 women whose mothers served as the sole informants also had pleasant associations with the menarche experience. Thus, regardless of the fact content and validity of the information imparted by the mother to the daughter (no woman in the study had received accurate or complete information prior to onset), *more women than not benefited when the mother was the giver* of information. In no other single or combined information category does this relationship occur. What was significant here was the human exchange in an area of experience common to all women. Perhaps the implicit message from mother to daughter was, "We are both female."

> My mother is the one who told me about menstruation. She told me that you have it monthly and bleed. This was not a frightening thing to me . . . It was the only good thing that she ever did for me, the way she told me about this. [Louise]

From some of the previous comments, it would appear that mothers and other adult female informants were more anxious and nervous about menstruation than their daughters. Erin, for example, who had learned about menstruation from girls at school and from books, felt "thrilled when it happened." She didn't tell her mother at first because her family had always acted "secretive" about menstruation, and everything else sexual. Her association with her mother and menstruation was always "dirty and messy . . . leaving soiled sanitary pads around the bathroom," and she had a fiercely negative reaction to her mother's use of the word "minstruate." She soon began to use Tampax, and dissociated the "whole thing from anything to do with Mother."

Such comments suggest a generational change of cultural attitudes: perhaps the mothers did not receive adequate instruction from their own mothers, and their consequent anxiety and lack of knowledge were in turn passed on to their daughters. These women, however, had the advantage of access to literature on the subject, which apparently helped to alleviate some of the anxiety.

Interestingly, 9 women recalled feeling very angry or disappointed with their mothers for not having treated the menarche as an event for celebration. Gloria observed that although she herself had looked forward to her menstrual period, it had begun on the first day she was to have appeared in a school play and her mother had "grumbled that it certainly was an inconvenient time for this to be happening!" Sara was

> very angry with my mother for not making more of a fuss. There was a family across the way, and when *their* daughter got her menstrual period, the mother would slap the face—which is an old Jewish custom—and for some reason, that impressed me as concern in this momentous time, and my mother simply took it for granted.

The narratives are strikingly barren of references to father's reactions, and no father or other male was cited as a source of information about menstruation. Only 2 women had any memory of their fathers' reaction to their menarche, and both were positive.

> I was so glad when it happened. It made me more like the other girls in school. When I told my mother that I had begun to menstruate, she acted matter-of-fact, blah. But my father acted real pleased and said something about being a woman now. [Jane]

To the above, I should like to add an observation related to the experience of at least 9 women who participated in this research and many, many more whom I have counseled. As "father favorites," they recall their fathers to have been quite loving and attentive during childhood: "My father would play games with me"; "I remember him taking me places on Sundays and weekends"; "He'd let me sit on his lap a lot," etc. Then, in one way or another, they all were aware that "something changed" in their father's behavior toward them. When asked at what age this change took place, they would answer invariably: "Oh I don't know—maybe eleven, twelve, thirteen —something like that." Always it was at the approximate time of the onset of menstruation, when the "little girl" became a "young girl" or "young lady," with all its attendant connotations.

My interpretation of this phenomenon (and it is conjecture, to be sure, for I didn't query the fathers) is that, noticing their daughter's development, the fathers became concerned about their feelings for these girls. A father responds to these "unacceptable" sensual feelings for his daughter with anxiety and denial, precisely at the moment when she is beginning to be aware of her own sexuality, with its concomitant conflicts and fears.

The difficulty created in this interaction is that the girl—up to this point accepted, now suddenly rejected—blames herself for the change that has occurred. "My father used to love me; now he doesn't. I must have done something wrong. Something changed about me—something bad. It causes him to feel very uncomfortable, and he now wants to push me away." While she does not understand the nature of the change in her father's attitude (and, most likely, neither does he), she associates the loss of a valuable relationship with her physiological change from child female to adult female. This factor may contribute to the difficulties many women have in accepting themselves as mature females. This would be another instance in which the adult (father), unable to assume responsibility for feelings that are socially unacceptable, causes the child (by default) to accept the blame.

PREGNANCY ASSOCIATIONS WITH THE MENARCHE

In order to evaluate the quality of the information the women received, I asked questions to discover if, at the time of the menarche, they understood the biological function of menstruation—that is, that menstruation was part of the physiological process of ovulation and that the function of ovulation was procreation. Did they in any way associate pregnancy with menstruation at the time of menarche?

No woman fully understood the meaning of menstruation, even if she felt "adequately prepared"; none received an explanation of its actual function and relation to ovulation and pregnancy. Seven women did not learn of the biological or physiological function of menstruation until early adulthood, and 3 did not understand it until they actually became pregnant.

> I never knew what the actual physiological process of menstruation was, and its actual connection with pregnancy until—I'm embarrassed to admit it—only five or six years ago, when I was about thirty-five . . . [Rachel]

(It is important to remember that all subjects in this study were highly educated women—one requirement for participation being a minimum of high-school education, while the majority of subjects had bachelor's degrees, master's degrees, or doctorates.)

Often in the preparation for menstruation, the dangers of pregnancy were stressed, but not explained. Even those who received oblique warnings to be "careful" about boys "from now on" were not given any clear physiological exposition of the menstrual-ovulatory cycle. The consequent misapprehensions, such as "If you go to bed with a man, you get a baby," or the assumption that one could get pregnant "even from sitting on a boy's lap," were common. As a result of these warnings and accompanying misinformation, many women associated pregnancy with "danger," "threat," "trouble," and some kind of "mysterious, uncontrollable phenomena."

> I don't think I knew about the relationship between menstruation, ovulation, and pregnancy at that time although I learned all about it a short time later, through reading. Even then it really wasn't brought home to me, the idea that *I* could get pregnant now that I had begun to menstruate—probably because I had already learned that nice girls don't get pregnant until they get married. Yet my sister got pregnant at sixteen and had to have an abortion. [Zoe]

> Nothing was ever really explained to me. Everyone seemed to ignore the whole thing [menstruation]. Just my sister used to make sneaky remarks like, "You better be

careful now not to kiss boys," and I guess I somehow connected menstruating with calamities like "getting in trouble." [Sarah]

Louise, who made the unusual comment that offering her menstrual information was "the only good thing my mother ever did for me," went on to say that, until the last one or two years, she had always experienced cramps with her monthly period—despite the fact that she had given birth to three children. She added, unsolicitedly, that her third pregnancy was unexpected, "I didn't even know I was pregnant until I was in about the third or fourth month." When I asked if she hadn't wondered about not menstruating for those several months, she replied, "Who thinks about menstruating when you don't enjoy sex? When you don't enjoy sex, I think you don't even think about any of the *results* of sex either."

PHYSICAL INJURY ASSOCIATIONS TO THE MENARCHE

About 37 percent of the women made some association during the interviews between the menarche and physical injury. This percentage represents 11 women, 10 of whom (including the 4 who were completely unprepared) evaluated the menarche as negative. Typical of their experience is the following statement:

Even though I didn't ask her, my mother gave me some information before it happened about menstruation along with some other "facts of life." It was all mixed up and my girl friend added to the confusion by telling me that when you menstruate, you begin to bleed and if you don't put on a girdle, you'll bleed to death. [Amelia]

Three women associated *both* pregnancy and physical injury with the menarche, and this constellation of feelings, carried over into adult life, expressed itself in intense fears of pregnancy.

INTERCOURSE PREFERENCE DURING THE MENSTRUAL PERIOD

Many women are aware of an increase in their sexual desires around the time of the menses, the feelings sometimes peaking prior to the period, sometimes during the period, and sometimes following it. Some women describe this increased sexual desire as continuous throughout the menstrual period, as well as just before and just after. In the present sample, 11 women (about 37 percent) expressed a preference for engaging in intercourse during menstruation, primarily because they believed that menstruation freed them from the necessity of contraceptives (although women have been known to conceive at the end of a period, due to early ovulation and sperm longevity). The majority of women (19) expressed feelings that ranged from neutral to disinterest to distaste.

Following are comments from some of the 11 women who expressed actual liking (preference) for sexual relations during menstruation:

> About sex during my period—well, I don't mind it if my husband doesn't mind. In fact, I rather like it . . . it's fine with me. Terrific, in some ways, because there are no worries about getting pregnant; also, I find that I feel strong sexual feelings in all phases of the menstrual period —that is, before, during, and after—although the strongest are before and during, and the least strong right after. [Rachel]

> I really like it then! I think I feel sexier then than at any other time of the month. But I wonder about it because I know that in some places women were considered "unfit" at that time. [Jane]

Twelve of the women expressed neutral feelings about intercourse during menstruation.

> I don't mind intercourse during menstruation, so long as it doesn't bother my husband—and he doesn't seem to mind. [Amelia]

A doctor taught me to use a diaphragm to lessen the excess flow during the early days, so now I don't find it so much of a mess. [Carol]

I don't know how I feel about it. I always thought that it wasn't good for a woman at that time because the flow comes from a sloughing off of the inner lining of the womb, and this always seemed like something rotting inside me. Also, you can get an infection at that time. [Gloria]

One woman had never had intercourse while menstruating because she believed it to be impossible, and 6 of the women definitely disliked having relations during their menstrual period.

I'm not crazy about it at that time—it's a messy, dirty time of the month with blood and all that and I'd rather not. [Rosemary]

I don't like it, and my husband doesn't either. It's messy and uncomfortable besides being dangerous for the man— he could get some kind of infection, you know. [Helen]

Nineteen of the 30 women, when discussing this topic, referred to menstruation as being in some way distasteful and troublesome, using repeatedly the description "messy." Yet 5 of them chose to engage in intercourse during their period despite the messiness. It seems that some combination of experience, partner's responses, personal habits, and proper information alleviates anxieties about the results and outcome of such relations.

MENARCHE EXPERIENCE PROFILE

Using the modal frequency (the highest number of like responses) as an index to the usual experiences and feelings surrounding menstruation, the following description is a profile of the "typical" subject:

She was twelve years, three months old at the onset of menses. She had some prior knowledge of the phenomenon, from her mother. Her expectation reactions were evaluated as positive by the researcher: she associated her first menses with neither physical harm nor pregnancy and was pleased at the onset. Her mother expressed no strong feelings of pleasure or displeasure at the onset verbally or otherwise and her father was silent. She expressed no preference for or against sexual intercourse during her menstrual periods.

CONCLUSIONS

Since the beginning of history, Dr. Katharina Dalton reminds us, human beings have been puzzled by menstruation. Month after month, women lost blood, and yet neither illness nor death followed; this mystified primitive man. Therefore, she explains, many supernatural qualities—both positive and negative—were ascribed to menstruation.[4]

Even today, the phenomenon of menstruation remains something of a mystery, and until, by means of further research, we learn much more about its physiology and psychology, some of the same supernatural qualities may be ascribed to it. However, one fact that emerges clearly from my own research is that the initial experience of menstruation need not be the "bloody trauma" symbolizing female inferiority that it is made out to be in the theories of some psychoanalysts. The findings cited above indicate that negative associations are a heritage of parental (particularly maternal) ignorance and bias. Neither the menarche nor the ensuing pattern of menstrual cycles need be disturbing, difficult, or psychologically painful if the young girl has been adequately informed in advance about the nature and meaning of menstruation.

The onset of menstruation is an unambiguous signal of a female's debut into puberty, regardless of her individual response to it or to femininity in general. A male may enter

[4]Dr. Katharina Dalton, *The Menstrual Cycle,* p. 27.

puberty without being aware of it (if he is not stimulated to ejaculation, he will not know that he has the capacity to ejaculate and that therefore he has biologically matured). But a young woman realizes immediately that she has entered adolescence: her body acknowledges it unequivocally. Obviously, this distinct rhythmic difference in the sexual cycles of males and females significantly affects their respective psychologies throughout their lives.

CHAPTER FIVE

SELF-STIMULATION/ MASTURBATION

Since we began to study the sex life of man, no other subject has been more frequently discussed, no other practice more roundly condemned and more universally practiced than masturbation.

—Lester W. Dearborn, "Masturbation"

I think masturbation is fine and natural, but what kind of mother would I be if I told my *child* that?

—Jane

Nothing human disgusts me, unless it's unkind or violent.

—Tennessee Williams, *Night of the Iguana*

ALTHOUGH OTHER CHAPTERS of this book report findings from this study pertaining to sexual experiences representative of a specific age bracket, this chapter is concerned with a form of sexual release that occurs throughout the women's lives.

Authorities report that the urge for self-stimulation is a universal phenomenon and perhaps one of the most common forms of sexual release. Kinsey and his associates postulated masturbation as the most significant measure of a woman's interest in sexual activity:

> Since the frequencies of masturbation depend primarily on the physiologic state and the volition of the female, they may provide a significant measure of the level of her interest in sexual activity. Heterosexual activities, on the other hand, are more often initiated by the male partner and, in consequence, they do not provide as good a measure of the female's innate capacities and sexual interest.[1]

One of the striking findings of this study was that, despite pressures toward greater sexual activity, cultural attitudes still attach guilt and anxiety to female masturbation practices. Most of the women in this sample expressed intense disapproval of masturbation, and their attitudes appeared to have little connection with whether or not they had ever masturbated, or the frequency with which they had done it.

This tenacious resistance to more liberated attitudes about masturbation seems to lie in the nature of the activity: masturbation entails a personal admission of, and responsibility for,

[1] A.C. Kinsey *et al., Sexual Behavior in the Human Female,* p. 146.

one's sexual feelings. Participation in interpersonal sex is rationalized on many grounds—love, passion, dating and popularity, marriage, pleasing one's partner, wifely duty, etc. —but masturbation can be considered only as the individual's direct expression of immediate sexual feelings.

With sexual self-exploration, the most overt form of sexual expression during infancy and childhood, comes the first confrontation with sex taboos. A child raised in a sexually repressive environment learns at an early age to regard all sexual expression as "sinful," "immoral," "wrong," and thus to be avoided at all costs. It is not surprising, therefore, that the repressive attitudes surrounding masturbation color most later forms of sexual expression and experience.

Relatively small percentages of subjects in sexual research have reported masturbating. The following comparison of this study with those of Kinsey and Davis gives the percentages of subjects who reported practicing self-stimulation in childhood and who attained climax by this means:

Davis: 24.6 percent practiced, 12.0 percent attained climax (unmarried sample, to age ten)
Kinsey: 19.0 percent practiced, 12.0 percent attained climax (total sample, to age twelve)
Schaefer: 43.3 percent practiced, 23.3 percent attained climax (total sample, to age twelve)

The larger percentage reported in my study may be a result of the interview method used. The in-depth, woman-to-woman interview may have enabled women to recall suppressed events and feelings in taboo areas that might not have been remembered under less intimate and intense contact. In fact, the most consistently repressed memories to emerge and become clarified in the course of the interview were those concerning masturbation.

The findings discussed below will suggest reasons underlying the wide differential between human biological capability and the actual practice of sexual self-stimulation.

AGE AND TYPE OF FIRST EXPERIENCE

For purposes of this study, masturbation was defined as any form of genital sexual excitation, which need not conclude in orgasm. Twenty-nine of the 30 women reported some masturbatory experience at some period in their lives. Thirteen reported their earliest experiences with masturbation before the age of twelve, 7 more reported such experiences during adolescence, and 9 reported initial experiences with masturbation as adults (over age nineteen). (One woman in the entire sample has never masturbated, in the sense of direct genital contact, but has—and does—experience orgasm exclusively through fantasy.)

Of the 13 women who reported self-stimulation before age twelve, 7 attained climax. Norma reported the earliest experience of orgasm through masturbation. At age four, she discovered

> the pleasure involved in exposing my genitals to the forceful stream of water in the bathtub. My mother seemed to be very angry when she caught me doing this and reprimanded me! She looked as though she was holding something in . . . but it was coming out in anger from her frozen face and stern eyes.

Despite awareness of her mother's disapproval, Norma continued the practice.

> I don't remember which came first, the faucet experience or this: I remember at naptime I would sometimes masturbate because I really didn't need a nap at age four. But my mother insisted that I stay in the room for an hour or so —it seemed a very long time, and it was a very light, bright room . . . their bedroom, as a matter of fact. I can remember her peeking in the door, and I would play possum. I was bored and was looking for things to do—and I found that. I remember having orgasms first with the water faucet, and I think that afterward whenever I did masturbate, I experienced orgasm.

Amelia recalled masturbating at age three but did not experience orgasm until age nine.

> At first there was never any orgasm; it was just kind of a pleasurable feeling. I imagine it would happen something like once or twice a week, varying on whether I was very busy in school or whether I was feeling sorry for myself, or depressed. I imagine these kinds of feelings had an effect on how often I did it, but I don't remember exactly.

After experiencing her first sexual climax through masturbation at age nine, she attempted to share her method for attaining this "great joy" with a young cousin, who reported the incident to their parents. Amelia was subsequently "forbidden to use that bathroom shower stall with the water tap that would make this wonderful thing happen." She explained that "once having known that kind of experience, it was imperative that I experience this, one way or another, each time."

Karen also had her initial experience with masturbation at age three. She discontinued the practice between ages five and ten, while she was involved in sex play with a boy her age. When she began again, around age eleven, she experienced her first orgasm.

> I remember how I learned to have an orgasm. My girl friend would have one, and I saw her behavior and then I understood that there was something further that I wasn't getting to. And it was a matter of finally—there it is, that's what it's supposed to be. Sometimes I'd do it even twice a day.

All 7 women who had experienced orgasm continued masturbating through adolescence and into adulthood, even if they were discovered or reprimanded. The other 6 discontinued the practice during childhood—5 of them not to begin again until adult life, and one never to masturbate again. Katherine Davis observed, in this context, that "a very large proportion of those who deny the experience of orgasm [in masturbation] fall in the group of those who have stopped the practice."[2] Apparently, for those who do not achieve orgasm, the pleasure does not outweigh the guilt feelings and negative external pressures.

Helen could not recall the exact age at which she began masturbating, but she felt that it was somehow associated with bathing with one of her boy cousins when she was about four. She continued the practice sporadically until about age eight, experiencing no climax during those four years. After a hiatus of more than twelve years, Helen started again in her early twenties, when she learned to masturbate to orgasm.

Celeste and Louise discovered masturbation in early childhood, but not to orgasm. They, like Helen, discontinued the practice until adult life when they became aware of orgasm through other sources.

Seven women began masturbating during adolescence or young adulthood but before marriage. Only 2 of them did not achieve orgasm. Cathleen, who first learned about self-stimulation from a book she found in the public library, reported:

> . . . at age fourteen I experienced my first masturbatory orgasm at the end of a very exciting evening. I was terribly aroused and didn't know why . . . I came home and had the sensation of not quite knowing what was going on—just feeling around to find out . . . and finding it felt so good that I just went on feeling, and then just exploded all over the place. It was a violent kind of feeling, and it happened so suddenly that I didn't know but what I was going over the brink. There was no holding back—all of a sudden I just had no control over it.

Nine women reported masturbating for the first time after the age of nineteen, some premaritally, some during marriage, some postmaritally or between marriages. Some continued this regularly during their marriages, some only when sepa-

[2]Katherine B. Davis, *Factors in the Sex Life of Twenty-two Hundred Women,* p. 113.

rated from their husbands, and others stopped. Among their recollections:

> I don't ever recall playing with myself until I was much older, after I had received my first orgasms. I was nineteen and engaged at the time, but not to my husband. We were standing, and he was kind of rubbing against me for a long time, and then all of a sudden my knees kind of buckled, and I experienced an orgasm, and that was my first time and it was different and wow! I loved it! He said, "I was waiting for that to happen!" And that's when I started masturbating because he explained it to me. I never knew that women could get those kinds of feelings! [Victoria]

> I never touched myself as a child that I can remember although I have a natural habit when I sleep of keeping my hands down at my genitals and when I wake up my hands will still be there . . . I couldn't bring myself to actually masturbate until I was in my twenties, until a friend said she did it. Up to that time, I did not know it was a possibility. [Eve]

As was noted, some masturbatory activity that began in childhood did not conclude in orgasm—and therefore was eventually discontinued. Yet only 2 women who began masturbating as adolescents or adults did not experience orgasm. Evidentally, this reflects a certain logic in human learning. These older women had obtained sufficient knowledge to expect orgasm from self-stimulation.

ANXIETY, GUILT, DENIAL

Lester Dearborn defined masturbation as "any self-stimulation of the sexual organs for the pleasure involved and for the release of tension."[3] The word "pleasure" must be qualified, however, by the negative experiences described by the women in this study who did, or still do, masturbate. Few, if any, of

[3] Lester Dearborn, "Masturbation." In Manfred F. DeMartino, ed., *Sexual Behavior and Personality Characteristics*, p. 239.

their autoerotic experiences were without feelings of anxiety, guilt, or shame. As Kinsey noted, "No other type of sexual activity has worried so many women as masturbation."[4]

Anxiety, which may be defined as fear manifested in a generalized, unspecific way, was expressed by the women in regard to self-stimulation in several ways: confused or repressed sexual knowledge and events; misconceptions about sexual experiences; phobias about touching themselves; fear of offending or hurting or losing their partners if they practiced self-stimulation. These anxieties are the inevitable results of childhood conflicts between an irresistible pleasure and a forbidding authority.

The fear of discovery was ever-present in the descriptions of masturbation experiences. But it was offset by the pleasure derived from masturbation and, more often than not, the pleasurable practice was continued in spite of the associated fears.

> I loved masturbation! I knew it was punishable and it would be definitely frowned upon, to say the least, and yet it was enjoyable, so I did it. It was comforting. [Karen]

Many of the young girls had sensed their mothers' disapproving attitudes toward sexual self-exploration, yet could recall no words or comments to this effect. They "just knew." Said Nancy,

> It seemed like I was masturbating all the time—oh, it's so hard to talk about it, even now! I remember once being with a girl friend and we were in bed embracing and kissing and I masturbated and she didn't even know it. I thought, if they catch me, they'll kill me and I guess I thought that girl would, too.

Others could recall the specific origin and content of an admonition against masturbating. Jane received her first warnings about the dangers of masturbation at parochial school: "The nuns said that if you touched yourself in your

[4]Kinsey *et al., Sexual Behavior in the Human Female,* p. 170.

private places, you'd go crazy. I don't think I knew what the hell they were talking about, and I don't think I really cared too much." Although the warnings seemed not to have an immediate effect on Jane, their imprint was evident in her comments about masturbation.

> I never talked about it. I think I knew that the other girls did, but I didn't admit to it. Even today, when somebody mentions masturbating, even the word, I get very upset. I always felt awful afterward, and I'd tell myself I'll never do this again.

Four events that had been totally repressed were recalled as a result of the stimulus of the interview. All were masturbation episodes.

Marion thought she began masturbating at age seventeen, when a man friend taught her how. But a memory occurred to her in the period between the first and second interviews:

> I've always slept curled with my hands through my legs. But I suddenly remembered my mother lifting up the blankets to look at what I was doing and I know damn well—I must have known even then—she was looking for *something*. And this took place when I was about six years old.

Susan reported her first orgasm experience through dreams during middle adolescence, and her first conscious experience of orgasm with her husband, at age 29. She reported no masturbation whatsoever—and no knowledge even of its possibility until her late twenties. She was almost totally ignorant of the facts of self-stimulation, but during her first interview she expressed great interest in learning what it meant to other women. At her next interview, she reported:

> When I went home after our first interview I told my husband about what the interview had been like, and the things we talked about. I told him that the questions regarding masturbation seemed to interest me the most.

And as I was falling asleep that night I remembered some-thing very vague—about age eight or so, being slapped on the hands and told not to do something. But I believe now that I must have been playing with myself. It was my mother who slapped me, and I have a feeling it had some-thing to do with her smelling my hands.

What Nancy recalled was an attitude about masturbation rather than an instance of it. Nancy had practiced masturba-tion to orgasm since age six. During the first interview she was reporting a nightmare that she had had several times during her adolescence.

The dream began with me and my mother going up in an elevator. Suddenly my mother looked like a witch, and said to me, "You know what you have, don't you? You have the hands of a devil!"

Suddenly she exclaimed:

I never really understood why that dream frightened me so much, but I think I do right now. I think I felt that my mother was saying that I had evil, masturbating hands!

Until the interview, Zoe believed that she first masturbated at age twenty. She had not realized that an experience she had at age eight was an orgasm.

I remember when I was in fourth grade, there was a playground with swings in it at school. The swings were hung across a horizontal bar and at the ends of it there were angled vertical bars. One of the things I liked to do was to swing hand over hand up one of these angled bars. I would do this and get such a great feeling between my legs that when the bell rang for recess to be over, I didn't want to stop doing it because it felt so good. So I would continue to do it until the last possible minute before being late, and then I would have an orgasm. I didn't know it was an orgasm, I didn't know what it was. I just knew it felt great.

Much of the confusion felt by many young girls about their genitals is related to anxiety about masturbation as well as to lack of information. Gloria recounted:

> When I was fourteen, I masturbated, and then I didn't understand it as being masturbatory because it was much more anal, I'd touch myself there, or put my finger there or something, but I would be involved in sexual fantasies. And I can remember at that time thinking that I didn't understand why the vagina would be more interesting to anybody because the anal thing was really sexual to me. I simply didn't know *what* to do with my vagina and the idea of putting something into somewhere seemed more feasible anally than vaginally.

As a child, Rebecca didn't seem to know the difference between the various functions of her genital and eliminative organs.

> From very early I had a concept of something being put in me anally from my mother using suppositories on me, but I had no idea of putting anything in the vagina. And I had no concept of putting my finger inside me because at that point I don't think I knew what was in there. I don't think I knew how a woman was built then, only when I saw things telling you how to use Tampax and how it can't get lost and all that.

The masturbatory method used during childhood and adolescence by most of the women was clitoral stimulation. Confusion about the function and existence of the vagina was one explanation the women offered; another was fear—sometimes vague, often specific: "I'd be afraid to put things inside me— afraid of germs, afraid I'd ruin myself." Karen also reported a fear of germs:

> I learned [about putting things in her vagina] from my girl friend, but I felt terribly guilty about it . . . My girl friend liked objects, but we had a whole thing about sanitation, and your hands seemed like a part of you so it didn't seem

like you'd get germs from them. I never liked objects. Objects were like foreign bodies.

Anxieties about masturbation were also expressed through various phobic reactions to self-touching. Sometimes these phobias were manifested in somewhat dramatic fashion, sometimes through reluctance, hesitation, and even ineptness in the use of the diaphragm as a contraceptive measure. Because of their feelings about masturbation, some women preferred sanitary napkins to tampons. Others disclosed their feelings through reactions to words or gestures that might, in some way, be reminiscent of masturbatory activity. Louise, for example, said that for twelve of her fifteen years of marriage

> I was never willing to have a diaphragm fitted, and to use one successfully. I think now that it was because I wasn't able to touch myself . . . I couldn't get it in or out . . . I didn't know where to put it. I could not figure out anything, and I didn't want to be bothered with it.

Rebecca, who was not fitted for a diaphragm until seven years after marriage, recounted:

> At the time I got married I had no idea where my vagina was. I had never investigated it. I went to bed believing there wasn't such a place, and some years later when I went to a doctor to learn to use the diaphragm, I couldn't learn. I didn't want to have any awareness or knowledge of this even though I was having sex.

Irene frequently had orgasms through sexual fantasies.

> But I literally can't bring myself to touch myself. I don't know why, but I can remember one time trying it, and it was just . . . too filled with some kind of feeling that it's something wrong, that it was something not very healthful.

Helen, who had difficulties in finding coital positions that would facilitate her orgasm with her husband, admitted:

> I know that if we lie on our sides, face to face, and I hold my thighs together in a particular way, I can have an orgasm in just a few moments. But I'm always ashamed to let him see me do this—because this is the way I used to masturbate, and I'm so afraid that he might recognize it as such—and then I'd feel so mortified.

Some women masturbated for a number of years before they learned that their activity had sexual connotations and constituted masturbation. So long as she didn't consciously recognize that a certain experience was of a specific sexual nature, or had a specific sexual name, a woman could allow herself to have it. With awareness came denial and even discontinuance.

Donna recalled:

> When I was about seven or eight, I had once figured out that if I squeezed my legs—or thighs, that is—together, real tight in a certain way, and did it long enough, I'd eventually get this absolutely terrific feeling.

She continued doing this for several years until her family hired a housekeeper, an austere and domineering woman.

> I remember her staring at me, very pointedly, one day and saying, "If you touch yourself there—that's called self-abuse—and you'll grow something ugly there." That's the first time I realized that what I had been doing was what they wrote about in books and was *bad!*

A related anxiety is concern about the expendibility of the male partner, should the female become too familiar with release through masturbation.

No woman in the sample nor, for that matter, among all the women I have counseled ever stated a preference for autoeroticism over heterosexual relations no matter how successful she was at masturbating to orgasm. In fact, some anxieties about masturbation grew more complex when the adult female became involved with a male partner. She frequently worried about what he would think of her, and if that anxiety were put to rest by the partner, her guilt found form in the idea that "sex without love" or "sex for release" was unacceptable, that self-induced self-stimulation was abhorrent.[5]

> I did it a lot even during my marriage because the funny thing was that the climax itself was much more satisfying, much greater than being with a guy. I felt terrible afterward, sick and then depressed because then you're alone and a lot of fun of sex is being with someone. [Jane]

Eve reported that since marriage

> masturbation has opened up for me more than before marriage. If my husband is away or if we're not having sex and I feel very hung up, I'll masturbate. I don't feel great about doing it because I feel I'd much rather have sex with him, and I even feel a little unhappy that this is the only way I can have any relief. But we've talked about it and both have been doing it and we both feel a little unhappy about doing it. Part of the reason I feel badly is that I know that masturbation keeps me in a self-sufficient system, which is my problem. It's always been my problem.

When I asked her what she meant by a "self-sufficient system," she said that the ability to masturbate made her feel both independent of her husband and detached from him. She found it difficult to have a feeling of closeness without feelings of compulsive dependence.

Despite her strong guilt feelings, Marion realized that, for a while, the experience of orgasm through self-stimulation was more satisfying for her than intercourse. She could experience orgasm with ease through either masturbation or coitus, but described her periodic preference for masturbation as a way of "staying in control." "I guess it was my way of not having to feel that any man could just have me at his mercy because of my sex needs." This troubled Marion as her feeling for her

[5]There is an interesting paradox here. In spite of anxieties about their expendability, many men find the vision of a woman masturbating (real or fantasied) extremely erotic. One man explained, "It's so terrific to see her wanting it as much as I do."

present husband grew stronger and the relationship more solid. She felt:

> I was taking his powers away from him—and some of his rights as a man. I felt guilty because I was delighting that I still had control over me. But at the same time, I loved the feeling that I was his woman, and all that implies . . . that he is the man that could staisfy me, and that I do need him.

Several other women expressed doubts about the benefits of masturbation in the course of a heterosexual relationship.

> I used masturbating for relief if I felt sexual desire and couldn't satisfy it in any other way. I can remember masturbating a lot when I was married the second time. I'd do it when he wasn't around. And I remember thinking to myself, "For Christ's sake! What's all this about?" It was very early in the marriage, I remember, and it made me feel so sad that I had to find sexual relief alone. I felt it should be different when one was married, that you shouldn't *have* to do this unless you're apart from each other for a period of time. [Zoe]

Of the women in the study who did not experience any kind of genital stimulation during childhood, 8 said they had not known that masturbation was possible for females. Among the relevant comments:

> I knew my brothers used to masturbate, and so did their boyfriends, I guess, but—you know—it never even occurred to me then that girls could! [Rachel]

> My brother could do it, and it seemed natural for him . . . it had something to do with rubbing his penis against the sheets. But I didn't have a penis, so I didn't think that I could do it. [Gloria]

Five of them expressed doubt about their lack of recall—because of what they had read in books, or because of the critical disbelief of others.

I don't remember ever touching myself genitally, or sexually, in any manner whatsoever when I was a child. But I suppose I'm blocking something out of my memory . . . I find it hard to believe, but even after six years of analysis I still haven't come up with any memories of masturbation. [Frances]

If an experience cannot be recalled even after considerable introspection, it probably never happened. Perhaps the first expressions and discoveries of sexuality in these children were discouraged at a very early age. This premise is supported by the absence in these women of the phobic manifestations that take root at a more mature age.

This denial of the experience itself is another manifestation of anxiety about masturbation. Girls who could figure out other sexual phenomena without any direct or specific information were psychologically blocked from discovering this one.

RATIONALIZATIONS

The women offered a variety of rationalizations in describing their responses to the masturbation urge, and appeared to feel that self-stimulation required complex justifications.

Sometimes, it's a way of "collecting myself." When I feel too many pressures pulling me apart there's something about the intensity of these sexual feelings—brief as they are—that helps me feel together again. It's no lasting gratification, and all it ever is is a momentary relief, but sometimes it's better than nothing. [Rachel]

Erin, along with several others, feels that masturbation "is always connected with loneliness." And Marion said:

When I was about eleven, I used to do it as a way of rebelling against my mother and father who I knew were having sexual intercourse. It was really sick. I wanted to stop myself from doing it. I felt that I would stop when I was wanted as much as someone or something else.

In some cases, during an adult sexual relationship the male either taught his female partner how to masturbate or gave her the approval she needed to overcome her enduring guilt feelings.

> I didn't have any masturbation experiences as a child. I have masturbated about five times in my life, and it's been since I've been married. I think I've been able to because of my husband's attitude toward it. He once said that masturbation is like mad money—you can always get home. Each and every time I've done it, I tell him, so as to get his approval. He's always very funny and light about it and always says something like, "Oh, that's great, now I'll screw you twice tonight as a reward"—something very approving and light. The last two times were very far apart, and I'd say I'm not going to tell him, but I always would because I wanted him to tell me how all right it was. [Della]

Some of the women, when questioned about their adult feelings toward masturbation, said they thought it was invaluable in teaching them about their bodies:

> I knew it was taboo—don't touch this area, don't touch, don't look—but I think my life is better because I did masturbate. In other words, I knew what to go for. I wasn't hung-up sleeping with a man and not even knowing what I'm supposed to get from it . . . [Karen]

> I think the experiences in adolescence helped my sexual relations, definitely. First of all, I knew what an orgasm was. Without masturbation, I never would have known anything . . . [Artemis]

> I think knowing about masturbation earlier would have made my life more bearable . . . the knowledge of masturbation improves a woman's sexual life because one finds out what the orgasm experience is like and some of the places in your own body that are stimulating. [Della]

But several others found that knowledge did not assuage their feelings of guilt. As Celeste put it:

> I'm still condemning myself for certain sexual practices that I apparently still feel are evil, like having a lot of men and masturbating. To me, masturbating still has certain underlying tones of being bad—Christ! even after all this knowledge.

CONCLUSIONS

The masturbation section of this research concludes with a question: Why is this most simple, personal, private, natural, educative, convenient sexual release so complicated, so tortured, so abused?

In most societies, according to Ford and Beach, masturbation by adults is considered undesirable.[6] It is therefore not surprising that all thirty women in this study—whether or not they masturbated or held "permissive" views on the subject—expressed anxiety about it in some way.

Why? Why are human beings everywhere overwhelmed by fears, anxieties, and guilts about masturbation? Probably because masturbation involves an admission of personal interest in sexual activity: it is the sex urge unadorned by the rationalizations that often accompany intercourse. It is nothing less or more than one human being's overt, direct expression of sexuality per se. Because it cannot be masked by "higher" motives, it has elicited the wrath of religions and social systems throughout history.

I think the fundamental cause of the extraordinary anxiety in this area is the result of the association between early sensual awareness and sexual exploration and concomitant early prohibition. The prohibition of infant sexual exploration is probably the first taboo experienced by a human being. The effect of this is understandably traumatic and will influence

[6]Clellan S. Ford and Frank Beach, "Self-Stimulation." In Manfred F. DeMartino, ed., *Sexual Behavior and Personality Characteristics*, pp. 274-75.

all subsequent experiences related to these feelings.

Early negative attitudes toward childhood sexuality discourages children from discovering themselves. This is, perhaps, the only childhood discovery of self not celebrated by adults in Western civilization. While the taboos prevail for boy children as well as girls, the effect is more deleterious for girl children.

> The structure of girl's genitalia makes it less likely that she will spontaneously discover . . . herself . . . and how to masturbate. . . . Unless she is taught by parents or older children, she may completely miss this learning experience. Yet parental attitudes in our society are geared toward hiding the possibility of self-stimulation from the period of infancy onward.[7]

When young boys are aroused they can recognize, via their erect penis, that something very specific has happened to them, even if they have had no previous education that such a phenomenon is natural. On the other hand, due to the covert nature of their sexual anatomy, young girls, unless educated, fail to recognize or identify sexual feelings. Females are discouraged from thinking about sex, from identifying sexual feelings, and from fantasizing—is this perhaps why so many women had difficulty recognizing sexual feelings? Does this explain why women had such difficulties in identifying the source and sometimes even the general phenomenal experience of orgasm?

Kinsey wrote, "It is doubtful if any type of therapy has ever been as effective as early experience in orgasm, in reducing the incidences of unresponsiveness in marital coitus and in increasing the frequencies of response to orgasm in that coitus."[8] Yet due to the prohibitions against all manner of sexual self-exploration and education, women are unlikely to avail themselves of "this type of therapy."

[7]Margaret Mead, *Male and Female*, p. 272.
[8]Kinsey *et al*, *Sexual Behavior in the Human Female*, p. 385.

Coincidentally, it is interesting to realize that women have been variously stereotyped as being slow to arrive at orgasm or as frigid if they didn't experience orgasm through intercourse in some prescribed fashion. Since sexual arosal is the function of the mental as well as the physical, and since women are discouraged from the use of their imaginations as well as fantasy, and discouraged from the discovery of the subtleties of their covert physiology, it is small wonder that they have long had difficulties with sexual satisfactions. Freud and some of his followers further added to the cunfusion in this area by describing "clitoral orgasms" (orgasms experienced exclusively through clitoral stimulation) as being "immature." The reason given for this appelation is that "clitoral orgasm" is equated with "masturbation" which, in turn, is equated with "infantilism." (It is of interest to consider that males, when children, masturbate in the exact same fashion and with the exact same organ as do male adults, and yet there is no distinction made between infantile and adult forms of orgasm for men.)

Considering the depth and breadth of this cultural bias against masturbation—in addition to the fact that all of the women expressed a definite preference for other sexual outlets —it is astonishing that women in this study masturbated at all! Yet they did: the ubiquitous force of this human urge is at least as remarkable as the strength of the taboos ruling against it.

CHAPTER SIX

INITIAL INTERCOURSE

The little girl is a virgin; after defloration she is no longer a virgin; something definite, identifiable, has occured that is very different from the boy's gradual experimentation with copulation.
—Margaret Mead, *Male and Female*

It wasn't painful, it wasn't pleasurable, no bells went off, none of those things I'd expected. And I thought to myself, "Is that what all the shouting was about?" And yet—with all of that—I kept wondering to myself the next day, if other people knew that I looked different!
—Amelia

Why did I do it that first time? Because all my girl friends already had, and I wanted to get it over with.
—Bernice [age nineteen]

Men are afraid that they will not be men enough, and women that they may be considered only women.
—Theodore Reik, from an article in *Psychoanalysis*

INITIAL INTERCOURSE was selected as the area of analysis most representative of the period in the interview guide designated as Late Adolescence and Premarital. This chapter will discuss the factors involved in the choice to have intercourse for the first time, and some of the ways in which conscious attitudes about intercourse conflict with actual situations. Some general questions asked in this area concerned early ideas and feelings about sexual intercourse, expectations of orgasm and pleasure and/or pain in the first experience with intercourse, and the promise of marriage as an important factor in the decision to engage in premarital intercourse. Anthropologists point out that in nearly every culture in the world except our own, there is some acceptance of coital activity for unmarried youth. Kinsey outlined the three primary factors militating against premarital intercourse in this country: 1) the sexual unresponsiveness of many young females; 2) the moral tradition in America; 3) lack of experience, and the individual's fear of engaging in an unfamiliar activity.[1]

Yet, in spite of the fact that 17 women in this present study expressed negative attitudes toward sexuality in general and sexual intercourse in particular, 23 of the 30 had sexual intercourse before they were married. (Social and religious prohibitions played a large part in the decisions of the other 7 women to preserve their virginity until marriage. Many expressed doubts about the marriageability of nonvirgins and fears of premarital pregnancy.)

[1] A. C. Kinsey et. al., Sexual Behavior in the Human Female, p.316.

Counterbalancing the many sanctions *against* premarital intercourse and the threats of "dire consequences" were physical desire and often a belief that the abandonment of virginity would bring sexual knowledge, confirm the girl's consciousness of her femininity, and imply a certain advancement, giving her a feeling that she belonged to the world of adults.

Erin, who had her first experience at age eighteen, with no expectation of marriage, explained that, among her peer group, "everyone was doing it." She added:

> The first time was not good, not bad. It wasn't much of an experience, but I was glad I had done it. I felt definitely that it was something that *could* eventually be pleasurable, and it felt good being as sophisticated and knowing as I thought the rest of them were.

INITIAL INTERCOURSE: PREMARITAL

Nine of the 23 women who experienced initial intercourse premaritally expected to marry their initial partners. Although only 3 of them actually did so, each of the remaining 6 said she certainly would not have had intercourse without some promise—however vague—of marriage with their initial partner.

> I had been going with this boy for about a year, and I was eighteen, we had intercourse because we were planning to get married. Afterward I remember lying in my bed at school thinking that I didn't really have too much choice in the matter of marrying him because I *had* slept with him. [Virginia]

The 14 women who had premarital intercourse for the first time without expecting to marry their partners gave the following reasons: 3 were eager to end virginity, to get the initiation "over and done with"; 11 perceived premarital intercourse as offering various kinds of gratification—personal sexual release ("for my sake"), gratifying the male in an effort to maintain a relationship ("for his sake"), gratification in the rebellion against authority symbols, or gratification through self-punishment (to absolve feelings of guilt).

Among the 3 women who wanted to terminate their virginity, to rid themselves of the fearful unknown of "doing it," the following experiences were reported:

> I had thought about it for so many years, it seemed, and I just wanted to get it over with. But when it happened, it was painful, and I was petrified all during the first time. I don't think I was ready—even though I thought I was impatient to get that first time over with. [Eve]

Nancy was frightened of intercourse, yet she remembers thinking:

> I *must* get this first affair over with, I must! The first time was easy—I was practically forced into it. We used to kiss a lot and pet, but this one time he pushed his penis into my vagina while we were standing up, and I made him stop. Then later he came to my apartment and told me to take my clothes off. I think I was afraid to say no, so I went into the bathroom and took my clothes off, and then was afraid to come out, but I finally did.

Artemis's choice of a partner for her initial intercourse experience was unusual. Because she did not want her husband-to-be to know that she *was* a virgin, she elected to have her initial intercourse with someone else first. She was eighteen, and had known the young man for several months; they had intercourse only once—enough to enable her to approach her fiancé as a "girl who had been around." She felt anxious and nervous although she knew the association would be limited, but the experience itself was unexpectedly unpleasant. Artemis feels, in retrospect, that she "just had to get this over with and he was the best one to do it with."

The expectation of sexual satisfaction ("doing it for my sake") was given by 6 women as the motive for initial intercourse. Della, for example, recounted:

The very first time I had a sex experience I thought that inercourse was if the man just penetrated the woman, that's all. And when it happened, I thought he was acting like a fool. And it was difficult for me to have intercourse the first time because I wasn't the least bit aroused. I was doing it out of curiosity. I just wanted to see what it was like, because there had been so many shady references to it. According to them, it had to change your whole life right away, but it didn't.

And Irene:

For my first experience I deliberately picked somebody I didn't love. I was seeing someone else then for whom I had love feelings but I felt I absolutely had to avoid him on a sexual level. But I was curious, so I threw myself into a relationship with someone who meant absolutely nothing to me. He was literally a seducer . . . very aggressive sexually, very dominating, he just filled that picture I had. He was even French. He didn't care anything about me, and I didn't care anything about him, so that left us a great deal of freedom. It was very exciting, and I certainly felt a great deal of pleasure from it. At the same time I was terribly frightened. I was either twenty or twenty-one, which was very late. I think that part of it had to do with just being terribly frustrated and feeling, why wait? He was on the make, and I looked like a very vulnerable target, and I was. He would take me out to dinner and would look at me over the table like I was the greatest thing in the world—a real kind of build-up. Since he was somebody I didn't care about, it was the perfect solution because I didn't have to worry about him hating me afterward—with all the other boys I'd been attracted to, my only feeling was that they were going to hate me if I went to bed with them.

I guess I've always felt enormously resentful about men and all the junk you hear about them wanting every woman to be a virgin, and they always want to be the first and only, and the greatest, and with everyone. I don't think they ever forgive you for not being a virgin, and it makes you feel just as angry as could be.

Five women chose to have premarital intercourse to satisfy the desires of their partners ("doing it for his sake").

The first guy I did it with told me that another girl laughed at him when they made love but that he wanted to do it with me because he felt I wouldn't laugh at him. I felt kind of sorry for him, so we did it. It was actually his *insistence* that we sleep together . . . not love, or expecting to marry, that decided me. [Erin]

When I was eighteen, I had intercourse with a non-Jewish boy I had been seeing for a few months. He was terribly attractive and considered me very intelligent, very smart . . . To this guy, I was very special. His parents felt some kind of pride that I was his girl, which suited me fine. He'd meet me after work, and we'd go have a drink and neck afterward. And then it seemed like the most obvious thing to do, to just go to the next step. With no fear, trepidation, doubt, hesitancy on my part—it just seemed obvious. The thing I most recall about it was not that it pleased me, but that it pleased him. That he expected it, and that's what he wanted, and it was all right with me. In fact, that's what I got out of it—pleasing him. [Sarah]

Six other women saw participating in premarital intercourse as a means to an end—a necessary condition to prolonging a relationship.

He told me that if I didn't have sex with him, it meant that I really didn't care about him. Actually, I didn't really love him—but I was afraid that if I *didn't* have this affair with him, he would leave me . . . and I couldn't stand the thought of being abandoned—even by someone I didn't care too much about. [Zoe]

I was mad about him. I would have done anything for him, and went to bed with him because *he* wanted to, not because I wanted to. Emotionally I was absolutely cold.

Felt nothing. Because I really didn't want to. I did it just to keep him interested. That first time was painful, emotionally more than physically. [Eve]

Among the women who gave rebellion against parental authority as a motive in the decision to engage in premarital intercourse was Marion:

I knew that if my mother ever found out that I was no longer a virgin—that I was sleeping with this fellow, and right in his own parents' home—she'd have a fit. Then, when he went back to college, we exchanged letters, very romantic, in which he would write a lot about how things had been with us sexually and all. Well—don't you know my mother discovered those letters one day? I thought I'd kept them well hidden from her. Now that I think of it— knowing how nosy and suspicious she always was anyhow —it seems strange to me that I'd have left those letters around the house at all. I must have *wanted* her to find out.

Marion's behavior expresses her guilty feelings about sex and her desire for punishment more clearly than some of the other women's actions, but the idea that genital sex for any reason other than legal procreation is wrong and taboo, and must somehow be punished, runs through the interviews. Irene offered this reason for her choice of her first partner:

I think, strangely enough, it was because I wasn't attracted to him. I have a feeling that when I experienced passion, there was so much guilt involved with what I felt that I couldn't *allow* myself the relationship . . . it seems I could justify what I was doing sexually only if I didn't really want it.

And Jane, explaining what type of boys she selected as partners for sexual activity:

The boys I dated and petted with were boys chosen from the wrong side of the tracks. They were more acceptable to the base and sexual side of my nature.

After her initial intercourse she experienced a sense of defilement, feeling that she had to marry the boy because she was no longer a virgin and "no one else would have me."

INITIAL INTERCOURSE: MARITAL

The decisions of the 7 women who chose to remain virgins until marriage were laden with varying degrees of conflict, guilt, and regret. Before the advent of the contraceptive pill, the possibility of pregnancy was an important deterrent to premarital intercourse. Obviously social and religious prohibitions also played a large part. Nevertheless, none of the women in the present study who chose to remain virgins until they got married had refrained from petting, and 2 invited their fiancés to have intercourse before the wedding date (in both cases the men chose to wait).

The following narratives express some of the conflicts and fears these women experienced prior to and following their weddings:

> My husband and I went together three years before we were married, but we never had intercourse, just a lot of heavy petting. I didn't have an orgasm with him until after we were married. I can remember feeling scared on our wedding day. I don't really know why because we'd gone so far with each other so many different times. I don't know why I felt so scared. [Cathleen]

All through her childhood and adolescence, Rebecca believed that it was imperative to remain a virgin: "Otherwise, the boys talked about you and wouldn't marry you." She also felt that a desirable man, "one who was looked up to by the society in which I lived," would not consider marrying a nonvirgin.

Barbara's parents impressed upon her the necessity of virginity at marriage.

> ... I was a virgin when I was married at age twenty-four, but my husband had had several affairs already. I really didn't want him to be a virgin. I felt if he knew other women, it would be better for me. He really didn't care one way or the other whether I was a virgin, but I did. I was very tense on my wedding night. The first time was not unpleasant, although it was disappointing.

Although her husband apparently didn't cherish virginity in his bride, Barbara agreed with her parents that "the majority of men in America do want to marry virgins."

The issue of virginity is yet another example of the specific way in which biological rhythms punctuate the lives of females. A woman's loss of virginity is a physiological as well as a psychological event. In contrast, when a man experiences his first intercourse, the event is purely psychological. Margaret Mead notes, "A girl is a virgin. After the breaking of the hymen, physically in case she has one, symbolically in case her hymen is structurally negligible, by extension she is not a virgin."[2]

One women, who was raised a Catholic and was therefore particularly concerned with the issue of virginity, described her adolescent confusion about the word "virginity" in relation to men: for a woman, the loss of virginity was clearly the breaking of the hymen, but for a man, "there was nothing to be violated."

Such different initiations into life's natural functions surely affect the psychology of male and female responsiveness. The issue of virginity is symbolic not only of the biological differences between the sexes, but also of the differences in the roles that society assigns to each. Margaret Mead further states:

> Stage after stage in women's life histories thus stand, irrevocable, indisputable, accomplished. This gives a natural basis for the little girl's emphasis on being rather than

[2]Margaret Mead, *Male and Female,* p. 175.

doing. The little boy learns that he must act like a boy, and prove it over and over again, while the little girl learns that she is a girl, and all she has to do is to refrain from acting like a boy.[3]

Society arranges sex roles so that the male is expected to prove himself constantly by performing and/or conquering: therefore, he has a vested interest in "getting her to give in to him." The female, conversely, has a vested interest in holding out, "not giving in."

Another fascinating aspect of initial intercourse is the factor of "choice," that is, the woman must choose how, when, and with whom she will alter her biological state. With menstruation, menopause, orgasm, etc., she has no similar choice: they are either biological facts, or natural phenomena, which she may or may not understand. This factor of choice causes enormous confusion and conflict for a young woman. She has been inundated throughout her life with sanctions and injunctions: "When you get married, sex is beautiful"; "Sex is bad unless you love the man"; "Girls who do it before marriage are not good"; and "Save yourself until the right man comes along." The effort to correlate the desires of her sexual self with the confusing admonitions of society (parents) and her conscience creates a veritable battleground in her ego. This intrapsychic warfare is particularly difficult because the young girl has all too often been given no firm foundation for making realistic choices.

EXPECTATIONS

For the women in this study, the actual experiences of initial intercourse, as contrasted with their expectations of orgasm and pleasure and/or pain, provide many poignant examples of disappointment, confusion, and genuine sorrow in their lives. The illustrative material that follows is striking because it

[3]Mead, *Male and Female,* p. 175.

demonstrates further how erratic and individualistic is the manner of introjecting sexual attitudes in the psyche. Perhaps in no other area so much as in the female's decision concerning her partner and the circumstance for her initial intercourse are the confusion, disparities, and irrationalities so glaringly apparent. (Among these are the confusions and separations between what a woman feels and what she feels she ought to feel.) One is struck by the unrealistic expectations: some women who had never experienced orgasm before expected it in their initial intercourse, while others who had experienced orgasm through other means for many years did not expect it in this instance. The inadquate knowledge concerning intercourse and pregnancy, like the expectations of pleasure and pain, were based on incredibly confusing information.

Eighteen of the 30 women had experienced orgasm at least once prior to initial intercourse, 10 through masturbation and 8 through petting, dreams, and oral stimulation. However, 7 of these 18 did *not* expect orgasm in the initial intercourse.

Amelia's early orgasm experience was through masturbation at age five and later through petting with her fiancé. She was a virgin, and had pleaded with her fiancé to have intercourse with her the day before the wedding, but he refused. Her expectations regarding orgasm, pleasure, and pain were completely realized in that she experienced none of them. She was anxious:

> I felt scared that I wasn't going to live up to his expectations, either in aesthetics or performance or in any way.

And rational:

> Well, of course. It's the first time and it said in all the books that I had ever read that orgasm wasn't going to be.

While not expecting orgasm in the initial intercourse, Grace did expect both pleasure and pain, but experienced only pain. It is of interest to note than when her sexual partner asked if she had had an orgasm, she thought:

> I didn't even know what that meant . . . What was an orgasm, I wondered? What does it feel like? I didn't realize that that was where you went, oddly enough—because in masturbating you achieved that orgasm but I somehow didn't know, or realize, how that should all work out in a real situation.[4]

She remembers being "terribly passive—really wooden."

Karen, in her initial intercourse at age sixteen, did not expect or achieve orgasm, but her expectation of both pleasure and pain was not fulfilled.

> I didn't expect anything like the stars turning purple and music in the background, but I felt terrible that we never really enjoyed it. I did feel, however, that it would be better the second time.

Despite the fact that they had no orgasm experience by any means prior to their initial intercourse, 2 women expected they *would* experience their first orgasm during the sexual act. Barbara, who had sexual intercourse for the first time on her wedding night, described:

> The first night was pleasant and the honeymoon, too, but I didn't have an orgasm. I think I was disappointed. I really didn't have too much information before I got married, and I can't say I was really afraid the first night, just terribly anxious . . .

Ten other women also had no orgasm experience prior to their initial intercourse, but they did not expect to experience their first orgasm then.

> I never had an orgasm with him. I didn't even know you were *supposed* to have one. I didn't know how to ask for anything, or what to look for, other than to experience what was happening. [Rachel]

[4]Kinsey has noted, in *Sexual Behavior in the Human Female,* p. 139, that many women who have difficulty with coital orgasm are unable to associate orgasm from one form of stimulation with orgasm from a different kind of stimulus. They do not recognize them as similar experiences.

Della, too, didn't know about orgasm until she experienced it while petting, *after* her first experience with intercourse.

> As far as orgasm went, I didn't know about this until my fiancé told me about it at sixteen, and he told me women were *supposed* to have them. [Della]

Sixteen women in the study expected pain from intercourse, 12 expected pleasure *and* pain, and 2 expected only pleasure. Of those expecting pain, 3 did not experience it.

> My girl friends were always telling me that intercourse was terrible. They would describe that there was a small place in a woman's vagina, and a man's big penis was supposed to get in there somehow . . . and because of a biblical sin, the woman *had* to endure pain. It is strange to me that after all those years of worrying about the painfulness of intercourse, I experienced no pain whatsoever from the first encounter. I couldn't figure out what all the commotion was about. [Rachel]

> The first time was not at all painful. As a matter of fact, so much *not* so that I wondered if all that stuff was a myth although I guess some people do have a bad time. [Cathleen]

Others found the pain bearable:

> The first time was very scary, and it hurt. His penis seemed so big, and I was frightened and couldn't figure out how it was all going to fit. The second time it was still painful, but gradually it just kept getting better and better as I stopped feeling so afraid. [Carol]

And others were disappointed:

> I didn't enjoy it at all, really. There had been a lot of preparation in terms of petting day to day, and I was curious to try it with him, but when it came down to it, I was nervous. I was never really aroused physically in relation to the experience. It wasn't particularly painful; it was just disappointing—very, very disappointing. I was

> very disappointed because I didn't love him, and I think
> I knew in the depths of my soul that I didn't love him, I
> really knew it. And I remember I cried. [Gloria]

Among the 14 women who did *not* expect to have pain
during their initial intercourse, 7 did in fact experience it.

> I did feel pain from this first time, but it was so mixed with
> sexual excitement that it didn't bother me at all. I do
> remember when I got up the next day there was blood on
> my pajamas, a little blood. And I wasn't due for a period,
> but I didn't connect this until much later with what it
> might have been. [Karen]

Melanie Klein has noted the anxiety that suffuses many
women's anticipations of intercourse, and describes how these
fears may be alleviated or transformed when a woman discov-
ers through experience that intercourse is not unendurably
painful.

> In making the sexual act a criterion of her anxiety situa-
> tions and thus submitting them to a test by reality . . . the
> alleviation of anxiety which she obtains through actually
> having sexual intercourse will give her strong enjoyment
> which considerably adds to the . . . gratification . . .[5]

Evidence from this study indicates that there is a qualitative
difference in durability between preconceiving sex as "dirty"
and as "painful." Pain is a sensate phenomenon; it can be
induced, augmented, measured, and *tested* in reality. Revulsion is a state of psychic being, exclusively subjective, not
easily measurable or testable.

The attitude that sex is base and lewd is not so easily
modified although it does not necessarily preclude pleasurable
experience. Indeed, the very "forbiddenness" of sex can be
stimulating to some individuals, adding to their experience of
pleasure in sexual congress. Grace recognized that her initial
intercourse at age eighteen

[5]Melanie Klein, *The Psychoanalysis of Children*, p. 289.

was more the *idea* of the thing. I had a feeling this was forbidden, and an awful lot of the pleasure I got from it was the simple fact that I was having *sexual intercourse.* It was a little bit painful . . . but it was thrilling.

Others reported no thrill—only shame and disgust.

As I recall now the intercourse itself was not only painful but also an unpleasant experience. I only did it because this was what he wanted, and I was sort of giving in. I don't remember it as being enjoyable at all . . . I felt disgusted and ashamed, really. In memory, it seems like his penis was *that* big around and pushing and it was just a very unpleasant kind of thing. I hadn't even heard it was painful; I really had no anticipations at all. The foreplay, the petting was pleasant . . . but it was almost like you had to pay a price (intercourse) for that pleasure before (petting). [Frances]

The first time I had intercourse was disgusting and painful, I think, because my husband hadn't been around that much, and he was very large, and I don't think I was really prepared for it. I remember it being terribly painful. I was petrified during it because I kept thinking of what people had said, that it was painful, and I must have tightened up even more. I don't think I was ready. It was as though I was saying, "Do it already and get it over with." I thought it would be just the first time that it would hurt. I bled a great deal, and I didn't like the first experience, and I didn't like the second experience. I didn't like it for a very long time. [Victoria]

REGRETS

Regret about premarital loss of virginity was expressed by 4 women (17 percent), a result close to that of Kinsey and his associates, who found that 12 percent of their sample of married women expressed some minor regret.

Regrets were inversely correlated with the extent of the promiscuity in the premarital activity . . . those who had confined their coital contacts to a single male (15% of the sample) seriously regretted their experience. On the other hand, of those who had extended coitus to something between eleven and twenty males, only 6% regretted their experience. It may be that experience reduces the psychologic disturbance, or it may be that those females who are least inclined to worry are the ones who become most promiscuous. It is probable that both factors contribute to these correlations.[6]

The 4 women in this study expressed their regret in the following ways.

Well, I was very sexually interested in him, but then we started fighting because I didn't want to sleep with him. I think I married him because I had slept with him, and I was no longer a virgin. And I felt very upset about that, and what was I going to do because nobody would want me. I was convinced that you had to be a virgin to get married. [Jane]

Afterward, I used to pretend that I was still a virgin. Whenever I had intercourse, I always said it was the first time, so I always maintained that illusion of myself. I felt terrible, not so much that no one would want me or that I wouldn't marry, but that it was shameful. That one was much more desirable if a virgin. I remember my feeling was—Oh, if I could only be a sweet, pure virgin. [Celeste]

Finally, I guess he got tired of me, and he left me. After the first time that we had intercourse it was quite a while before I had another date with him. Then he just stopped calling. And that made me feel very guilty and bad. It seemed never to be the same again. I wasn't the same person; I had been sinful. Somehow I was ruined for life, and I could never undo what I had done. [Frances]

[6]Kinsey *et al., Sexual Behavior in the Human Female,* p. 317.

Even later, when I decided not to marry him, I thought I'll just have to lie about my virginity . . . because nobody will want to marry me if I've slept with anybody else. Of course, I did have intercourse with other guys before I finally did get married. I was and am capable of intense physical desire. When I would start an affair, I would make the man my "boy." I was very loyal, and I'd think in terms of marriage. Then it would hit me all of a sudden that this person was not at all everything I had told myself he was,and I really didn't love him and I would get almost a feeling of nausea and I'd think, if I see that person again, I'll throw up! [Virginia]

Virginia displays here an American behavioral characteristic described aptly by Margaret Mead:

This ability to block out the past, to enter each new situation, be it job or love affair, with the kind of innocence that it seems to Europeans could only be acquired by amnesia from a blow on the head, is a peculiarly American characteristic, bred of the need to be both poised for flight and firmly rooted in the immediate landscape . . . Past loves, past experiences, are named over to be, by that very act, eliminated. Each lover brings . . . a conviction that this is the real thing . . . if it fails, then it is not the real thing, but the next experience may be.[7]

Three women regretted the choice of their initial partner, but not the premarital intercourse experience itself. Erin recalled that the factor of "premarital sex" was

not a great issue then—all the [young people], everyone I knew then was doing it. But what I regret was the person I had sex with first—he was very ugly to me physically— that is, I found him so unattractive, even repulsive.

But I had no other regrets at all about having sex before marriage. I would never want to marry a virgin, and I didn't think, afterward, that a man would want to marry

[7]Mead, *Male and Female*, pp. 352–53.

a virgin either. And this way I know from my own experience what to do to have sexual satisfaction.

Grace exemplifies the 16 women who experienced no regrets whatsoever at their decision to have premarital intercourse.

I don't think I cared a bit about not being a virgin any more. I did feel this though—I felt that it was a prize. And I still have never forgotten him because I felt the way I did about him, and I felt no sense of loss. It was more kind of a celebrational feeling than anything else.

Among the 7 women who remained virgins until marriage, 3 felt some regret at not having had intercourse experience, as Barbara illustrates.

I really regret that I didn't have premarital sex. I felt I offered my husband so little, and he had to show me so much. American men want virgins, yet they want their wives to know a lot about sex. I feel today that I cheated myself because I allowed my parents to influence me with their values and conflicts, and thus I denied myself.

INITIAL INTERCOURSE PROFILE

Using the modal frequency (the highest number of like responses) as an index to the expectations and experiences of these 30 women concerning their first intercourse, the following description is a profile of "typical" attitudes and responses:

She first had intercourse when she was about 18.5 years old, having already experienced orgasm at least once through masturbation and had petting experience. Her first intercourse was premarital with no expectation of marrying her partner. She did not expect to experience orgasm during her initial intercourse, and in fact she did not; she half-expected pleasure but did not experience it; she expected the experience to be physically painful and it was.

Her earliest awareness of the existence of sexual intercourse was through information from other children. At the time of her initial intercourse she had relatively little factual knowledge about pregnancy and contraception.

CONTRASTING STATEMENTS FROM CURRENT GENERATION

Virginity was an important issue for the women in this study, born in the 1920s and 1930s. In order to contrast them with the generation of girls born since the early 1940s, I am including here some accounts of initial intercourse experiences of 7 of the 15 girls under the age of twenty-five, whom I have interviewed and counseled.

> [*Age seventeen*] At around thirteen I finally said, Oh fuck it! I just decided that it was now or never—or rather, now or next week. I figured if I got pregnant, well—I'd run the risk. I guess I felt kind of guilty about losing my virginity, like I really *shouldn't* do it but I might as well. About pregnancy, well, everybody worries about it all the time, not just now and then. But I think he used something the first time. After that, it was that he'd use something or pull out.
>
> I thought it was going to be painful, and it was, but not too bad. It seemed to last about two minutes. Afterward, we got up and dressed real quick in case my father got home. And my boyfriend was very gentle, asked me was I hurt or could I walk.
>
> I just decided I was old enough at the ripe age of thirteen. My best friend Janet had done it, and that probably had something to do with my decision. From her, I learned just that it would be good.
>
> I think premarital sex helps. I'll be a much better lover and I also think it just helps my attitude. I mean, I wouldn't want to get married and just have slept with one man my whole life.

Once or twice I had regrets. Just the average feelings—I should have "saved" myself. Well, I *was* brought up in America!

[*Age twenty-four*] It happened when I was twenty . . . on our third date. I really felt I liked him, and I thought he *wouldn't* like me if he thought I was a virgin. A lot of my friends had done away with their virginity, and it didn't seem to be a traumatic thing for them. I really had no use for my virginity, anyway . . . I don't remember being afraid at all until we actually got into bed. He had no idea I was a virgin, so I just went through the motions as though I wasn't.

It was painful, and I had been told that sex was pleasurable. If I hadn't been told this, I don't think I ever would have tried it again. My whole culture had told me that sex was pleasurable, but I don't *know* that it is. What I really think is that I enjoy sixteen-year-old sex . . . that is, non-intercourse sex.

[*Age twenty-three*] When I was sixteen, I was at a slumber party with a bunch of girls, and they were talking about intercourse, and I thought to myself, I've just *got* to get it over with. I didn't start dating until I was sixteen, which is quite late. The guy was in high school with me, a splendid fellow who had never been to bed with anyone before either. We decided together to get it over with, and it worked out perfectly. It was beautiful! I had an orgasm and everything! After that one perfect time, we went back to acting exactly as we had before, just dating. And we never slept together again after that. We'd accomplished what we'd set out to do, and maybe we were afraid it wouldn't be any good again. Also pregnancy fears got to me, and I didn't have any way to get contraceptives at that age.

[*Age twenty-five*] I was twenty-three and he was thirty-three and a drunk. I'd gone with him a few months, and

I thought to myself, Oh I might as well, I'm going to do it now. I'd had orgasms from masturbating, and I'd petted a lot but when it [intercourse] happened, there was no feeling at all. It was just like putting in a Tampax. The guy didn't mean a shit to me. This happened in the afternoon, and when he said that night that he couldn't come over, I pretended I really cared, but I didn't.

He was older and good looking and had a good sense of humor, but I never thought I'd marry him. I expected it to be pleasurable, but it was nothing, and I didn't like it. It just didn't *feel* good. Anyway, I stayed with him a few months after that, but it was never any good, although I used to pretend it was. I didn't expect to have an orgasm the first time. I really just wanted to see what it would be like.

Shortly after this, I met my future husband, and sex with him was very good, and I had an orgasm with him very, very soon.

[*Age twenty-one*] I was seventeen and at college. I had never necked or petted with anyone before, only kissing. He was the first one who paid so much attention to me. He had a very strong personality and a lot of status on campus. It seemed to happen gradually, from petting to his putting it in me a little bit, which I really liked a lot. In fact the sex feelings were very thrilling. Then one night in the back seat of the car, he penetrated all the way. My first reaction was to become very angry that he had fooled me into going all the way. Even though we had relations, I felt I didn't really *know* we did.

I expected it to be pleasurable and it was. I didn't expect pain, and there really wasn't any. I didn't have an orgasm the first time, but I did later while we were petting, before intercourse. Now I'd rather masturbate than make it with guys I don't care that much about.

[*Age twenty-four*] I knew this guy three days and just wanted to do it . . . I thought I would continue to see him and maybe might marry him, but I only saw him for a month afterward . . . the act itself wasn't particularly pleasurable but being in his arms was wonderful . . . I knew about orgasm because I read about it somewhere . . . I've had several affairs since that first one, but I haven't had an orgasm yet.

[*Age twenty-five*] I was twenty the first time . . . It was a matter of curiosity and a peculiar kind of social pressure . . . more from within myself than from my friends . . . Something I felt I *ought* to do already . . . It wasn't painful like I expected but the greatest pleasure I got from it was from the idea that I had done it . . . I'd had an orgasm from petting before this, and somehow petting made me more scared than actual intercourse.

CONCLUSIONS

The current generation of young women seems as anxious about admitting "sex hang-ups" as the previous generation was about admitting premarital sex. Ironically, many girls of the present generation who are told not to feel guilty about premarital sex find themselves feeling guilty *because* they feel guilty. The unmarried girls of the previous generation insisted that they were virgins—whether they were or not—and the girls of today's generation insist that they are experienced— whether they are or not. The female orgasm has become a kind of status symbol and, consequently, women today are often more concerned with whether they will be orgastically "adequate" than with whether they will be virgins at marriage.

There is a prevalent misconception that the current generation of late adolescents and young adults enjoys more sex, and enjoys sex more, than older generations. I believe that these young people engage in more sexual *activity* than their elders; however, I have found that the feelings attached to this activity are not much freer of guilt, confusion, or contradictions than the feelings of their parents' generation.

The easiest, although perhaps the least rewarding, path is always to withdraw from the responsibility of making one's own decisions. In the past, decisions concerning sex were relatively simple for a girl to make, and her reasons for making them were undisputed. She desired sex, but she was required by society to deny that desire and its fulfillment. She knew the rules and she could deal with them as she chose. She could follow them dutifully and be proud of her will power and reputation—or rebel against them and feel regret for her "sins" and her lowered social standing.

Today, however, a young girl faces two sets of rules: the old rules endure tenaciously, while a new set of rules—which dictates that she must desire sex and fulfill her desire—gains increasing acceptance. There is no way for her to figure out and conform to "contemporary standards of sexual behavior," because those standards themselves are in a state of flux and mutual contradiction.

The issue becomes further complicated as technology advances and traditions recede. Yesterday's "reasons" for the choices a woman has to make in her sexual life are quickly disappearing. She can no longer hide behind the traditional reasons for remaining chaste: pregnancy fears, venereal disease, loss of her reputation—or even the eternal damnation of her soul. The more thoughtful woman will realize that she must become her own authority in matters regarding her sexual conduct. She is obliged to create reasonable rules for herself. She must weigh every edict, liberal or conservative, and discard those that do not make sense for her life. The only alternative is to succumb mindlessly to the latest fashions in sexuality—which may be as repressive as earlier, orthodox styles of sexual abstinence, and may introduce anxieties considerably more difficult to dismiss.

Human beings unfortunately are not born with an innate ability to enjoy satisfying sex lives. Each of us enters the world with a capacity to experience pleasure, but the *what* and *how* of its development depends upon interaction with the unique circumstances of our particular environment. As young girls, the women in this study were told, in so many *words,* that for nice girls, life—and sex—could be beautiful. But they were told, in so many *attitudes,* that life and sex are dangerous, and (for nice girls) taboo. Influenced by such admonitions and attitudes, they often entered into their first experience of sexual intercourse with great expectations—and trepidation. It was rarely wonderful. Most women were fearful, tense, and embarrassed, and, afterward, disillusioned.

> The sexual act which brings about the loss of virginity stands out sharply from all subsequent sexual experiences. The apprehension that goes with it and the fact that it is an invitation demand that certain rites be observed and that the feelings that accompany it be rich enough to constitute its emotional justification.[8]

Perhaps with a new contraceptive technology, free choice will be more feasible. These women, and subsequent female generations, may have greater opportunities to select their own values, and to express their sexuality in their own terms.

[8]The French Institute of Public Opinion, *Patterns of Sex and Love: A Study of the French Woman and Her Morals,* p. III.

CHAPTER SEVEN
ORGASM

The truth about female orgasm will never be fully known until women themselves give us their own detailed accounts and studies of what transpires in their heads and bodies when they engage in sex relations.
—Albert Ellis, from his introduction to *The Housewife's Handbook of Selective Promiscuity*

I feel about orgasm, no matter where it's from, or what you call it—when you have it, you know it. Some are better than others, but that's the only difference, as far as I'm concerned.
—Karen

Being geniuses of the orgasm is far more demanding than Calvinism.
—Walker Percy, *The Last Gentleman*

ORGASM WAS SELECTED for analysis as the area of experience most representative of the age period "Marital and Adult" in the interview guide.

Female orgasm has been a controversial subject in both theoretical and empirical literature. Some of the major confusions, contradictions, and disagreements about the nature of female orgasm focus on the following issues: the relative merits and "maturity" of "clitoral" and "vaginal" orgasms; the percentage of the female population that experiences orgasm and the frequency of the experience; whether the orgasm is necessary to sexual satisfaction and/or marital happiness; whether failure to experience orgasm is related to neurosis and psychosomatic symptoms or is of physiological or genetic origin; and techniques and procedures for the treatment of psychosexual and orgasmic inadequacies.

This study differs from those conducted by Kinsey, Chesser, Terman, and others in its primary purpose—to discover how women feel about the sexual experiences they have had, and those that they have *not* had; and to have women describe their own orgasm experience. How did they learn about the physiological phenomenon of orgasm? How did they feel during the experience? What did it mean to them? Were there frustrations or resentments when it did not occur?

In my opinion, the controversy about the sources and physiological manifestations of female orgasm has been definitively settled by the monumental research of gynecologist-obstetrician William Masters and his associate, Virginia Johnson.

Masters and Johnson conclude from their observations that "the human female's physiological response to effective sexual stimulation develops with consistency regardless of the source of the psychic or physical sexual stimuli."[1] Her responses, they declare, are essentially the same whether the orgasm is mediated through psychological stimuli, clitoral stimulation, vaginal stimulation, or any combination of these. Furthermore they discovered that, in contrast to the male, who has a single primary sexual response—erection of the penis—the female undergoes multiple primary and secondary sexual responses. Masters and Johnson divided the female's genital sensory cycle into four sequential phases:[2]

1) Excitement: varying from minutes to hours, depending on sensory receptivity. This phase is characterized by vaginal "sweating" within the first ten or twenty seconds after the onset of stimulation, distinctive physiological changes in the vagina, cervix, and uterus, and increase in the size of breasts, clitoris, and labia.

2) Plateau: a relatively brief phase, during which "the female integrates psychological and physical strength from mounting sexual tension," in preparation for the third, or orgasmic, phase.

3) Orgasm: lasts three to eight seconds, during which there are four to ten rhythmic and involuntary contractions of genital muscles that occur at the climax, and other generalized muscular contractions that occur throughout the body.

4) Resolution: begins immediately after orgasm and is characterized by general detumescence.

ORGASM: INITIAL SOURCES

Kinsey stated that orgasm should not be the sole criterion for sexual pleasure, since other aspects of sexual arousal and the

[1] W. M. Masters and Virginia Johnson, "Orgasm, Anatomy of the Female." In Albert Ellis and Albert Abarbanel, eds., *The Encyclopedia of Sexual Behavior*, vol. 1, p. 792.

[2] Masters and Johnson, "Orgasm, Anatomy of the Female." In Ellis and Abarbanel, eds., *The Encyclopedia of Sexual Behavior*, vol. 1, p. 788.

sexual relationship can also be pleasurable.[3] Yet most scientific sex researchers have used orgasm as their criterion because it is the most precise and measurable indicator of sexual response. For purposes of this study, orgasm was defined as the spasmodic, highly pleasurable feeling with which the sex act concludes; the feeling—or feelings—that are the peak of sexual excitement and pleasure.

Some of the questions the women were asked were: age at initial orgasm and the means by which it was achieved; orgasm experiences subsequent to initial orgasm; difference in types of feelings during variously induced orgasms; necessity of orgasm as a condition for pleasurable feelings during sexual activity; motives for and feelings about pretended orgasm; and occurrence of dreams in which orgasm was experienced.

The 30 women experienced their first orgasms at a wide range of ages (from four to thirty-eight), and in a great variety of circumstances. Ten of them experienced their first orgasms through masturbation during childhood or adolescence; 2 through dreams during childhood or adolescence; 9 through premarital petting; and 9 through intercourse.

Petting as Source of First Climax

Petting is recognized as a nearly universal practice among American youths, and is almost always a source of concern to those engaging in it. Although the statements of these women may not seem contemporary, they are historically important. They reflect the attitudes of women in one of the last generations to whom contraceptives were not readily available premaritally. In considering the following data, it is well to keep in mind that the daughters and sons of these women may attach totally different meanings to the phenomenon of petting—meanings that these women find difficult to comprehend.

[3]A. C. Kinsey, *et al., Sexual Behavior in the Human Female,* p. 371.

Of the 30 women, 27 had petting experience prior to initial intercourse. The 3 who had not had their initial intercourse experience before they were married. Nine women reported having their first orgasms as a result of premarital petting, 3 with men whom they subsequently married. (Other women in the sample experienced orgasms through premarital petting as well, but it was not their *first* orgasm experience.)

Three of the 9 women who experienced their first orgasms through premarital petting had already had some intercourse experience. (The intention to marry was present in each relationship.) Virginia, for example, experienced her first orgasm through petting *after* she had had intercourse with a previous lover.

> . . . we were in the back of the car, necking and petting, and I don't even remember exactly what we were doing, but suddenly everything stopped! I was so stunned, and I thought, "Oh my gosh—I mustn't let this get out of hand!," and I tried to stop that feeling, but I couldn't. It was only *after* I experienced that orgasm that I knew how much I had missed before, and the crazy thing about it was that I thought all along I *had* been having it . . . Up until then I guess I didn't even know what it *was!*

Celeste experienced her first orgasm through manual stimulation with her husband, after three months of intercourse.

> He masturbated me and that's when I had my first orgasm. I felt very shook up and also very out of control at the same time. I knew that I'd had an orgasm and I enjoyed it, but I didn't permit myself to have this again . . . even though my husband tried very hard for me.

Celeste had experienced intercourse at age fifteen (not with the man she married), had petting experience with many other males, and had had many sexual encounters of various kinds and intensities, none of which concluded in orgasm until she was thirty-eight years old. When asked why she made no effort to repeat the experience that had occurred that one time with either her husband or ensuing lovers, or even in masturbation, Celeste replied:

> I couldn't ask a man to do anything. It had to come from him and if it didn't, then I felt that I just had to suffer. I did make some effort at masturbating thereafter, and I guess it's significant that the fantasy that would usually accompany this was one of being attacked by a male—and me being the helpless female.

Dreams as Source of First Climax

Two women reported initial orgasms through dreaming. Rebecca was twelve years old.

> At the time it was happening I made no connection that this was something sexual. I thought it was like any other dream that I had had; common dreams like flying down a flight of stairs. It was a dream that repeated itself and it gave me a pleasurable feeling. It never aroused my curiosity or interest to think about this kind of dream as being different from any other kind of dream.

Later, in her courtship with her fiancé, Rebecca was reminded of her dream experience.

> I can remember that the first time we petted and I let him touch my vagina was after the engagement. It was at his house and that was the first time that I experienced an orgasm that reminded me of my dreams. And after that, this was the way we continued to make love during the engagement. And I enjoyed it and he enjoyed it.

Susan stated:

> I don't recall the content of the dreams, but I know I got very excited in them and I would wake up right in the midst and be going through the whole motion of having sex.

Neither of these women recalled any conscious masturbatory incidents in childhood or adolescence, and in their adult life both women continued to have orgasm dreams.

Intercourse as Source of First Climax

Nine women first achieved orgasm through intercourse. Two experienced their first orgasm in premarital sexual relations with the partner they did marry; 3 with a partner they did not marry. Four experienced their first orgasm after marriage, 2 with their first husbands, 1 with a later husband, and 1 with an extramarital partner.

Carol experienced her first orgasm at age twenty-four in premarital sexual relations with the man she later married. She recalled:

> I wasn't sure what it should or would feel like, but afterward I know I felt relaxed and at ease and wonderful.

Rosemary's first orgasm occurred during her first marriage at age seventeen. She had been married several months before actual penile penetration was accomplished, and orgasm did not occur until about a year after the wedding:

> When it finally happened to me, I was surprised. I felt a sensation of sort of losing consciousness briefly.

Upon considering the initial orgasm experiences of the 30 women, what seems particularly striking is how different they were. Orgasm occurred with and without previous information, through a variety of sources, after just a few efforts in some instances and after an extraordinary amount of effort in others.

ORGASM: CLITORAL, VAGINAL, OTHER

The controversy among writers and theoreticians in the field of female sexual behavior as to the relative merits and "maturity" of "vaginal" and "clitoral" orgasms rages on and on. Freud held that these were two distinct sexual experiences. The clitoral orgasm was an immature reaction of girls and young women because, according to Freud and his followers, the clitoris is the sexual organ that young girls use for masturbating, and masturbation is infantile. Freudians contend that the "immature" clitoral orgasm should normally give way at some point in a woman's sexual and emotional development to the more "mature" vaginal orgasm.

The clitoris in the human female is in some ways the counterpart of the glans of the penis in the male. But the clitoris has only one function: sexual stimulation (pleasure). According to G. Lombard Kelly:

> The head of the clitoris is composed of erectile tissue and possesses a very sensitive epithelium or surface covering, supplied with special nerve endings called genital corpuscles, which are peculiarly adapted for sensory stimulation that under proper mental conditions terminates in the sexual orgasm. No other part of the female generative tract has such corpuscles.[4]

Perhaps this area of the female body is demeaned because its sole purpose is pleasure—and pure pleasure is suspect in a sexually repressive society.

It would appear that the myths perpetrated about female sex responses are so twisted and confused that what women may have been attempting to achieve for so long is unrealistic, to say the least. Moreover, the myth of the vaginal orgasm causes difficulty for men as well as for women. Many men feel at fault if the women they are with do not have the "correct" orgasm.

Ellis has stated the case most cogently: the "vaginal" orgasm is misnamed; it should be referred to instead as "orgasm obtained through intercourse (or through other methods of intravaginal stimulation)."[5]

Because women have so seldom described their *own* feelings about sexual climax, the personal statements presented here should be both useful and enlightening.

Cathleen stated:

[4]G. Lombard Kelly, *Sexual Feeling in Married Men and Women*, p. 35.
[5]Albert Ellis, "Is the Vaginal Orgasm a Myth?" In Manfred F. DeMartino, ed., *Sexual Behavior and Personality Characteristics*, p. 354.

I can have orgasms that are clitorally stimulated, and these to me are like high C on a keyboard . . . there may even be a uterine contraction response, but a vaginal orgasm is more of a full pelvic feeling. It's not localized. It's like the difference between having your pelvis on fire and just having a clitoral bonfire going.

Grace explained that she does not have difficulty in experiencing orgasm—whether clitorally or vaginally stimulated—but

if I were more psychologically in tune, I feel I would have fuller climaxes, and they would happen more quickly . . . if I didn't feel so generally threatened by men, I think I might not need clitoral stimulation at all . . . However, in regard to vaginal orgasm, it seems to me that the sensation is so very sensitive that any *negative* thoughts can really get in the way. But the clitoral stimulation is *so* direct that not much can get in the way of that!

Nancy felt

nothing vaginally until two or three years ago. It used to feel like just an intrusion—that was the most distasteful part of intercourse to me. Once I had an orgasm [stimulated manually or orally via the clitoris], that was it. No feeling after that at all. Yet I knew that something was terribly wrong.

After four years of psychotherapy, she began to have vaginal sensations,

which had never happened previously, I feel, because there was a psychological barrier in my feelings toward men which prevented orgasm through penetration.

Jane reported that she often felt stronger orgasmic sensations from masturbating than from intercourse.

I don't know if it feels like it's in a different place. The feeling is just so much more intense on the outside that what I usually do is just keep inching up so . . . [he] will be where I want . . . [him] to be . . . I don't usually have any trouble reaching an orgasm, so it's not a big thing in my mind.

Celeste stated:

When I could only have a clitoral orgasm with some manipulation, it made me feel as though I were participating in something unilaterally. It's as though I'm on the receiving end exclusively at that time. In a vaginal orgasm I feel very much as though I am participating with somebody—so that's the biggest difference to me.

As to the site of Celeste's orgasm experiences,

well, with a clitoral orgasm it starts at the focal point—at the clitoris, that is—then it spreads . . . until it is a brain thing—a visual, almost total sensory kind of response. Then I become almost aware of a sensation that makes me feel as though I'm seeing something—a peach, or a big round ball, or a red light. Or something that makes me feel as though it's not isolated—although the center is focused on the clitoris still, it radiates out and reaches all my senses. With a vaginal orgasm I'm very, very conscious of my skin, as well as the vagina. I get the sensation—I don't know if it's before or after—that my entire skin is involved. But it's much more my skin then than when I have a clitoral orgasm—tremendously sensitive. Almost as if I had a billion different nerve endings over my skin.

Frances was asked to describe her orgasmic feelings, and whether she felt differently when the orgasm emanated from different sources.

I don't feel there is any difference. At least I'm not aware of any. The time I have an orgasm is an intense kind of experience, it doesn't matter if it's vaginal or clitoral—after it there's an immediate release and relaxation for a moment. I don't think there's any difference. In one evening I might have both kinds—if there *are* two kinds, because much of the time during foreplay, I'll have some orgasms, and it'll be the same kind of experience then as when he inserts his penis. I don't feel any difference. I think there's more of a feeling of fulfillment when he's inside but I don't know if it's from the closeness—the psychological closeness . . . but I have more of a feeling of satisfaction with intercourse. Maybe it's also some feeling that this is the way it is supposed to be—I think we're given a feeling that this is the way it's supposed to be, so we feel it's more right if it happens with the penis inside.

Karen thinks that orgasm involves some kind of clitoral stimulation—that the clitoris is bound in some way

to be touched. If you're having intercourse and even if the penis isn't touching the clitoris, it's bound to be moving around there. That baloney about simultaneous orgasm— two people don't *have* to have a climax together. I think it's another one of those myths and lies. As long as it happens, what does it matter if you come first or he comes second, or you come twice, or he comes once—sometimes maybe you don't even come at all.

Amelia noted that "there is an additional area of important stimulation which is the crest of pelvic bone where the outer labia meet." For her this area and the clitoris are

augmentation spots . . . even slight or momentary stimulation at these points, especially when the pressure of my husband's body builds up vaginal spasms and a kind of vaginal hunger for the penis—that is, if it isn't already there. And from the vaginal spasms, waves radiate all over, inside and out. It feels like being part of the universe —an orbital or whirlpoolish sensation. I used to think of some sensations as being in my stomach, but I've realized from things I've read that these must be in my uterus. Sometimes even muscles in my feet get involved in the contractions.

As for simultaneous orgasms, my husband and I have that happen sometimes—although it's more likely to be an overlap with his orgasm beginning when mine is nearly

over and then mine either continues or there are several
more. I can't really tell which. But sometimes it can continue a very long time—almost as though there will never
be anything but this ecstasy. When we do have simultaneous orgasms, there's something different about it because
it's great to know you're both in the same kaleidoscope,
and I feel sort of flashes of alternating awarenesses like,
"I'm here, we're here, I'm here, we're here."

Grace, at forty, prefers clitorally stimulated orgasms.

I would say that clitoral orgasm is some shivery something
that kind of runs out along the nerves . . . but with my few
and far between vaginal orgasms, it's somehow something
deeper . . . a deeper physical feeling. There's some kind of
weight about it. One is along the nerves, the surface of the
body, and the other has this, I don't know what . . . a kind
of thing you get more submerged in feeling fully. And I
recall that feeling as very overwhelming, washed over by
something, that crying or sobbing was really the only
place it could go to express itself. If it's a true vaginal
orgasm, I can see where the quality of surrender is greater,
and I'm not so good at it because I can't surrender that
fully.

Although Masters and Johnson claim that the *physiological*
phenomenon of orgasm is always essentially the same, regardless of the source of stimulation, these women perceived striking differences in the sensations of various kinds of climax
experiences. These felt differences may be due to past experience and habits, or to the female's failure, for various reasons,
to appreciate the physical potentialities of her sexuality. That
is, women need to have the freedom to learn *what* and *how*
they can feel. Many books and theories of sexual techniques
and responses that have claimed to educate and liberate have,
instead, shamed and deprecated people by laying down rules
of what is right and wrong, ideal and not ideal, about sexual
responses and relationships. Those women who do not fit what
authorities consider "healthy" or "mature," or whatever the

current terminology for sexual adequacy is, hold themselves in low esteem and feel like sexual failures.

Kinsey wrote:

> . . . if the female is disappointed because of her inability to accomplish *what she thinks she should,* she may develop a sense of inferiority which further reduces the possibilities of her ever having satisfactory relationships.[6] [Italics mine]

In other words, instead of orgasm being an experience, it becomes an achievement or a test of competence. Some touching examples of this were the feelings expressed by 3 women in the study. Frances, in stating her reasons for participating in the study, commented:

> Previously, talking about sex was something which was difficult, very difficult, for me, and therefore, I felt I would learn something from this experience. However, I also think that the fact that I felt I was having satisfactory sexual relations enabled me to volunteer. If I felt that my sex life was something that I was ashamed of or something that was not satisfying, then I think I would have been more reluctant to talk about it. This way I felt there was nothing to hide, so I can talk about it.

Two other women who had not experienced orgasm through heterosexual intercourse until some time during the two years prior to the study stated—independently and voluntarily—that if this had not happened, they would not have agreed to participate in the study. Each said that she would have felt ashamed to admit what she considered to be her sexual inadequacy or "neurotic deficiency."

MULTIPLE ORGASM

Masters and Johnson's research verified that the human female is physiologically capable of experiencing multiple or-

Kinsey et al., *Sexual Behavior in the Human Female,* pp. 371-82.

gasm. Yet, only 8 women in the study reported experiencing multiple orgasms. The accounts of Frances and Zoe were typical.

> Usually when my husband and I are having sex, especially in recent years, I may have five or ten orgasms before my husband ever has one, so it's never a question of my not having an orgasm, but rather it's a question of how many I have before he has one. He is able to continue going for a long time and he is able to hold off until, well, until I've had enough. It may sound like I'm bragging, but I'm not. It has reached the point where in one evening there can be ten orgasms, and each orgasm has a little discharge and then I'll sort of collapse, and he'll go ahead and have his and that will be all. And almost invariably while he's finished, I'll have another one, even though I'm too exhausted to move. [Frances]

> When I was thirty and separated from my second husband, I had an affair with a young man about twenty-two. We were making love and he rubbed against my clitoris during the foreplay and caused me to have an orgasm. In a few seconds, he entered me and we began to have intercourse. At that time, I had a second and even greater orgasm. I was amazed because the second one followed so closely upon the first one. I didn't know at that time that women were capable of having more than one orgasm in a short time period. When I later read about multiple orgasms I experimented when I was masturbating to see just how many I *could* have. It was really wild! I got very tired of counting after twenty-two and just continued until I absolutely could not move one part of my body and all that was happening were the spasms inside. [Zoe]

THE NECESSITY OF ORGASM FOR PLEASURE

Why do some women care more than others about orgasm? The noted Kinsey group considered three important factors in analyzing the considerable variation in female responses to orgasm: the stimuli, the capacity of the responding individual, and the nature and extent of her previous experience. Obviously some women, like some men, are more interested in or oriented toward sex than others. There is variety in the ability to have orgasm, and even variety in the wish to have orgasm. Some women have more sex more often than others; some women let themselves get more stimulated than others; and perhaps some women have more sensitive nerve endings.

Masters and Johnson found that when a woman sufficiently stimulated and aroused to reach the "plateau phase," during which the organs of the pelvic area are engorged with blood, experiences orgasm, these organs return to a state of detumescence within approximately ten minutes. Without the release of orgasm, however, the process takes approximately three hours. This condition probably accounts for feelings of discomfort, tension, aches, and certain disappointments of many women who experience high arousal *without* climax.[7] Therefore, some women need orgasmic release psychologically *and* physiologically. Others don't want or need or allow themselves to get very much stimulation in the first place.

There were women in the sample who had no difficulty experiencing orgasm, but whose ability to have warm and intimate human relationships was impaired. Conversely, there were women who had sexual or psychological difficulties experiencing orgasm yet seemed able to establish and maintain satisfying heterosexual relationships. Psychological problems are not always reflected in sexual responses: one woman may have a sex response problem, while another has a relationship problem.

Several women in this study used orgasm not as a way of

[7]This finding also increases our understanding of the chronic pelvic congestion some women experience. First described in 1949 by Dr. Howard C. Taylor, Jr., chronic engorgement of the blood vessels of the uterus and associated pelvic organs seems to be related to a number of gynecological problems. According to Dr. Taylor, it is traceable in many instances to a constantly recurring pattern of sexual arousal with no orgasmic release.

sharing a deep experience with a man, but rather to diminish the intimacy of sexual encounter. Jane and Karen explained that they experience orgasm very quickly, in order to avoid feeling any deep or prolonged commitment to their partners. (This presents an interesting contrast to those women who—according to men, and probably in fact—deliberately "refuse" to have orgasm.)

Eve, who complained about lack of orgasms with her husband, was reluctant to engage in extensive foreplay with him. It is not surprising that she was unsatisfied, since she would not allow herself to be aroused. For many women, orgasm is not only not always a necessity, but is sometimes frightening. Eve could not admit to fear of her own sexual feelings and thus arranged matters so that she could blame her husband.

Gratifications other than orgasm impel some women to continue to engage in sexual relations. These gratifications are individually perceived and variously described.

> I often have sex with my husband when he feels like it although I may not feel like it. I will have sex with him just because it is pleasing to him, and I like to please him. Also, I know that if I do feel like having sex and experiencing an orgasm, I can always do so. Really, I think that for me the only thing that affects the pleasure at all is my psychological state, which I sometimes understand and sometimes do not. But whether I understand it or not, it has the very most to do with how much I enjoy the sex or how much I *can* or *want* to involve myself. I find that it is very possible for me to have sex just for my husband, and feel very much with him and feel that he is very much with me, and enjoy the sex. [Rachel]

> Sex is the means by which one feels closeness and satisfaction, and I can overlook other things if there is a feeling of affection about the act. I'd say my sexual appetite has not so much to do with sex itself, as with the need for affection. I'll go through with the sex act not because I want it, but for that feeling of affection. [Rebecca]

Grace stated that if she can

> accomplish an orgasm through oral stimulation—which is quite easy and fully pleasurable—then I come close to, at least, some kind of emotional orgasm after insertion. Then there's a fuller feeling about the whole thing. Sometimes I have even sobbed from the accomplishment of that full feeling, it was so overwhelming. But even so, even without orgasm it's enjoyable to be with my husband. He's very good to me, and I like doing things that give him pleasure.

And Norma:

> If we have intercourse—which is rare, because my husband usually prefers oral sex or something other than screwing—then I'm so glad to get back on this track, and I'm pleased and feel good whether I have an orgasm or not. It's all extremes. If I feel that he has tried to communicate with me and give something to me emotionally, that he's enjoying me and I'm enjoying him, then I don't care whether I have a climax or not. It's not that important. Of course, I wouldn't like to go every night without one. Then I would feel very frustrated and want something more.

Some of these statements bear out Dr. Elkan's contention that "orgasm has little to do with happiness and may, or may *not,* enrich a woman's life."[8] But the accounts of other women suggest that the degree of disappointment or frustration experienced is equal to the degree of expectation. Sarah for instance finds that orgasm is

> absolutely necessary for me each time I have sex. Without it I feel unfinished and deprived. This has always been true for me. I could never just feel, "Oh well, next time," or "It's nice anyhow."

---

[8] E. Elkan, "Orgasm Inability in Women," *International Journal of Sexology* 4 (1951): 243.

Certainly, some women are more sex-oriented than others; they permit themselves to become stimulated easily and therefore require orgasmic release. Women who expect to experience orgasm and do not are both *un*satisfied and *dis*satisfied. As one woman in the study put it, "If you have your mind set for it and it doesn't happen, then you're frustrated. But if you're not expecting it in the first place, then there's no letdown."

PRETENSE OF ORGASM

Orgasm is too often thought of as an accomplishment rather than an experience. Seventeen of the women reported that they had pretended to have orgasms with their partners at various times and for various reasons; that is, they simulated the orgasm when they weren't in fact experiencing it. Twelve women never pretended, and 1 woman felt it necessary to pretend *not* to experience orgasm with her husband.

Of the women who pretended, Zoe explained:

> I wanted him to feel that he had given me complete satisfaction, which in a sense he did. He couldn't have given me anything else, and I wasn't grinning and bearing it; I was enjoying it, what there was of it. Sometimes I pretended to have an orgasm just to get it over with, when I knew nothing was going to happen with me.

Barbara reported that she began pretending orgasm after her husband accused her of being frigid.

Donna used to pretend

> in the early years of our marriage. I thought he would have a feeling of failure if I didn't have an orgasm and that he would feel that he had disappointed me. I did it to protect his feelings—but I must admit I also did it to protect mine—that is, I was afraid he would think I wasn't very feminine or sexy if I didn't have an orgasm each and every time.

Karen stated:

> Sometimes I pretend to have an orgasm because my hus-
> band gets upset if I don't. I've often told him that I can
> enjoy giving *him* pleasure and being close to him and that
> it isn't *always* necessary for me to have a climax. But you
> can't ever make a man believe that!

Among the women who never pretended, Nancy reported
feeling "very badly about pretending what I don't feel. I can't
imagine doing such a thing. I'd feel like such a fake." Amelia
felt that to pretend orgasm would be a form of

> hypocrisy and contempt toward the man, thinking that he
> would believe it. Also, you're not considering that an
> orgasm is something you're entitled to and should be en-
> joying. I don't remember any man ever asking me if I had
> had one, but I imagine I would have told him honestly but
> kindly, "No, but that's all right, I like you. Otherwise I
> wouldn't be here with you."

Irene's husband refused to believe that she *did* experience
orgasm.

> . . . when it did happen he said he didn't believe me. He
> thought it was disgusting and horrifying, so I learned to
> cover up those feelings with him. I don't know why he had
> this need to accuse me of acting, or making it up—I
> believe now that it must have to do with his strong moral-
> istic attitudes.

The most common reasons given for pretending were: 1)
self-defense, against the accusation of "inadequacy" in this era
of the "cult of the orgasm" and 2) a wish not to hurt the
partner's feelings (many men appear to feel that it is a reflec-
tion on *their* adequacy if the female partner does not come to
orgasm, and find it difficult to believe a woman's stated feeling
that it is not always important for her to experience orgasm
at every union).

MALE AND FEMALE

Men's understanding of female sexuality is perhaps no greater than women's understanding of male sexuality, but since the male view of sex has been predominant for as long as we can remember, its failure is more apparent as scientists and humanists uncover at last the real facts of life.

Some of the differences that promote our failure to understand the experience of the opposite sex are physiological. Masters and Johnson have observed that the type of stimulation most conducive to orgasm is "consistent friction." The act of intercourse itself generally provides this for men: the friction involved in penetration and sexual movements inevitably stimulates the glans of the penis; but it does not necessarily provide such stimulation for the clitoris. Consequently, men usually experience orgasm through intercourse whereas women may or may not.

Timing of sexual response is another apparently significant difference between male and female sexuality, although it may have more to do with technique and psychology than with physiology. It is commonly believed that men take less time than women to reach orgasm: women are blamed for being "too slow" and men are ridiculed for being "too quick." Yet, many men learn to control and delay their sexual climax, and many women reach orgasm when they are relaxed and adequately stimulated. Another factor in the timing problem is that men have traditionally initiated the sex act. Thus, by the time a man approaches a woman, he is already somewhat aroused psychologically if not physiologically; that is, males have a head start in the process of sexual stimulation. This head start does not necessarily imply that men have fewer sexual anxieties; but rather, that their anxieties have a different focus. Men's fears of sexual inadequacy generally relate to the beginning of the sex act (erection), while women's fears are more often concerned with the end (orgasm).

The orgasm itself is quite different for men and women, as

described earlier, and is therefore another area in which one sex misunderstands or is unaware of the other's feelings. Carol, for instance, feels that she always knows when her husband has an orgasm, but that he does not always know when she does. And Rosemary reported:

> I don't believe that men know when women have orgasm because I have pretended and they didn't know the difference. I also think that women often can't tell when a man has one. There are some men who absolutely lose themselves, to the point of making some kind of sound, a groan or something. And there are some men with whom I never knew when this was happening for them . . . There were no sounds or actions that I could identify.

"Intercourse," says Webster, is communication. A great deal of communication is necessary for a male and a female to reach each other from their entirely different experiences. They have to let each other know *how* they prefer to communicate, and find a means to indicate their preferences—in terms of frequency, duration of various phases of the union, positions, technique, and any of the other subtle, often fragile, wishes, desires, and habits that are crucial to the effectiveness of a relationship.

Many women had great difficulty telling their husbands what sexual positions and experiences they liked. Della described experiencing orgasm through manual or penile stimulation prior to intercourse, but

> even though I knew that I could *always* have an orgasm that way, it still seemed like a chancy thing . . . because you see I could never *tell* my partner what worked for me, so if a guy just happened to know about this, then he would satisfy me, but if he didn't know, then I could never ask or tell him.

Roxanne admitted:

> . . . I know that my breasts are very sensitive to stimulation, and yet wouldn't let my husband do anything like this for me.

Zoe found, when she did become able to express her desires, that her husband couldn't accept them.

> Before we married sex was very pleasurable, even though I didn't have a climax. I was too embarrassed to tell him the only ways I knew that I could have orgasm—that is, orally or by rubbing the penis against the clitoris. But later in the marriage, I found a position where I could be on top of him and simultaneously stimulate the clitoris and have an orgasm during intercourse. But he didn't like me to be on top of him, said he didn't like what he thought it signified pschologically. Then eventually he told me all I ever thought about was sex. I never had the feeling he was satisfied even though he had an orgasm. He was like a spring that couldn't unwind. It seemed that, sexually, the more I was able to enjoy him, the less he was able to enjoy me. It finally got to the point where he simply would not sleep with me at all.

In the matter of frequency of relations, 22 of the women reported that they were in accord with their mates' wishes, or that their mates' desires were generally in accord with their own. Three women, however, desired sexual relations more frequently than their husbands. One woman's husband approached her as infrequently as once a month; her first solution to this difference was self-stimulation, later an extramarital relation, and still later, a divorce. For the other 2 women, the disagreements about frequency were mainly reflections of other problems in the marriage. The remaining 5 women wanted less sexual contact than their husbands.

Many of the women in this study found the general psychological climate of the relationship to be at least as crucial a determinant of sexual responsiveness as adequate physical stimulation. Amelia said that she and her husband could be stimulated by talking or reading poetry to each other, while Catheleen said that for her,

> the best foreplay is if I have had all day to be with my husband . . . It doesn't matter where we are, we just have all day to respond to each other, to look at each other . . . and the kind of give and take which can go on in a day is to me a very important part of foreplay. It doesn't have very much to do with technique, or the specifics of foreplay that you read about in a sex manual [but] in general with how much I feel that I've being given in life.

Orgasms that resulted mostly from good technique (in her previous marriage) were "not so totally full. The physical response would be there . . . the orgasm would be there as such. But it wouldn't leave me filled up emotionally."

Rosemary believes:

> The best in sex always comes out of that kind of contact when we just feel good toward each other . . . the natural result of that kind of feeling in sex. I just have this kind of bookish feeling that that's the way it should be. And the best times are also when I can let myself be involved, and not be afraid. It seems when we have lots of time to relax, and peacefully enjoy our surroundings, and the privacy and all—times we've gone out to the country for the day or a weekend—we just build up so much closeness to each other, and that's the best kind of situation for having sex. It seems more psychological than physiological, doesn't it —but that's the way I experience it.

And Karen reflected, concerning her responsiveness to the psychological feelings and stimulations:

> I really think that sex so reflects every other single feeling that there is no separating it from other parts of the relationship. If I'm angry with my husband, if I feel hurt, rejected, demeaned, then I don't want sex, and if I do have sex, then I won't have an orgasm. If I feel good about myself it's a joy at all times. If, on the other hand, I'm

feeling depressed and the depression is not directly related to my husband, but rather a general depression, then I can have sex with him just for his needs. It's not that it's a great pleasure then—it's just a function. Other times it can be very pleasurable even without an orgasm. It just so much reflects what's going on with me.

PERVERSITY

Ten of the 30 women considered various sexual activities or techniques "perverse." Five of them felt that any kind of acted out sado-masochism was perverse ("hitting" or "being hit"), 4 named homosexuality as a perversion, 2 anal intercourse, 2 mentioned bestiality, 1 child-parent incest, 1 masturbation, and 1 "intercourse without orgasm." While 20 women considered no sexual activity perverse, some of the others named more than one.

Invariably, those who specifically mentioned sado-masochistic sexual actions as perverse had—and sometimes still have—relationships in which psychological sado-masochism was an integral part. Yet they did not regard their own behavior toward their mates—or their mates' behavior toward them —as perverse.

EVALUATION OF MARITAL VS. NON-MARITAL INTERCOURSE

Ten women participated in *extra*marital sexual relations while living with their husbands. Seven of them *preferred* extramarital intercourse to marital intercourse, mainly because of poor sexual relations with their husbands.

Louise was never able to experience orgasm in her marriage and felt ashamed: "I don't know—maybe my husband was too much like my father." She reported, however, that with one lover she had "strong sensual feelings. I actually *felt.* And I was able, for the first time in my life, to experience orgasm."

Roxanne reported that her lover is "the first person who has been able to satisfy me consistently in intercourse."

Five women felt that their premarital sexual relations with their husbands were better than their marital relations. Celeste reported experiencing orgasm with her husband premaritally

> but I certainly didn't permit myself to have many after that, even though he certainly tried very hard for me. Once we were married, even though I enjoyed experimenting sexually, I quickly lost interest because he was no longer the "illicit male," and therefore he was no longer exciting.

Zoe stated that the sexual relations changed in quality after marriage and a similar feeling about her husband's withdrawal after marriage was expressed by Rebecca.

> No matter what was going on, he seemed not to be there. There was a singular absence of presence in him and it was like he was going through the motions, even enjoying them, but *he* was absent.

CLIMAX PROFILE

Using the modal frequency (highest number of like responses) as an index to the usual experiences and feelings about orgasm, the following description is a profile of the "typical" woman's responses:

She experienced her first orgasm through masturbation when she was well into her sixteenth year. She began masturbating before her first menstruation at age twelve and continues to have guilt feelings about it. Although somewhat familiar with the feelings of orgasm, she did not expect nor did she experience it during her initial intercourse, which occurred premaritally. She did not regret the loss of her virginity and did not expect to marry her initial partner.

She continued to masturbate at times after her marriage, but preferred intercourse with her husband as a means of sexual release. Although she usually experienced orgasm during intercourse, when she did not, she could also derive satisfaction and pleasure from the physical and emotional closeness of the sexual act. On occasion, she pretended to experience orgasm during intercourse, primarily to spare her partner feelings of "failure."

She recognized an increase of sexual desire around her menstrual period and had intercourse during this time. In general, she and her husband agreed on the frequency and technique of intercourse. She never engaged in extramarital relationships.

She never experienced orgasm while dreaming, nor did she experience multiple orgasm during intercourse. She was not aware of having fantasies while masturbating.

Although at some time prior to her initial intercourse she perceived sex as somewhat lewd, she does not now consider any sexual practice perverse.

CONCLUSIONS

A serendipitous finding emerged from the data of the 30 women who volunteered for this study: all 30—sooner or later—experienced orgasm through heterosexual relations. Yet orgasm adequacy was *not* a prerequisite for participation in the study. This unexpected universal led me to wonder about various other traits that might possibly hold true for orgasmic women.

From the personalities and responses of these 30 women, it appears that the factor of orgasm experience does not in and of itself signify anything more than a physiological response. Whether orgasm was necessary or gratifying or difficult or easy or frustrating or fulfilling seemed to be a matter of each women's motivation.

But if orgasm is not a biological universal, what is its role in human evolution? Does it, in fact, serve any purpose at all?

In spite of the variations in response discussed above, orgasm apparently does function for many people as a psychosexual incentive to relate to each other—whether or not these relationships result in reproduction. A century ago, women were told that marital sex was merely a dark necessity to be endured. They were not expected to enjoy sexual relations for, as wives and mothers, they had other sources of gratification: economic security and unquestioned respect for serving a clearly defined function in society. But as women's roles changed, their expectations became more uncertain, and their sense of identity more ambiguous. Consequently, they began to search for something to replace the satisfactions that psychosocial evolution had destroyed. A few theorists believe that for females the orgasm became a reality only very recently and that it will become a much greater one as their traditional domestic gratifications decline.

Biologists point out that in the animal world there is little evidence at all of orgasmic response among females. However, almost all male animals are so structured physiologically that they clasp the female securely for a period long enough to complete copulation and impregnation. In effect, the mating urge brings them together and physiology permits them to interlock. Besides human beings, there is only one other exception to this style of sexual intercourse: a particular family of swans that does not have the capacity to "clasp." According to observers, at the end of copulation, the female swan, often emits a "cooing" sound, indicating some kind of pleasure.

Dr. Elkan, in an article describing the etiology of the orgasm, made the point that men and women need something to bring them together.[9] When the incentive is not physiological, it is something else: status or security or even pleasure.

[9] E. Elkan, "Evolution of Female Orgastic Ability: A Biological Survey," *International Journal of Sexology* 2 (1948): 1–13.

CHAPTER EIGHT

INTERVIEW: JULIA

It is lamentable that women have done so little thinking and writing on their own behalf and have accepted so meekly the passive role which men in Western civilization have stamped upon female sexual interest.

—Helena Wright

I didn't know until this experience how much I was like anybody else.

—Eve

If a woman wishes to test the validity of another's feeling, she must bring her own feeling into play. . . . But the feelings she brings must be her true feelings or they will not form a true standard by which to measure, and she will remain ignorant of the other's reality.

—M. Esther Harding

THE FOLLOWING complete interview will demonstrate the kinds of information elicited by this research procedure and interview guide. It has been edited only to facilitate reading and to protect the woman's identity.

A dear friend once commented that, to him, people are like snowflakes: "They look alike but each one is different." In this sense, Julia is not typical of these thirty or any other woman. Typicality is obviously too circumscribed a concept to apply to the human experience.

Julia is a very attractive woman, and is exceptionally intelligent and articulate. Tall, with long, darkish blond hair and a slim, graceful figure, she seems very feminine. She has a soft speaking voice, and at certain moments, especially when she talked about her early childhood, I could easily picture her as a little girl. At the time of the interview, when she was thirty-four, Julia was a nursery school teacher and planned to become a child therapist. She had been divorced for several years, but shortly after the interview met a man she later married.

Our sessions took place on consecutive Sunday mornings during the winter. There was a special quality to the quiet atmosphere of a Sunday morning that heightened the intensity of our concentration.

FIRST SESSION

JULIA. I was reading *The Source*, by Michener, which is about a dig, and I got to the part where they dug up a little goddess called Astarte, the goddess of fertility. I

looked at the drawing they had made of her, and it was
the nicest thing because I identified with this beautiful
little goddess, this funny ginger cookie little drawing. I
said, "My God, she looks just like me and she's 1320 B.C.
I identify with her completely." Her whole shape was
fundamentally, totally feminine. I looked at it in amaze-
ment, and it was the greatest feeling to be able to identify.
I had to tell you that before we started.

LEAH SCHAEFER. As you were talking just now, I got the feeling—and maybe it's because of where we are in therapy or
because you were thinking about the interview—that you
had taken yourself back to the beginning of your life . . .

J. I've had a lot of rebirth thoughts lately. I feel like a baby,
in a sense starting totally anew.

L.S. Since we've known each other for over two years, I may
already know the answers to some of the questions I am
going to ask you, but I will ask them again for the record.
I will ask them as though I haven't asked them before,
for two reasons. The sequence is important: talking about
one thing helps you think differently about what follows.
You will probably find that some of what you talk about
you yourself will see differently, or that you will learn
something new about yourself. As you are gradually led
deeper into your memory you will make all sorts of associations and connections. When you repress a sexual
memory you repress a lot of peripheral memories with it
and when you dig it up, you dig these up also. They help
to reconstruct the memories of the evolution of your life.

Incidentally, if you want any of these tapes destroyed,
I will do so. If you want to keep them, you may. I have
them typed and keep a copy myself, for my own information, for my research.

What I want to ask you first are certain facts we both
know. How old are you?

J. I'm thirty-four.

L.S. Do you have brothers and sisters?

J. I have two brothers.

L.S. How old are they?

J. Alan is thirty-three and Ben is thirty-two.

L.S. And you were all born in the United States?

J. I was born in New York, Alan and Ben in Europe, in our house. I saw Ben when he was one day old.

L.S. Did you see him being born?

J. No, I don't think I did. I was just over three. It was a confusing period in my life because we were all in Europe, and I remember that we were staying with friends of my mother's. And the next thing I remember is going to the house in the country, and my father taking my brother and me upstairs to see the new baby. He was in a kind of blue Moses basket, and you know I loved my little brother immediately. I remember—maybe it's a fantasy —that I thought he smiled at me. And that was just the greatest thing in the world.

L.S. How old were your parents when you were born?

J. My mother was twenty-four and my father was twenty-six.

L.S. How long had they been married?

J. I think about three or four years.

L.S. Now, your mother is American and your father is European. How much schooling did each of your parents have?

J. My father went through college and got a B.S. And my mother just went through high school and never went to college. She met my father while he was at college.

L.S. Did your mother's family have money?

J. Yes. Not masses of it, but they were very comfortable.

L.S. Did his family have money?

J. They had money but, well, I guess at that time they still had it because it was pre-World War II. Although I don't think they were as comfortably off as they had been before World War I.

L.S. What was your father doing in the United States?

J. Well, he went to M. University. I don't know why he went there, but that's why he came here. And then he got a job with an American firm. Politically, I don't know what was happening then, but that was the early thirties. He must have seen the handwriting on the wall in some way, because he did get an American job and he did start to do something about citizenship.

L.S. You were born in 1936, right? And then how long after you were born did they move back to Europe?

J. I think they did so first when I was six weeks old. Then they came back here. That's a very confusing three years. I remember that the winter of '37 I was in Europe for Christmas because I have seen photographs. And my brother Alan was born in '38 and he was born in Europe. The summer after that, before Ben was born, we were in Europe. I can remember crawling into the water there.

L.S. Did your father speak with an accent?

J. I think it was more of an intonation. He had a very definite way of speaking. So you weren't quite sure what was his accent and what was his own particular way of talking. And we spoke German at home anyway.

L.S. Did you speak German before you spoke English?

J. Yes.

L.S. Did your mother speak German also?

J. She spoke it fluently but badly.

L.S. How did she learn it?

J. She learned it in Europe. The year before she got married she went over to Europe for the winter to get to know my father's parents. She must have taken some German lessons. And she had already learned enough French to speak it pretty decently. She just picked up languages naturally.

L.S. Just tell me several more vital statistics. Your father died when you were what age.

J. I was seven and a half.

L.S. And he died during the war?

J. Yes, he was killed in action.

L.S. He was a flyer?

J. Yes, a fighter pilot.

L.S. And your mother died . . .

J. You know, it's very hard for me to remember the date when my mother died. It was '65. Around Eastertime, March. She died at home, at my grandfather's. She had been living in New York, and when she knew she was sick, she said she wanted to go back home and she wanted to be taken care of there. And she died two months later.

L.S. How long after your father died did your mother return to the United States?

J. He died in January, and she came back around August of the same year.

L.S. And then she remarried just the one time. And when did she remarry?

J. It was the same year. And that was always very nebulous. Because I think she got married in Europe. In fact, I know she did because my grandfather told me. She had gotten married in April over there and what she told us was that she got married when she went to visit my stepfather's mother in Canada in November. And I've never been quite sure what really did happen. My stepfather was Canadian and was in the army. She said they got a cablegram at his mother's house that he was coming back that very weekend and she said they got married then. That was in November, Thanksgiving.

L.S. I don't know whether to ask you this now or save it for later, but I think I'll ask you now because it's on my mind. Did you have any strong feelings about her remarrying that soon after your father's death?

J. I kicked up such a storm about it that the household could not rest for days. Because what happened was that she had come back at the end of the summer, and we were at my grandmother's summer place near the Cape. And it's a great old shingled house and Granny had been brought up there and everything. After lunch we had to have a rest. One day, I can remember, my mother was putting me to bed, and I noticed she had two wedding rings. I said, "Why do you have two wedding rings?" She had been telling us about this fabulous Uncle John who was going to come and stay with us, and ride and swim and all these great things, so I was sort of looking forward to meeting Uncle John. But then she said that she was going to marry Uncle John, and instead of giving her an engagement ring, because it was the war, he had given her a wedding ring. And I was simply livid. I thought it was an incredible betrayal of my father. And I can remember screaming that I didn't want to have any more little brothers and sisters, especially if they didn't have our name. I think it must have taken my nurse and my mother and my grandmother about two or three days to get me calm.

L.S. As you look back on your life, as far back as you possibly can recall, what is your very, very first memory of anything that has a sexual connotation? Now, that doesn't have to be an actual event. It can be a feeling, something you oversaw or overheard or believe you saw or overheard, a sensation. And in fact to an outsider it might not have a sexual connotation. But if it feels that way to you, tell what it is.

J. Well, there are two things that come to my mind that have always interested me. One was—I think they were about the same time, I was probably three or four—I was walking through the house with my father, and a friend of his was staying with us, Uncle Max, and we walked into the bathroom and Uncle Max had just been taking a shower and had no clothes on, and I remember pointing at his penis and looking at my father and saying, "What's that?" And I remember knowing perfectly well that I knew what that was because I had two little brothers— I just wanted to see what my father's reaction would be.

And he answered me perfectly matter-of-factly, and that was fine.

L.S. What did he say?

J. He said it in German, a *Schnecke,* which means a snail.

L.S. Is that the German word for penis?

J. I think . . . No, it isn't. Because my sister-in-law doesn't use that word. It must have been a family word or something. But I don't think it's typical . . .

And the other thing I remember was about the same time. I was in my room standing in my crib and the butler, whom for some reason I didn't care for particularly—maybe he frightened me, I don't know—came into my room when I was with my nurse. And I had no clothes on. When he came in, I didn't want him to see me without any clothes on, so I remember trying to wind the apron to my little dress around me so that he wouldn't see me. I was used to people seeing me with no clothes. It was just him I didn't want to see me.

L.S. Because you didn't like him.

J. Yes. These stand out in my mind because there is some kind of awareness of male/female, being aware of sex and difference. And the thing that amuses me is that I was already so aware by this time.

L.S. Do you think that the butler memory happened before the memory of your father and his friend in the shower?

J. I don't know why, but I think it happened after. But I have no rational reason to say that.

L.S. Do you think they happened near each other?

J. Within two or three months.

L.S. Do you have any recollection of ever having seen your father nude?

J. I don't, which is interesting because I'm sure that I must have.

L.S. It's also possible that you might not have?

J. Well, my family always walked around with no clothes on. But my father was away a lot. And because I was so small, it's possible that I didn't see him. I remember seeing my mother. I used to go in when she was taking a bath.

L.S. Do you have a sense that throughout your childhood nudity was treated casually?

J. Yes.

L.S. For anyone?

J. No, not by my father's family. But my mother's family! My grandfather was very modest, and my grandmother was always streaking around with no clothes on. And my mother. But as children, we were always bathed together. And if Mommy were taking a bath or if Granny were, they practically had seances in the bathtub. It was a very social time.

L.S. Would you take baths with them? Or was it the children with the children and the grownups separately?

J. Children with children and the adults by themselves.

L.S. I think this is worth a little bit of looking into because of your interpretation of the question you asked your father about his friend's penis. You felt that you knew because of having little brothers, and yet often to children, a male child's penis and a male adult's penis are quite different. The size, the pubic hair, etc. And yet . . .

J. You're right, because the feeling I had is that I knew what it was. So maybe I had seen my father, but I just don't remember.

L.S. It's possible that you had seen your father. And it's possible that you had had to suppress that memory because of what you now say about his family's attitude. If his family's attitude about nudity is a suppressive one and you had ever seen your father, by chance or whatever, the feelings that he communicated to you might have been suppressive.

J. That occurred to me when you were asking that.

L.S. It could have been a very clever way to make known to yourself what seemed unknown about your father, since your father would not have looked like your brother. Do you think that the answer he gave you was a family euphemism? I mean, if you think of the associations that you make thinking about the word "snail"—I don't know what that suggests in German.

J. It's called that, I think, because it looks like one. Isn't that why it was called that? My mother always called a penis a "turtle." And I think that was purely her own word and was based on what she thought it looked like.

L.S. Well, if you think of everything upside down, if you think of the snail coming out of the shell, it's like the penis.

L.S. I see, I see . . . There are a lot of Yiddish words that are like German words, and there's a Yiddish word for penis, although it's often used derogatorily.

J. *Schmuck* . . . Do you know what *"Schmuck"* means in German? Jewelry. So to me it means jewelry—that is, the best you've got—and when I heard it used for penis, it seemed such an interesting word play, because in common parlance it means just the opposite. And I thought how very funny because it truly should mean what I think it means—jewelry. You know that I don't know what the German word for penis is.

L.S. Well, if the euphemism for it is snail, or *Schnecke,* then I thought there might be a relationship between that and the word *"Schmuck."*

J. There may well be. I know my sister-in-law calls it "her-spatsie," whatever that means. Whether different families have different names or . . .

L.S. Do you have any other very early memories from that time other than those you mentioned?

J. I have a feeling that that was also the winter that I saw my parents most. Let's see, winter of '37 we were in Europe. You know, staying in Europe meant staying in a huge house with long, winding corridors. So that meant we hardly shared my parent's private life at all. Now the house in the country, in England, was much smaller and

I was older and we could wander around it. I can remember seeing my mother taking a bath and brushing her teeth and I was slightly disgusted. Isn't that interesting? She was kind of wobbly, and for some reason I didn't like that.

L.S. What else do you remember around then?

J. I was just thinking of a story my mother once told me. What had flitted through my head was that I was envious, you know. Because the story is that I was trying to get into the bathroom, and I couldn't reach the door handle. So she helped me or sombody helped me get in, and I said to her in German, "When I have a long nose and breasts like you, Mommy, I'll be able to open the door." And that was the same winter.

L.S. What did the long nose mean? Did your mother have a long nose?

J. Yes. It just meant a grownup, I guess. I was always teased because I had a *Stupsnase;* it turned up. I'm sure people thought it was rather cute and I'm sure it got tweaked, etc.

L.S. Did that make you feel different from your mother?

J. Yes.

L.S. Did the long nose make you feel different in a way that you didn't like?

J. I think I thought it was rather impressive to have a long nose. I think I wanted to have one. And that was the winter that Ben was born. My mother had a midwife, and gave birth to him at home. I always felt my little brother was the one my mother cared about the most, that he was the one who seemed to her to be a real baby. I think that there must have been some jealousy involved . . . I have a very strong memory of seeing him for the first time.

L.S. What did he look like?

J. He wasn't a blue baby, but he wasn't exactly pink and white. A kind of gnarled-up little baby with dark hair and just lying there. But for some reason, I really liked him.

L.S. Has he always been your favorite brother?

J. There was a time when he fell out of favor. But now I've become close to him all over again.

L.S. What you were telling me were associations to the fact that what you wanted was something that your mother had. You saw her as an idealized creature. Maybe the fact that she had your father made her seem to you the favored one . . . (I hope I'm not reading into this. If it doesn't seem right, let me know.) It's almost as though your father was the favorite parent and she had him. It must have seemed possible that if you could have what she had, you might get him, among the treasures.

J. I think you're right. I remember reading last year or the year before about Oedipal and Electra complexes. And I thought to myself, oh my God, you're the prime example. I can remember being very angry after Ben was born. My mother for some reason had been in bed and she was coming down to dinner and my father carried her down the stairs. It made me furious. Why was he carrying *her?* I was the baby, and I was the one who was supposed to be carried. I must have been terribly jealous of her. This was all the same period of time.

L.S. It's interesting that you would say that you were the baby, why wasn't he carrying me, since you weren't the *baby* baby. But I suspect you were never a baby and would have liked to have been.

J. You see, I know, for instance, that my mother nursed me for something like three weeks. I also know that in the hospital I had a nurse who was very devoted to me, and after three weeks she left. And that's when my other nurse came. So there must have been a big change at three weeks.

L.S. Is that Louisa, who stayed with you all the time? Who was very tough and unloving?

J. Yes. She did love me very much but she didn't demonstrate much affection. And she was also very tough. You know, I was thinking about this the other day. When I think of what examples of femininity I had to identify with, I think it's lucky I'm not in a mental hospital by now. Because Louisa was like a troglodyte. She was about 5′2″ and built like a pack poney, very solid, heavy, very masculine, always out cutting trees, exhorting us to get out in the freezing cold air and do some kind of physical activity. Not organized, not gymnastics, the sort of thing a lumberjack does. And it's funny because she had two brothers. I remember staying at her family's house, and I loved her younger brother. I remember him picking me up and carrying me around. And I thought he was splendid.

L.S. What recollections do you have concerning toilet training?

J. I don't really have any. I must have been very repressed. I can remember sitting on the potty, aged three, and trying to move around with the enamel potty beneath me, seeing how far I could move around the bathroom.

L.S. So what associations do you have?

J. Somehow that I was always being put there and that I didn't have to go, but they put me there anyhow. I never wanted to go when they put me there.

L.S. Whom do you mean by "they"?

J. Louisa. We always were supposed to go right after breakfast. And I never had to go after breakfast. I would have to go probably around ten. So after a while, I trained myself so that I would go after school, not wanting to go in school, being a Virgo and private by nature. And that still stuck to this day. But somehow I associate going to the toilet with Shredded Ralston because we always had breakfast upstairs, not downstairs or even in the kitchen, at my grandparents'. It was always brought up by Louisa and it was always cold cereal, which was O.K. if it was Puffed Rice, but half the time she would give us All-Bran and Shredded Ralston. And I just hated it. And then we were stuck on the toilet. And there was no time anyhow. Then you were put into the car and sent off to school. I just hated the whole thing.

L.S. Was all of this area of your life, toilet training, etc., supervised by Louisa?

J. By Louisa.

L.S. Do you remember any feelings of pleasure of distress associated with toilet training?

J. I think now that I look back that I felt like a failure. Not a horrible failure. But you were supposed to, and I didn't perform. Whereas if I could do it by myself on my own time, I was perfectly happy.

L.S. How did you react to the fact that you couldn't go to the bathroom when they expected you to? Did you expect to be punished? Did you have to tell fibs about it? How did you handle it?

J. No, it wasn't like that. I don't remember telling fibs about it. It was one of those wierd things. I think Louisa knew that I went whenever I did go. And I wasn't punished when I didn't go. But it was just one of those things you were supposed to do, and I couldn't do it and it went on every day. For instance, I never liked the taste of milk. It was a real job for me to get it down. So Louisa sometimes would put tea in it, and I could drink it with no trouble. However, sometimes she didn't. And I was made to drink a glass of milk every night and you couldn't leave the table until you finished your milk. I finally got myself into a system where I would eat my whole meal and slurp it down as fast as I could and my whole dinner would come up. But they still kept giving me a big glass of milk. When my mother came back from Europe she said, just don't give her milk. And after a while I got so that I could drink milk. But it was the same kind of thing as with the toilet training. It had no sense, it was just there.

L.S. Did you have any sense of your mother's saving you?

J. Yes, from that and from fish on Fridays. For that I will

be eternally grateful to her. I used to be sat at the table for hours and hours and hours and I had three things, the milk, the fish, always the most horrible kinds, and also gristle on meat—I just couldn't eat it, and that's all. And at school we had horrible meat three times a week. And I just couldn't eat it. Once I found a piece of willowware in my food, and that did it. I couldn't eat anything else. But they insisted on keeping me there. So I would sit there while everyone else was on the playground or in rest period or story period. And I would sit there and sit there. Then I think they must have relented a little bit. And, of course, once they relented I would try a little. But I never could eat the meat, and I would just eat the rest.

L.S. This trait of yours seems to show up so interestingly, doesn't it—that you always seem to have a sense of what is expected of you and even of the right thing to do. And you *will* do it so long as nobody is *forcing* you, so long as you are left to make your own decisions about the matter. You know, there is a kind of grandness, a kind of independence about your approach to everything, and a willingness to assume responsibilities—but just so long as nobody is pushing you. Someone should have told your family that they had the prehistoric goddess in their midst. They might even have chewed up your food for you—to say nothing of not daring to tell you what to eat, eh?

Incidentally, it will be interesting to talk later on about how this particular trait of yours manifests itself in your sexual and social-sexual relations with men in your life today. These personality traits always show up in some fashion.

J. My God, that's so interesting . . . I never thought about it like that before.

L.S. Do you remember the first time during your childhood that you heard or saw written what we call dirty or obscene words?

J. The first time I remember being aware of them was when I was nine years old. We had moved to a farm out West, and my stepfather had hired a farmer and his wife to work for him. They had five children. And my brother started to talk about shit, which didn't make any impression on me because I didn't know what it meant. But then my mother said, "Don't say that," and of course I asked what it meant, and she said it was a word that nice people don't use, it meant manure or bowel movement or whatever. And also I remember about the same time, maybe a year later, rhyming words, and I arrived at piss and I realized that something was wrong. My mother and my tutor were there and my mother said that that was something we didn't say. And I remember that I was embarrassed.

L.S. This was about age nine?

J. Yes, before that, at school, I can't remember . . . I'm trying to think what we considered dirty then. Oh yes, I remember, when I was five, at school it was considered a gas to pee down the drain, and one day a little girl was doing it when a teacher walked in and that ended that game. And I remember being very glad that it wasn't I who was doing it.

L.S. Do you remember what word you used for pee?

J. "Tee Tee."

L.S. And for bowel movement?

J. "Ta Ta." "Tee tee" and "ta ta."

L.S. Do you remember what words were used in your family for genitals?

J. Well, my mother used the German word for "turtle." And do you know, I can't remember any word for a little girl. My mother would always call it your little pussy, but earlier . . . (I'm trying to remember what my nurse called it. Totally blocked that out . . .) There must have been something.

L.S. Did your family have a concern about enemas and things like that during your childhood?

J. My grandmother was the most anal woman that lived. She called a bowel movement a "movie " *(laughter),* and she would say, "Did you have your movie, dear?" and it was none of her business because Louisa took care of that —by that time we had established the system—so I would tell her no or yes. And I felt she always had a sort of prurient interest in the timing, etc. She always did have this. In fact, one of my last memories of her involved this. She had cancer, and she always insisted on having a bowel movement every day no matter how little she had eaten, and the medicine caused her to lose control, which upset her. I remember one day coming in, and she had had an accident and gotten it all over herself, and she said rather pathetically, because I cleaned her up, that she hoped this wouldn't be my last memory of her. It's rather sad. But she did have a kind of concern about all of that. I don't know . . . I just remember being rather scornful of that.

L.S. When your brother was born, did you have any idea how babies were born?

J. I don't think I had any idea. I was told I was going to have a baby brother or sister. I of course wanted a sister because I already had a brother. I don't remember any-thing about breast feeding either, if my mother breast fed, which I'm not sure about . . . I don't remember knowing anything about how babies were born until I was in the first or second—no, the third grade. I had a beloved second grade teacher, and I remember my grandmother saying to me, "Your teacher will be having her baby soon," and I remember saying, "Is that why she looks as though she swallowed a pillow?" Then, I was sort of interested when I saw other ladies who were like that.

But, you see, as far as I'm concerned that whole period of early childhood was totally devoid of seeing adults being affectionate because we were so separated from them all the time.

L.S. Do you remember when you first learned how babies were born?

J. My mother told me. I'd been nagging her to tell me about it because we had goats and the goats had babies. I was about seven, and I guess my nurse must have told me that the goat babies grew in their mother's stomach, and then I'm sure I wondered how they got out.

L.S. You never asked how they got in . . .

J. No . . . You see, we drank the goat's milk, and I knew that was for the baby goats, and we had chickens that laid eggs. It seemed to be natural. So I don't feel that I was terribly questioning about that side of life at all. But the goats did have to be taken to be bred, and that's when I'm sure I asked what that meant.

L.S. What did your mother tell you?

J. She explained it very well. She said we took the goats to be bred, and that the billy goat had a turtle, and that he had sperm, and that he put that in an opening in the female goat—so then I thought that must be the opening where your pee came out and she explained no, it was right next to it—and then the sperm traveled up a little tube, and that's where it started to grow. You know, it was very rudimentary. And she explained that it was a special time because the goats go into heat. And I knew about goats going into heat, I had heard about that from my nurse, and I never questioned it. You know, flowers bloom in the spring, goats go into heat . . .

L.S. At what point in your life did you make a connection between what the goats did and what humans do?

J. Well, then my mother told me that that was the same with human beings, and then I was shocked!

L.S. It seemed O.K. for the goats. . .

J. But not for us!

L.S. What was your feeling of shock like?

J. My feeling of shock was that a penis was for peeing and what did it have to do with making babies? And by that time, I still didn't know about dirty words, but I can remember people giggling in school about "wee wee" and "pee pee," so it seemed a very strange way for people to get together to have a baby.

L.S. Did you think then that perhaps your parents did this?

J. Yes I did, and then I think I quickly forgot about it.

L.S. I wonder if there is any association between thinking that your father did this with your mother and why you didn't want your mother to have more children?

J. I was trying to think . . . It was before I learned that that I didn't want to have any more brothers and sisters . . . So I don't know how to put that two and two together. But I played bride and groom and we had dolls for children. So I must have assumed that children came after you were married.

L.S. She told you so perfectly about the animals, but when telling you about people, she left something out . . .

J. You know what she left out with people? She left out any kind of love. She could talk very romantically about my father, but it was sort of tacked on afterward.

L.S. The only other thing I want to talk about today is language. For instance, when we were talking about the word for genitals and the word for toilet functions, etc., and you told me all the euphemisms. The fact that you never heard a word for vagina until way past seven . . .

J. I know what we called it. I called it the same thing as urine. I called it my "tee tee." I guess that's not so uncommon.

L.S. No, it's not so uncommon.

J. That's probably another reason I was shocked by the stories of the goats.

L.S. Because the words you were taught were not really special for vagina but were actually toilet function words.

And your fantasy of how babies were born was that one swallowed a pillow. You thought it had to get there through another orifice. Now how did you think it got out?

J. I think I must have thought it came out the belly button. Because I knew it was called the navel, and I knew it had something to do with babies, but I wasn't quite sure what. So I have a feeling that I thought that opened up and out came the baby.

L.S. Well, we'll have to finish for today. You know, usually I try to cover childhood up to prepuberty during the first session. But your early childhood is filled with so many memories. Many people either can't remember so much, or have repressed it too deeply—or maybe simply aren't so sensitive to the importance of some of their recollections.

As Julia was leaving, and we were standing in the hallway, she spoke of a realization she had come to during the interview: that her positive feelings about herself as a female come from men rather than from the women who had been her gender models during childhood. Her nurse was a very masculine, tough sort of women. Her maternal grandmother was a "very anal" kind of woman. Her mother was actually very feminine but, in her competetiveness with her daughter, she did not really allow for any kind of identification or cooperation, or any kind of communication of friendliness or camaraderie in this particular area.

SECOND SESSION

J. I've had such good feelings about our interview. It made me feel very strong. And I kept thinking about the lack of emphasis there was for me on being a female when I

was little. It was just underplayed in a subtle way. Everything was really masculine. What we were supposed to do
culturally were much more little boy things. And I realized that I felt very good about myself in a way. I had
hung onto something that was mine. I preserved it in a
way, and it gave me a good feeling about myself. It gave
me a feeling of personal dignity that, even as a little girl,
I knew what was me and I hung onto it.

L.S. It's true. You were able to hold onto something, despite
the fact that everything around you put women in a
caretaker role. Your nurse was a domestic and masculine,
and she was one model. Your grandmother was strong
and long-suffering and anal, and she was also a model for
you. One thing I thought was interesting was your memory of your father carrying your mother downstairs and
your sense of outrage. It's especially interesting that you
saw your mother as the baby and that your father was
picking the *wrong* baby by not picking you. You didn't
see your mother as the woman of the house, having a role
separate from you.

J. As a little girl I don't remember seeing my mother active.
She was always sitting still, and she also spent a lot of
time in bed. She wasn't passive by temperament, but she
like to be served.

L.S. For some reason, I am now reminded of something which
I feel might be connected. When you came back from
Europe last year you told me about a married man in
Paris who was interested in you. You had had a really
marvelous time. And one of the things you were so
pleased about was a chance to be the "other woman."
And when you were talking before I was thinking about
your mother having the glamourous role in the
household.

J. *(Laughter) She* was the "other woman."

L.S. Right, in the glamour role. She was the desirable one.
You were in the *mother* mother role, the caretaker—

which is, in fact the role you played with your ex-husband. Did you have any other memories up until age
seven, when your mother came back to this country?

J. Yes, there were a couple of things that happened. One of
them was: there was a little girl when I was five who was
also a refugee, so to speak, like us. She always wanted to
play doctor, and I didn't like it at all. It wasn't so much
that I was afraid my nurse would come walking in, it's
just that I didn't dig it. I was quite disinterested in the
whole thing.

And then, when I was thinking about that, I remembered going there, one rainy day, and her foster father
came in and gave her foster mother a kiss, and I was very
embarrassed by that. I never remember seeing my parents
kiss. It was a totally foreign experience, and also something I thought should belong to them and I shouldn't
see. I didn't think it was bad; it's just that I thought I was
looking at something that was private . . . Now, perhaps
I have repressed an earlier memory of my parents kissing.
But I don't think so because we were always so removed
from them.

L.S. I wonder if there was something different about their
relationship, that it was somehow a more affectionate
kind of relationship that you were used to seeing, that it
had a kind of meaning or intention that you had not seen.

J. I think so. Well, it must have had a sexual connotation
to it, which is what I think made it seem foreign to me.

L.S. What about your stepfather and your mother—was their
relationship more affectionate?

J. Yes, it was a much more affectionate relationship. John
was an affectionate man. He was a teddy bear kind of
person. And I was very affectionate with him, and he was
with us. He was a kind of tease and very lovable. I was
about nine, ten at the time because they were away the
first winter mother was home, looking for land in the
West.

L.S. How long were they married?

J. Six years, and then she divorced him.

Oh, there was one other thing I wanted to tell you about during this period, up until seven. We had a pediatrician and I remember going to him (I always hated going to the doctor). He used to open up your legs and say, "I'll just see how you're growing," and take a look, and then shut you back up again, and I hated that. That was an intrusion on my privacy.

L.S. What do you think your feelings were during that period? It must have been a very complex period, and you must have felt like an outsider. For instance, here's Louisa, who's a Nazi, who privately defends Hitler. At the same time you come back to a country that is totally against Hitler, and also your father is killed in a war fighting Hitler. I wonder what effect all of these discrepancies had on you.

J. It was totally confusing because Louisa was the person who took care of me, whom I trusted fully to do anything. I think I repressed thinking about what she thought about or what she believed in. She wasn't allowed to come to the seashore with us in the summer because she'd signal a submarine or something. So I knew that about her. And I knew that the governesses we had in the summer hated her and that she hated my grandmother —oh my God, I mean, it still boggles the mind to think about it. What it does is make me not trust anybody.

L.S. Yes, think of it: she's the woman that your mother chose to bring you back to the United States. At the same time, your mother stays on in Europe to keep your father company and he is participating in a war on the side your mother believes in. Yet your mother chooses Louisa as her representative to take you home to the United States. And Louisa substitutes for your mother all the years your mother's in Europe.

J. I just got a ghastly feeling about two minutes ago—like,

what do you *really* believe in? What do you believe and who are you and where are you?

L.S. I hadn't thought about this before either, in the active terms in which it was lived.

J. And you know, at school, the little boys were always gunning me down as a German, and here I had this thick, thick accented nurse at home. It made us very different.

L.S. How long did Louisa stay?

J. Until I was nine. And then my mother sent her back. She started to turn us against my mother. She'd say things like, "Why do you want to stay here, don't you want to go back to your grandmother?" and stuff like that. There were times when I did want to go back to my grandmother. My mother was sick a lot . . .

I can remember weeping when Louisa left. But at the same time it was an incredible relief.

L.S. Do you remember when your mother told you about menstruation?

J. She told me during the whole conversation about the goats. She told about how goats went into heat. Then she explained that people also had a special time. And I got confused. I thought that menstruating was like going into heat and that that was the only time you could have children. It seemed kind of funny to me that the sperm didn't get washed away. I think my ex-husband Chris cleared that up for me by telling me about ovulation.

L.S. So what did you think menstruating was?

J. I thought it was the fertile time.

L.S. Do you remember how your mother explained it?

J. I was seven and a half at the time. She said women have a special time of the month too, and that they bleed. And she told me that you could use Kotex or Tampax, and that her mother had called it being unwell and she called it the curse because it was inconvenient. That didn't bother me. I was looking forward to getting it. I thought it would be something marvelous. I wasn't afraid about it.

L.S. What did you think would be marvelous about it?

J. Being grown-up . . .

L.S. And being grown-up seemed marvelous . . . ? I was remembering that the reason *I* liked getting my period was that it was the first thing that happened to me that let me feel like other girls.

J. I felt pretty different from the others. I had had the experience of having someone very close die. And no one else had had that experience. And also I had had the experience of seeing my mother and stepfather divorced. Now, other girls had seen divorces, but they hadn't been in on them. Because I had been the buffer in a lot of fights. I can remember being cranky and upset a lot of times at school, and an older friend of mine said, "Oh God, you're feeling so sorry for yourself." And she didn't understand, she couldn't, so I just shut up. And that was an awful feeling. And I knew my mother could understand, but I didn't want to talk to her about it because it was her problem and I knew she didn't want to be reminded of the incident or whatever. And I didn't want to talk to Granny about it because I would have felt that I was being disloyal to my mother. So it all stayed bottled up.

L.S. Why would it have been disloyal to discuss it with your grandmother?

J. Telling her how unhappy I was that the marriage broke up. And telling her how awful my mother had been to my stepfather. I suppose I wouldn't have had to tell her that, but that was in the back of my mind.

L.S. What was the worst argument that you ever heard between your mother and stepfather?

J. There are two things that I remember. One was, we were upstairs and my mother was washing milk pans in her bathroom upstairs. She was having a fight with him, and I don't remember what it was about, but the milk pans were clashing and banging. And it was awful, like they were beating each other up. And My little brother came in and asked what was going on and was very scared and upset and wanted to climb into bed with me. And another time, they were having a big fight and my mother was in bed screaming that she wanted my father, and I thought that was a terrible thing to say, so demeaning.

L.S. You mean her first husband? Your real father?

J. Yes. There were also a lot of put-downs.

L.S. So your view of the mother was of the woman being stronger than the man.

J. That's right. And she used to tell me how he went off to parties and got drunk, which she thought was terrible. And she really did everything she could to poison me against him, which you see goes back to my nurse turning me against her.

L.S. Do you recall ever seeing your mother and stepfather in any kind of sexual situation?

J. Once in the middle of the morning I walked into my mother's bedroom, and she had only underpants on and she was rolling around on the bed laughing. My stepfather had his clothes on because he had just come in from outside. So I quickly shut the door and walked out.

L.S. What did you think was going on?

J. Well, I knew what happened by then, so there was no bewilderment. And I felt slightly embarrassed to have walked in there because I thought it was a personal thing.

L.S. When you learned how babies were born . . .

J. I was very interested and asked a lot of questions.

L.S. And how were you told?

J. I was told very mechanically. But I was never told it was great to have a baby. I was told where the baby came out and that you have contractions, etc. As a matter of fact, my mother did not have a very difficult time having children. I was born within three hours, and the water broke with the boys and she had some kind of shot to speed it up. But, I never heard an "Oh wow, it's great to be a mother," etc.

L.S. So you first learned about babies being born at the same time that you learned about menstruation.

J. That's right.

L.S. Where were you when you first got your period?

J. I was at my grandparents' house. It was a school night. And I remember during the day having a pain in my stomach and thinking I had diarrhea, but I had cramps. But I didn't really think about it. Before I went to bed, I went to the bathroom and I noticed. I went running to my mother and I said I had the curse, since that's the name I had learned from her. And she had said how exciting, and I guess she had some Kotex. And I was very excited and told all the kids at school.

L.S. And then you didn't get your period for six months?

J. Right, and I was scared to death that it meant I was like those cousins.

L.S. Tell me about those cousins, and the aunts and the aunt-in-law.

J. Maria was the cousin that my grandfather's sister discovered had never had a menstrual period. She took her to the doctor and found out that she was one of those people who don't have any female insides. I don't know why my mother told me about it particularly, but it was just before I got my period. It may have been that I was asking her some questions. We may have been talking about my aunt, and maybe got into this thing about her having an immature uterus and having had trouble having babies. And I don't remember dwelling on it.

L.S. How did she talk about Maria?

J. I think she said she had no female insides. I think my mother was talking about how Aunt Janet was so stupid for not having taken her daughter to the doctor earlier.

L.S. How old was she when she took her?

J. In her twenties.

L.S. It seems, then, that she had the hormones to develop

breasts but not to develop female insides. And she had no vaginal incision either, is that right?

J. Right. I remember talking about this in therapy group one night. We had a beautiful white goat and under her tail where the incision should have been was a little red mark, and the vet looked at her and said, "Never going to be any good, she's a freemartin," and I asked what that was, and he said she was a little goat who couldn't have kids. So I don't know what happened, but I think they gave her away, and I was heartbroken because I loved her very much.

L.S. How old were you then?

J. Nine or ten. That must have been on my mind. And then what happened was I got my period—I was delighted— I was thirteen and a half. But I didn't get it again for six months. So I was in a cold sweat that whole time.

L.S. Did you tell your mother?

J. Yes, I did, and she said, "Oh don't worry, you'll get it again." Nobody knew how scared I was. And then I thought that I'd go to a doctor and he'd tell me that I was like my cousins. I finally did go to a doctor and told him I was irregular, and he said not to worry, that I would straighten out and of course I did eventually.

L.S. Was there any kind of physiological problem with your four aunts?

J. No, but none of them ever married. And when I got to know them they were kind of strange looking, old and wispy and whiskery, and very ugly.

L.S. A preview of coming attractions . . . And there was your mother, beautiful and glamourous, and your grand-mother . . . I remember your telling me that you felt like a wallflower during your adolescence. Can you talk about it?

J. Well, before my mother got divorced she sent us East for two winters to go to school, and we went to a progressive school. I skipped a grade, and all the girls were wearing nylons and going out on dates, etc. I had been taught at home except for the last half-year when I went to a boarding school. But I had been taught at home with a boy who was a year older than I was, and I adored him and we had a great time, great pals. And I had crushes on his two older brothers. But I was very naïve; I was very young. We lived on a farm and I wore blue jeans and played tag at night—we did our homework together and it was fine. But when I got to school, we had this sort of artificial structure put on boy-girl relationships, and my mother said, I think you should go to some dances and have a long dress and all. And I guess the first winter some boys danced with me and I found them a total bore. And then I can remember going to socials: because the school we went to was a boys' and a girls' school. And the glee club was together, etc., but classes weren't. We had to go to these horrible dances, and I didn't really know any of the boys. We'd been going back to the farm during the summer and by that time, there were no boys there. So I didn't know anything. I didn't know about batting averages, I didn't know how to sail, I didn't know how to play tennis, and it was a very WASP school. And I was just the supreme wallflower.

L.S. Until what age did you feel that your social, sensual life was somewhat barren?

J. Seventeen or eighteen—it's the most miserable feeling. You know, I used to think I was boring and ugly, and yet another part of me knew that that wasn't true: I was much smarter, much more sophisticated than a lot of those boys. And I knew that I wasn't any uglier than a lot of those girls who were more popular. Later on, I blamed my mother. But at the time, I just knew that I was different, had been different. It was like, no matter what I did, I was never going to make it.

L.S. To what did you attribute your lack of social appeal?

J. I thought I wasn't lighthearted enough, I wasn't funny

enough. I guess that I wasn't pretty enough. And then—and this is typical of my mother—the summer when I was fourteen going on fifteen she took us on a trip to see our old relatives. I was upset anyway because we weren't going to the farm, which was terrible because I loved the life there, and I knew we weren't going back because that was the summer my mother got divorced. And I knew we weren't going to see my stepfather again, and he was kind of erased from our memory by our mother. That was such a terrible thing to do—go visit relatives when every other kid was going sailing, etc. Then when I was fifteen, she arranged for me to work as a counselor on a ranch, but I must say I loved that summer. I was furious before I left, but it was a very good experience, although I was probably the oldest one. There was one other girl my age, but the boys were all younger. They were cowboys, and they thought I was a terrific rider and they liked me very much, and that somehow did something.

L.S. Can you remember what it felt like when you went to a dance and weren't able to dance?

J. It was sheer agony. Sometimes, I would come home and cry. And it goes back to that thing of just feeling closed out. A happy world all going in front of you, and you're an outsider. And you must look queer. Let alone act queer, stand queer. It was like sitting on that porch at school waiting to be picked up, waiting to be saved.

And I remember my mother was always saying, "Why can't you go to dances?" She didn't know what she was going to do with me. Mind you, she had brought us up in the wilderness like little children of God, and then we're plunged into the nylon stocking-lipstick set and supposed to adjust to it just like that. And then just as I was adjusting to it and having dates and fun, she switched into her religious act and life had a purpose, one was supposed to live purely, and then she wanted me to become a nun! Then she would make me feel guilty because

I enjoyed going to parties. And there was a feeling of guilt. I lived with my mother the year I came back from my junior year abroad, and she was always talking about the higher life, and she aroused a feeling of guilt in me.

L.S. Well, you and your mother were never on the same track at the same time.

J. Yes. And if I went out, she never met the people I went out with, there was no interest on her part.

L.S. At what point did you know about intercourse?

J. Oh, of course I had forgotten all about masturbating when I was thirteen. So of course I knew about it before that. And I guess I read . . .

L.S. You read . . .

J. I used to read anything I could get my hands on because I was home all the time. So I read everything in the library, and of course there was a marriage manual there.

L.S. Do you remember what it was?

J. Van der Velde, *Ideal Marriage.* And there were some sort of junk paperbacks. So I had a pretty good picture of it. And then I used to have these fantasies and masturbate, and I did that for about a year, when I was thirteen.

L.S. How did you learn how to masturbate?

J. Someone told me. A little girl I played with asked me if I ever tickled myself down there. And I said no, and she said I should try it, it's great. So I did. And it was great.

L.S. How did you feel about it?

J. Curious. And I didn't have any horrible guilt feelings about it. But I did think that older people didn't do it— that is, people over twenty. And I found out in school that other people my age did do it. I decided that I would not like anyone to find me doing it. And I didn't know why that was. I didn't know what the word masturbation meant until years later.

L.S. What did you call it then?

J. Tickling myself, I suppose. When I got to boarding school, I just stopped. What happened was, I was too busy—we had a lot of homework and I was sharing a room, so I couldn't do it then. I just totally lost interest in it.

L.S. Did you masturbate to orgasm?

J. Uh huh. And I figured out that that was an orgasm. I mean, I just knew it was.

L.S. How long did you masturbate before you had an orgasm?

J. I had one the first time, I think.

L.S. Well, what did you think was happening to you?

J. Having an orgasm.

L.S. Where did you hear about orgasms?

J. Probably read it in Van der Velde.

L.S. What did you feel about it?

J. That it was a neat feeling.

L.S. Now, if you thought it was such a neat feeling, why would you stop?

J. It had something to do with the fact that I thought that other people didn't do it. And . . . oh, I'll tell you what happened. I did it when I was just over my period. And I thought my period had started all over again, because there must have been some aftermath, and after that I thought it might not be too good to fool around again. And I . . . that probably scared me off. I just knew there was something taboo about it.

L.S. But you didn't know what.

J. No.

L.S. During the year you did it, were there any particular conditions, times, moods that would move you to masturbate? . . . For one thing, the year that you masturbated was also the year that you menstruated. Also, you stopped menstruating for six months.

J. Right, but I was still masturbating that whole period, and after about six months, I got my period again. I would say that I had been masturbating about a year when I did it that time when I had my period. Now why I did it . . . I suppose sex was on my mind. You know, I had gotten my period, I was concerned about it, being in school with boys . . .

L.S. Did you do it in the bathroom, your bedroom?

J. On my bed. I'd be reading, you know. I'm sure if I were reading some kind of romantic book or something, I'd be more inspired. And I used to have a fantasy about two people doing whatever they were doing to each other.

L.S. What were they doing? What word did you call it?

J. I can't think of the word, It wasn't fucking, it wasn't making love. It must have been sleeping together. That was what my mother called it.

L.S. Before we finish this morning, I'd like to tie together a few thoughts. Masturbation is very taboo, apparently, but so long as you called it a different name, it was easier for you to let yourself do it. I wonder whether you in any way connected masturbating and not having a period for six months after you had the first one.

J. I just remembered something. At that same age I got some kind of vaginal irritation. And I wonder if I didn't associate that . . . I mean, I had to tell my mother I had an itch. And she didn't send me to a doctor, but told me I was probably over-alkaline or acidic and told me to douche. So I did. Well, I didn't know how to use a douche, and I remember her saying, "Don't get excited," which seems rather a strange thing. So maybe I thought I got the itch because I was masturbating. Then when she said that . . .

L.S. What a strange thing to say . . . Some of the pieces do fall together, in a way . . .

J. Well, my mother obviously disapproved of sex.

L.S. Especially for you . . .

J. I don't remember incidents, but I had the feeling you had to be in love to have sex. So to be alone and have a great pleasure was wrong. She communicated the feeling that that was wrong. Unless sex was sanctioned, there was something wrong with it. And when I was getting married, she told me that a red hot affair was all right but it didn't last, and one should marry someone whom one was comfortable with.

As Julia was leaving, we talked about the picture of her mother that seemed to be emerging. During this session Julia realized for the first time that her mother had many fears about sex. I thought this might have accounted for her having allowed Louisa, a more-than-sick woman, to take her children back to the States. It was a way of putting a control on their possible outrageous and unacceptable sexuality. At this point Julia added that perhaps her mother was concerned about being "bad" because she had wanted to wear lipstick and high heels, of which Julia's grandmother very much disapproved. Perhaps she was determined to have a "good" daughter to make up for herself. This is probably also why she became religious at the end of her life.

THIRD SESSION

J. The other night I started to put something together. After our session I went out to lunch with an old friend, actually my ex-husband's first lover, although that lasted a short time. We always stayed friends, and I didn't know at the time. And now we're better friends. I don't think he sees Chris. He is married and quite successful. We went to lunch with a couple of men, and we were slightly drunk. What happened was that the guy this friend of mine said was dull got very turned on to me and we had a ball. We were talking about children, about other things, and we never stopped talking. We really related. My friend walked me home, and he said that he had never seen that man like that, that I must have turned him on. So when I got home I was thinking about the afternoon and our session, and all of a sudden I felt rotten. I was trying to think about masturbation and getting more and more frustrated. Then I thought about lunch and realized that that guy was very seductive, and then I realized I had been seductive. Whichever came first, his being so or me, it doesn't matter. Then I got this image of my mother looming in the doorway, and I knew it wasn't a real image —it was like a fantasy. Like she was twice her size, and she could just walk in the door any time.

L.S. She was there without even opening the door? . . .

  J. Right . . . and I was thinking about being seductive, and then I realized that I had been very seductive when I was young, that I adored my father, and that that made my mother furious. And I was petrified of my mother all my life because I always felt that I had done something wrong. And then another association . . . I was over here at your house and I met your husband, and he invited me to come over sometime. And you know what passed through my head: what happens if we get together, supposing he liked me, and I remember thinking, well, for God's sake, she can handle that one. And I dealt with it very rationally. Then I thought, why would that have occurred to me, and I realized that since I do think of you as my "good mother" it was like a repetition. But the terrific thing is that I could talk to you about it. And in another way, it's terrific I could feel that way because then we're equal. So I was thunderstruck by all of that.

L.S. I just thought of something . . . Considering the age at which you left Europe and that you probably didn't really know about the war, I wonder if you felt that you were being sent away from your parents, and especially your father, because of that.

  J. That occurred to me . . . and also that I might have felt some guilt because he was killed . . . With my mother and stepfather I always had to be the buffer, so that was the reverse role, of pulling them together.

Then there were a lot of things that my mother did later on that fit into that pattern of those adolescent years. I can remember her having a dinner party, and after the dinner party, the men went to the living room to drink their brandy, and the women stayed behind. And I stayed with the men. I was ten years old. There was an old friend of my father's who was there, and he was funny, and told me all kinds of stories and I just loved it. The next day my mother told me that you just don't do things like that. The men are to be alone, to tell dirty jokes if they want to. She made me feel I'd been rather a trollop, and also as though I had inflicted myself on them.

And then I thought of another odd thing when I was about ten. My mother was still getting along with my stepfather and I thought that it was great that she had company all night long and that she had a double bed. And I was saying how terrific that must be to her, and I was going on and on, and all of a sudden she said, "All right, you can spend the night with him." So my stepfather spent the night with me and it was rather miserable and I tossed and turned, but it seemed like sort of an odd thing to do. I'm sure I had not been asking to spend the night with him, and I got some vague feeling that there was something demeaning about it.

L.S. Demeaning to both of you, I think, because it seems she was always degrading him. It's almost as if she didn't really want anything to do with him, so she said to you, "If you think it's so hot, why don't you try it?" What's really so interesting is the element of competition, the triangle type of competition—it's such an important factor in everything that happens to you. And it's significant that you could experience that feeling you had about my husband and talk about it and free yourself of the anxiety. In the past you always got so uncomfortable in these triangle situations. Then, it couldn't be another woman.

With Chris, it was a man. And with Fred, since he's an alcoholic, the bottle is the competition. But not another woman. And that terrific feeling you expressed about your trip, that finally you could be the "other woman." And all triggered off from the statement that your mother made, "Don't get excited."

J. It's fascinating to me how frightened she was. And she had a big thing with my brother Alan. He was a very sexy little boy, and he was tremendously attracted to her, and I remember her saying she couldn't stand to have him crawling over the bed. For one thing, he was very like my father, and I'm sure that bothered her. But there was something else. There was a kind of repulsion concerning that infant sexuality.

L.S. Do you know how long your parents went together before they were married?

J. About a year.

L.S. Do you think she was a virgin when she married him?

J. Yes, she used to rather stress that, and she would always say that you could tell when someone wasn't a virgin any more.

L.S. The thing to try to understand is what you started to say when you were leaving Sunday—the different picture of your mother that is emerging. Because, actually, the picture you had of her was of the last years of her life, when you were a young adult and were—at least consciously— least frightened of her. Interestingly, they were also the years when she was least sexual, and without a husband. It's as if when she freed herself of her fears, you were also less fearful of her.

We're near the end of this session, so I want to ask you some other questions to make sure we've covered all the areas in this age period.

J. Do you know one thing that crossed my mind? The only person I can remember asking anything about sex was my father—that one question about his friend in the shower.

My mother told me things, but I don't remember having the freedom to ask when I was really curious about something that really confabulated me about sex. Actually, later on with Chris I felt perfectly easy asking about sex, so it's interesting that in a way I felt freer talking with men about sex. The most valuable information that I ever had about it, aside from you, was from men.

L.S. That'a terrific observation. After you discontinued masturbating, did you start again?

J. No.

L.S. Did you ever know about other children masturbating?

J. Not really, except for having heard two people at school talk about it.

L.S. Do you have any recollections of overseeing or overhearing adults in any sexual situation?

J. Not during childhood, except for that one time with my mother and my stepfather. And then one time when I was about sixteen. We were staying with my mother's friend in Switzerland and I went upstairs to go to the bathroom and opened the wrong door and the cook and the butler were in bed together. I was absolutely horrified, and I told my mother the next day. Actually the cook was very sweet about it.

L.S. Who do you feel was the most affectionate person in your childhood?

J. I feel that my baby nurse was. I feel that I got a good start. And then my father in his own way. I can remember him taking my hand and bringing me dolls. I don't remember my mother being that way.

L.S. Well, you didn't really see her as a mother, and the reason for that is that she wasn't acting like one.

Did we talk about at what age you put together intercourse and babies being born—and also the relationship between intercourse and pleasure?

J. Well, we did talk about that the first time. When my mother talked about the goats, she said that there was pleasure from sex and that this was maybe the greatest kind of pleasure you could have. And I remember that impressed me, but I also remember feeling that something was left out because it was expressed in terms of physical pleasure, and there was no association to mental involvement or affection. She might have talked about those things at another time . . . So I was able to understand it intellectually.

L.S. You might have heard it, but I don't think you took it in because I don't think that she ever quite took it in . . . Is it difficult or easy for you to imagine your parents engaging in the sex act?

J. I can't imagine it, and it's not because I get Peeping Tom feelings about it—it's because I don't remember them ever having been affectionate.

L.S. During what is called the latency period—ages seven to twelve, approximately—do you recall having any memories of a sexual nature? Freud suggested that children's sexual concerns are dormant during that period.

J. Oh, yes. In fact, with me it increased because I had learned about it, and also because my stepfather was around, and there hadn't been a man around for a long time, and I had two brothers. I was always thinking about babies and how they were born and when I would be married.

L.S. Do you remember ever having sexual or sensual dreams?

J. In adolescence I was always dreaming about horses. *(Laughter)*

L.S. Do you remember any daydreams of a sexual nature?

J. Well, it was always meeting someone marvelous and getting married.

L.S. Did they involve real people or fantasy people?

J. Well, if there was someone on the scene, then it was probably that person. If there wasn't, then it was probably a fantasy.

L.S. Which adjectives would best describe how you felt when

you saw your father's friend nude, or a female adult nude?

J. The first word that pops into my mind is fright. For no reason . . . a feeling of being overwhelmed. I was kind of small looking up at that . . . the scale.

L.S. During the period you masturbated, do you remember any fantasy that you had?

J. Yes, I would fantasy myself with some faceless, nameless guy or two people, man and woman.

L.S. The woman might or might not be you?

J. Right.

L.S. You experienced orgasm the first time you masturbated?

J. Yes, the very first time.

L.S. In your recollection, how long did it take?

J. I don't know, maybe about ten minutes, not long.

L.S. What do you think motivated you the very first time?

J. I told you, my friend had told me about it. And I can't remember whether or not I went home that day and tried . . .

L.S. You told me about one experience of homosexuality.

J. You mean the little girl who wanted to play doctor and I didn't like it?

L.S. Right . . . was there anything else?

J. I can remember something when I was thirteen or fourteen and my stepfather was away, and I spent the night with my mother and it was like a big deal because we would talk and all. I know I had pubic hair then and suddenly she leaned over and felt me and said something about it was so interesting in comparison to her. And, well, I was shocked. And I don't remember her saying anything more, but it just seemed like an odd thing to do. But I think it might have frightened me.

And then I went to that first boarding school, and a lot of the young girls had crushes on the older girls, and the expression was "fag for them." You did little things for them, and it really was a rather innocent admiration. And then at boarding school proper, when I was older, lesbianism was the big issue. I had a great friend, I adored her, and we were quite inseparable. But it was never physical.

L.S. When was the first time you ever thought about the idea of homosexuality?

J. My mother told me about it first, when I was about eleven, in a conversation about somebody. She told me that some men instead of liking women like men better. I remember not being terribly concerned about it. And then I realized that lesbianism was the female counterpart of homosexuality.

L.S. Did you feel differently about lesbianism and homosexuality?

J. Yes, because it was a big topic at school and also because lesbians are women, and men were more removed.

L.S. Did it arouse more feelings of anxiousness?

J. Yes, because I remember wondering whether I was a lesbian because I was a wallflower, and I wondered whether the fact that boys didn't like me showed I was a lesbian.

L.S. Does the idea of homosexuality or lesbianism for yourself seem abhorrent, acceptable, repulsive, strange, interesting?

J. I would say that it doesn't seem threatening any more. The other day I was thinking about it when I was thinking about my mother, and for the first time it didn't seem threatening. It didn't seem vitally interesting, either.

L.S. Do you think that other people's opinions have a strong influence on that?

J. No, I think it's private. People's opinions are part of it, but there's a private disinterest in it that has always been there.

L.S. When you were in your early adolescence, who if anyone did you feel yourself able to talk to?

J. My mother. I would have asked my mother anything about having babies, biology, but when it came to the nitty-gritty about what it was like, that I couldn't do.

L.S. Was there anyone you wish you could have been close to?

J. No, because I realized I wanted the experience, and I sensed that no matter how many questions I asked or books I read, I still needed the experience to know.

L.S. If you could live your childhood over again, do you think you would have acted differently about any part of your sexual experiences or the choices you made or about masturbating?

J. I don't think so, because I did learn one thing from masturbation. I learned that genital sex was pleasurable. I also realized it would have been more pleasurable with another person. So I can't really see wanting to change that. Maybe I would have masturbated longer if I hadn't felt guilty.

L.S. Well, would you rather have been able to do that?

J. No, not necessarily, although it's funny, I never realized how much I got out of masturbation until we talked about it now. I hadn't realized how it did help me to look forward to having sex with someone else.

I wouldn't particularly want to go through my childhood again, but if I could choose a life, I'd choose mine.

L.S. Actually, what I meant was, do you think your present life would have been richer had you known certain things?

J. I think I wish that as a small child there had been more awareness of sexuality, and also that there had been more affection. Do you feel that way?

L.S. I don't know. I think if I had had more knowledge, I wouldn't have been as driven to find out more about sex, or even, for instance, to do this study.

At what ages did you see yourself as a "wallflower"?

J. I'd say fourteen to eighteen. I was going to boarding school. I started to get out of it my last year of school. And then when I went to college, I started to go out. I went to college and I stayed for two years with a woman

who boarded two girls and two boys. I was just seventeen.
That was a good experience. Then I went to Europe my
junior year, and that was the breakthrough. I associate
this also with my menstrual period. You remember, after
the first one it stopped for six months and then it started
—but still it was quite irregular, and I would get it about
seven months out of the year, until I was nineteen. And
when I was nineteen, I was in Europe traveling with two
boys and a girl, and I said to myself, "I'm going to get
my period every month," and after that I got it every
month. But it had something to do with the fact that I
was alone, away from home. I had had a marvelous winter in Paris. I'd been going out with several boys and I
had cousins in Paris who were about twenty-seven,
twenty-eight, and who took me out a lot and who were
darling to me. And also the boys I was traveling with that
summer were terrific, and I know it must have had something to do with that—feeling accepted and at ease with
men and feeling acceptable as a female.

L.S. You used the word "gray" when you described yourself
during the wallflower period, and I was reminded of the
first time I met you. That is the one adjective I would
have used. The difference between then and now is start-
ling! You haven't changed anything specific about your
appearance, and yet you *look* like a different person. Over
a period of time, it's as if everything about you has come
to life.

J. Well, it was the same kind of feeling. I again felt out of
control, terribly rejected in a female sense. I had the same
feeling of hopelessness.

*What emerged from this session was Julia's realization of
her mother's feelings of competitiveness with her. In the
area of looks and success with men, her mother insisted on
seeing herself as better than Julia. In the area of intellectual and mothering capabilities, however, Julia realized*

that her mother was willing to let Julia express herself. During our after-talk, Julia came to the realization that her mother was unwilling to let her be a separate and independent person: she wanted Julia to be her extension in those areas where she (the mother) could not or would not function.

FOURTH SESSION

L.S. This is the last session of our interview. I've been thinking all week about what a fascinating experience it has been for me, and I hope for you too.

J. It's such a fantastic experience! And it's one I can't really explain to people because I feel that they will expect me to be like someone out of *McCall's* magazine, the before and after. You are supposed to be totally transformed. Actually, it's an inside kind of transformation. It's a very female kind of trip, a slow transformation. It's made me feel very good and it's somehow made my life easier, I think because of that whole mother thing. I think I let something go. There's somehow an acceptance of my self in a sexual way. Reading *The Source* was the start of it, and then this opportunity to look back over my life. I saw, for instance, how hard I fought to hold onto parts of myself. I get a tremendous sense of my own strength . . . It's like some kind of chain falling off.

L.S. From the time you were in Europe until the time you met Chris, did you have any significant relationships with men?

J. I had one that was my first great love. Superficially, the guy was like everything my family would have wanted, very handsome, etc. His name was Paul. I met him at a friend of mine's. He had been in the service for two years and prior to that he had been at Harvard. His family was very close to good friends of my family. Anyway, he and his father came over to the friends' house in New York. The girl I was staying with didn't like Paul, so I decided to give him a hard time. And I did give him a hard time, and the next thing I knew he was asking me out. Then, I thought he was a dream: he had a Mercedes, we went to the Harvard-Yale game, a typical Miss Teenage—the whole deal. His father just adored me, and I know that his father just couldn't wait until he put the ring on my finger.

What happened was—and I'll never forget it—we went out to dinner and to the theater with his sister, who was married, and she said something about my going to a christening with them the next day, which I had been planning to do, and Paul said, "She's not coming," and I was kind of thunderstruck. But we went to the theater, and it seemed like a perfectly nice evening, and yet I didn't see him again. I talked with him on the phone a couple of times but never saw him again. But I was too upset by the whole thing, and too unself-confident to call him up and say, "Look, what's going on?" . . . My mother was very nice about it. I told her about it and she said, "He must have cared about you a lot." And she told me about a friend of hers that that had happened to, and the guy came back after about a year, and I think eventually married this friend. By that time, I knew that I would never have wanted to marry him, because a lot of the things I liked about him were very superficial. He did write me a postcard about a year later, and I just didn't answer it.

L.S. You never figured out what it was?

 J. Yes. I think that his father inadvertently put a lot of pressure on him, and I don't think that he was in any way ready to get married, or engaged, or even to think about it. And I think he just got frightened. I think I was shoved down his throat.

L.S. That was the most important relationship before Chris?

J. Yes.

L.S. What were your sexual or sensual outlets during this period?

J. I used to neck a lot, not with everyone I went out with, but with just a few of the boys.

L.S. What kind of outlet did you get from that?

J. It really turned me on.

L.S. Did you feel like you had to neck with someone if you wanted him to go out with you again, or that you would have to "handle" any fellow who might want to have sex with you?

J. I was brought up to believe that you just didn't . . . and I think most of my friends were brought up that way. I always had a fear, or rather an anxiety, of being with someone who really liked me, whom I didn't care for and therefore didn't want to kiss. I was always upset by that —I didn't do it.

L.S. When you went with Paul did you ever go farther than necking?

J. Petting, but not farther than that . . . "nice girls" don't do that.

L.S. Could you ever pet to orgasm?

J. I think I probably did a couple of times with Paul. I remember getting very strong feelings, but I am not sure whether I reached an orgasm. It wouldn't have upset me to have an orgasm, but I think that in my mind I thought you couldn't have an orgasm without intercourse or masturbation, that is, without some kind of physical manipulation.

L.S. Petting didn't take that form with you?

J. No, down to the waist was O.K. I knew that it could be below the waist, but I thought that it would lead to trouble very quickly. (Laughter)

L.S. Then there was no orgasm experience between the age of thirteen, when you stopped masturbating, and this time in your life.

J. I think I might have dreamed to orgasm. Every now and then, and this still happens to me, I wake up and I'm having an orgasm.

L.S. What were your feelings about virginity, about the necessity of virginity for marriage?

J. From my background I had strong feelings about virginity—thought I ought to be a virgin until I got married. After I met Chris, I reconsidered. Although by the time I decided to with him, I think I knew I was going to marry him.

L.S. Were you sorry you waited?

J. No, I'm not sorry I waited. When I think now of the people I would have had love relationships with, I don't think I missed out on anything. And I think that the initial experiences with Chris were so good. Knowing the other people, I don't think it could possibly have been as good with them. So by waiting for Chris, and it being so good, it set a tone for sex which I'm very grateful for. With me it has to do with the relationship—and sex is merely the expression of how I feel inside. In fact, I notice that right now—with Jeff, it's always good—how *fantastic* it is depends on how close we've been with each other recently.

L.S. Then Chris is the first man you had intercourse with?

J. Yes, I must have been twenty-two. I was twenty-three when I married him.

L.S. How did you meet Chris?

J. I was interviewing for a job. This was after I had finished college. And when I was being interviewed, I saw a very attractive man moving furniture around, and that was Chris. We became very good friends. I was going out a lot, and having a very good time. And one day he said, "Why don't you get married?" And I remember thinking, that means him, well, maybe I will marry him. And I didn't think about it again. Well, finally he did ask me out, and after that it was hot and heavy. Then we got engaged, and, oh, he asked me to marry him on New Year's Eve, I remember that. It was two or three months later that we had sex.

L.S. How did it happen?

J. He was over at my house one night—my roommate was away—and he was sort of pushing for it all the time, but I had all these ideas about your wedding night, and all that. And then I thought about it a lot, and I thought, well, what's the difference, and it would be much better to do it when you felt like it instead of having it be a "must" on one particular night. And I made up my mind that the next time I felt very turned on, I would. Which is what did happen. And I remember that I was terribly disappointed . . . thinking, what's so great about it? I didn't have an orgasm. But I wasn't upset about it. Before it happened, Chris had gotten out all sorts of books to explain what happened. And he was really terribly sweet. When I said, "What's so great about that?" he laughed and it didn't seem to bother him, and it didn't bother me because I knew enough about first times, etc. It wasn't terribly painful but it wasn't exactly a dream, either.

L.S. Did you expect it to be painful?

J. Yes I did. And it was painful, but not as painful as I thought it would be.

L.S. Did you expect it to be pleasureful?

J. Yes, I thought first there would be pain and then there would be pleasure. But it wasn't either one of those things.

L.S. Did you expect to have orgasm?

J. I didn't know, but I figured if I didn't have one that time, I'd have one another time.

L.S. How long after you began to have sex did you experience orgasm?

J. I think maybe two or three times. It got easier each time.

L.S. In the period of time that you were with him, did you

experience orgasm all of the time, most of the time, some of the time?

J. Ninety-nine percent of the time.

L.S. Do you think that your having orgasm so early in the relationship, given the fact that you had little petting experience, is attributable to his knowledge?

J. No. I attribute it partly to him because he wasn't nervous about it and was very reassuring, but I also think that I worked at it myself. I wanted to have one, and I did have some control over my muscles.

L.S. What knowledge about yourself did you apply?

J. Well, in the first place, I was in love with him. Also, I am very ticklish. I enjoy all kinds of tactile sensations, so it doesn't take long to warm me up. I didn't know how important the clitoris was, but I would just maneuver myself into the position, and Chris would know how to stimulate. And I also was able to control my muscles.

L.S. You were very fortunate to have someone who had physiological knowledge, and knew that it was important to understanding sex.

J. Yes, I remember his showing me diagrams as being a very nice part of the whole experience.

L.S. Does it seem to you that the pattern of your sex life changed after marriage?

J. Yes. We got married about six months after this initial experience—before it was infrequent, my roommate was around, I went to Europe, I didn't see him that often.

L.S. How long were you married?

J. Seven years, eight years.

L.S. How long were you married before you became unhappy and realized that your husband was changing toward you?

J. Three years.

L.S. During the three years, how would you describe your sex life?

J. It was very good. We never had a gymnastic, exhibitionist sex life. We had a very intense one. If you asked who was the aggressor, I really couldn't tell you. We would both just do it. And we really loved each other very much, I think.

L.S. When things between you were getting bad, the quality of the sex didn't change, but you just wouldn't have it as much, is that right?

J. That's right, exactly.

L.S. So the quality stayed the same, but the quantity changed.

J. And then, you see, after three years there was a whole incident with a guy. Then he decided he didn't want to be with that person any more, and wanted to be with me, and we had another very good two years. And we were even closer after that incident than before.

L.S. How long did that incident last?

J. I would say about seven months.

L.S. During that period, did you and he have sex?

J. Sometimes we did. Other times he would feel tremendous guilt, and at those moments he couldn't really face me.

L.S. Was there ever a period of time when he might be having sex with someone else and with you too?

J. I don't think so, really. You see, his boy friend was living in New York. So I would be out of the picture totally when he went to see him. But if he were working on a project and I was around, we would make love, and it would be good if we were in tune.

L.S. Did you and Chris have the same feelings about what you liked sexually?

J. I think so, yes. It's interesting—he never did sixty-nine. That must have scared the living daylights out of him. The quality of the most ordinary kind of sex was very nice. And we often had simultaneous orgasm.

L.S. Did you practice oral sex with your husband?

J. I tried it on him.

L.S. Did he enjoy that?

J. He didn't indicate that he particularly did. And then later on, he asked why I didn't rape him, and I realized that he was talking about oral sex. But he had never indicated that before, so I think he must have had some problem with it.

L.S. Perhaps he liked it but was unable to say so. Did you ever know what his particular patterns were in homosexuality?

J. No, never. At the time I just couldn't face it.

L.S. Did he ever have an affair with a woman that you knew of.

J. I don't think so. There was one particular woman I think he was using as some special way of getting at me.

L.S. Why would he have to get at you some more? Hadn't he already done so with his homosexuality?

J. I think he felt very torn. He did have moral feelings—and I think he did care for me. But he also must have hated me because he felt bound to stay with me.

L.S. Do you know why?

J. Some personal belief. He was married. That did mean something. One of his friends told me the other day that he was still in love with me. And I said yes, in a very unrealistic way. I think he feels terrible guilt about being a homosexual, and that's why he is so confused. In a way, I am the angel who could save him. And in his way, he does have a real love for me. And I love him, I still do. It saddens me very much to see him because I remember the remarkable thing that we did have. It is like having someone die and seeing him reincarnated in another form. But I don't feel that I am always waiting, that he will be there to go back to.

L.S. During the time that you were married to him, did you have any sexual contact with other men?

J. No. And I still think that that is true of me. I can't scatter myself.

L.S. Was Fred the first man you knew after Chris?

J. I had that one experience with Ted. But that was just a

bust. We had a nice evening, made love, and in the morning it was as if it never happened.

L.S. Was the one time with him pleasant?

J. Not terribly. I was self-conscious because it was the first time since my marriage. So Fred was the real awakening. I got so much from him, so much sexual confidence. He came to visit me one time after it was over and wanted to spend the night, and I said no. And later we were talking, and he said to me, "Well, I did do something for you, I gave you the ability to say no." He is perhaps the most brilliant man I have ever known. I always see Fred as a troubador or a minstrel, someone in the Middle Ages. When he gets drunk enough, he can be very poetic. And it is almost as if he falls into something he doesn't consciously know about.

L.S. I have some more general questions. Were you ever pregnant?

J. I think I was, and had a very early miscarriage.

L.S. Did you want to be?

J. Yes. In fact, if I make love with someone whom I really care for, I always want to have a baby. It's like something has been so great that there should be a reminder of it.

L.S. Did you ever have sex with a man who was a virgin?

J. Never.

L.S. Would that appeal to you?

J. No. I was brought up to think that men should have experience. If it were someone I really liked, it wouldn't much matter.

L.S. Do you have any feelings about sex during menstruation?

J. No. Except that during the first two days, the flow is heavy, and I have cramps or am sore, so I wouldn't enjoy it.

L.S. Do you think that men know when you have an orgasm?

J. I don't think they do until they know how I react.

L.S. Did you ever feel it would be necessary to pretend that you had an orgasm when you didn't?

J. Yes. I'd rather not. With one guy, until I got to know him better, I felt that he would have felt very rejected if I didn't have an orgasm, and there were a couple of times when I didn't. When I got to know him better, I told him and it didn't matter.

L.S. Can you usually tell when men have orgasms?

J. I can't usually feel it. My nerves are so stimulated that I can't really feel it.

L.S. What kind of contraception do you use?

J. A diaphragm.

L.S. Have you always used that?

J. No with Chris I used foam. And I have used the pill, but I don't like it. It makes me feel awful. I gain weight; I lack energy; I feel uncomfortable.

L.S. What made you change from foam to a diaphragm?

J. I went from foam to the pill to a diaphragm. A diaphragm is simpler.

L.S. What do you think about the psychological differences between the pill and a diaphragm? A diaphram is used directly in conjunction with the sex act and indicates a willingness to have intercourse. The pill you take daily.

J. Yes, and that's the annoying part of a diaphragm. Supposing you're dating someone, and you're in his apartment, and you don't have your diaphragm.

L.S. Would you carry it with you?

J. I suppose I would in those circumstances. It's also a drag to start making love and have to stop to put the diaphragm in. But it doesn't bother me that much. I can't say that it does.

L.S. What has been your experience with masturbation in your adult life?

J. I don't really, much. If I want to, I can think up some fantasy, but usually I don't. Usually when I am not in a relationship, I am working very hard, and I put that energy somewhere else. I prefer to be with someone.

L.S. On occasions when you have, what has been the motivation?

J. A purely physical thing. That I just felt like it. Perhaps physical tension.

L.S. In the periods when you and Chris didn't have sex, would you masturbate?

J. No, because I think at that time I was very closed in. I was wiped out sexually. After I separated, I went through a period when I did.

L.S. What do you think made you able to do it only after separating from Chris, and not before? After all, there must have been enormous frustration.

J. I think that as long as there was a possibility that I might be able to do it with someone, I clung to that. And also, at that time, I felt very unsexual. I was repressed.

L.S. This might be a clue to what caused you to stop masturbating as a child. I was thinking about when your mother told you you shouldn't excite yourself, and your memory of Fred saying that what he gave you was the ability to say no. Your leaving Chris was giving yourself the ability to say no. Almost as though when you were with him, if he didn't give you sexual recognition—

J. Yes, that's what I was going to say. It's almost as if he took my femaleness away. And when we split up, I realized I was still alive.

L.S. It was as if the less important you felt to him in a sexual sense, the less important you in fact were . . . I want to ask you before we finish—what is your personal opinion about the so-called clitoral/vaginal orgasm?

J. Personally, I do think there is a difference because even though it may be the same nerve endings or whatever, there is a difference between having something inside you and having nothing inside you, and I prefer it internal. I feel closer to the person.

L.S. Can you experience orgasm from oral sex?

J. Yes.

L.S. Does that feel different from intercourse orgasm?

J. I know that the orgasm feels different. With intercourse it's as though there were nerves and muscles in the lower area and as though somehow higher up there was also something happening. It does feel as if there is something happening inside, whether that's in my head, or whether it's physiological.

L.S. Well, the physiological phenomenon is the same.

J. I think that when it's internal with me, I must work harder with those muscles inside, and that gives me a stronger orgasm.

L.S. And your working harder gives you a different kind of response feeling? Could you describe in words what an orgasm feels like?

J. I always think of a fountain of water with bubbles, jets that go up, and although it's a genital-vaginal contraction, the feeling spreads throughout my body. It's as if I almost black out—not quite, because I am still conscious, but it affects my whole being. It's almost as if a whole lot of oxygen is being shot through your system.

L.S. Is there anything particular you like especially about the way someone has intercourse with you. Do you like foreplay, etc.?

J. I like foreplay, I like kissing, I like it all. I don't think that really affects it as much as being very much in tune with the person and feeling that he is with me that makes it particularly pleasurable to me.

L.S. In your opinion, does it make any difference to you as to the size, the width, the length, of a penis?

J. Not if I like the man. I have noticed differences in penises, but that doesn't make a difference about having orgasms, really.

L.S. Do you have any particular feelings about having known a man before you have intercourse with him, or does that make any difference?

J. Now it does. Now I feel that I would like to know a man

quite well before I have sex. In my last two relationships, I got involved very quickly. But in my next experience, I would like it to be profound, and I would like to know the person quite well. I don't like one-night stands. I used to feel—there were times when I was worried that I didn't make physical relationships easily—and I was afraid that I was deficient in some way. But recently I've had a couple of experiences that—yes, I now know I *can* do it just for pleasure . . . but unless it means something very intense, I'd like to put that energy somewhere else. And I think in a way I've always known this. I think that sex is such a profound experience—that is, bed sex—and for me it is such a very enjoyable experience, that I would be very reluctant to have casual experiences from now on. Rather than being deficient or thinking that sex didn't mean much to me—on the contrary, I feel now that it means a terrific amount to me. And that's why I'm very selective about it.

L.S. Before we turned the tape on, you were saying that you had a dream that you felt came out of what we had been talking about.

J. I woke up about 7:30, and I didn't write it down. I dreamed that I met my mother. I had to go to the toilet, and I had diarrhea, and something seemed funny. Well, when I flushed the toilet, the whole thing overflowed and went all over. And I thought, now here's all this shit to wipe up. And then a friend of mine came onto the scene. She often represents my mother in my dreams. And I explained to her what happened and she was much better about it than I thought she would be. And I realized that I hadn't broken the toilet, that the toilet must have been broken before I started. And she said, "Well, never mind, here is your doll, and you can make some dolls' clothes for it." And there was material and everything. I liked the dolls, but I had no idea how to make dolls' clothes. She had just left me with this whole thing to do, and I had no idea how to do it. And I was bugged, simply frustrated. And that was the way the dream ended.

The first thing that came to mind was that at school the children don't call them the dolls: they call them my babies. And they were the dolls we have at school, black dolls, white dolls, etc., and they generally have their clothes off. And the whole thing about mopping up the shit, that it was my fault that the thing didn't work, but it really wasn't my fault. The toilet had seemed in perfectly good working order. No one had said not to use it, and there I had to go and mop it up. The plumbing thing is interesting, because my brother always used to say that so-and-so was having trouble with her female plumbing.

L.S. I associate it immediately with what you talked about when you were thirteen. That was the year your mother told you about your cousin's plumbing, and you were afraid that yours was like that, and that was the year that you got your period. You had all kinds of associations with masturbating that year, including your mother telling you to be careful. And also your feeling that it was your fault, which is why you were being sent away from Europe when you were three. And I thought of the dolls as the baby in you, which your mother didn't take care of.

J. What I thought was that she was saying, yes, go ahead, grow up, have children, but you have no model . . . Figure it out for yourself.

L.S. Right . . . grow yourself up. It was a bitter philosophy in a way. That is, if you clean all the shit up, then you can have the dolls to play with. But the fact is nobody helps you clean up the shit, and no one told you not to use the toilet in the first place, and as a reward you're given the dolls, and you don't know how to make the clothes. No one is helping you, and no one is teaching you.

J. It's an interesting dream, because usually dreams have to do with the future, but this one had to do with the past.

I wasn't anxious about something that was coming, but irritated with someone in the past.

L.S. I think it also comes from the fact that you are finally able to see your mother through your own eyes, and not just now, but as you saw her in the past. In a way you let yourself see that she failed you.

J. Oh, she certainly did. What I do think is how terribly frightened she must have been about having children.

L.S. And she really needed you to help her . . . Do you see anything else in the dream?

J. No. I think that's what it was all about.

L.S. Did you have anything that you wanted to add from the last time?

J. No . . .

L.S. The last part of the interview has to do with general opinions and attitudes you hold today that don't necessarily relate to specific experiences in your life. At this time in your life do you consider any kind of sexual adjustment, or any particular kinds of expressions of sexuality, to be perverted?

J. Some kinds of sadism, masochism, of which I know very little—anything that involves pain—that to me is perverted—like the Boston rapist. But so far as homosexuals, lesbians, I don't feel that I would care to do it, but I don't feel a stigma about it. I don't think it's harmful.

L.S. Do you think your attitudes about this have changed over the years?

J. Yes, certainly they have about homosexuals.

L.S. Do you know what caused the change?

J. Therapy, time, exposure too. I realized that some things work for some people and other things work for other people. So it doesn't have to be black and white. And also, homosexuality was very threatening to me because of Chris. But I don't think it would be again.

L.S. Do you have any feelings about stimulants during sex?

J. I know that if I am attracted to someone and I have a

couple of drinks, I am even more attracted to him. When I started the relationship with Fred I used to smoke pot, and at first it was great. But as I got more secure, I liked the pot less and less. Because what happens to me with pot or liquor is that I get so relaxed that I don't have as good an orgasm. So I would prefer to be straight. But if it were the first time, I would probably feel more relaxed after a glass of wine.

L.S. When you first started to see Fred, what were you afraid of?

J. I thought I would be a total dud in bed because I had only slept with one man. Somehow, with him, I got over that.

L.S. Do you have any feelings about lights on or off during sex?

J. No. When I started with Fred, it made me nervous to have the lights on.

L.S. Did the lights on or off affect you with Chris?

J. No, I was very comfortable with him.

L.S. Do you have any particular sex position that is always more satisfying for you?

J. Yes, me under. I can put my legs anywhere as long as we're both close enough for me to have clitoral stimulation. The other way around I can enjoy, but it doesn't seem to work as well.

L.S. Have you ever experienced multiple orgasms?

J. Yes, I have.

L.S. Do they follow one right after another?

J. No, I have to wait in between.

L.S. What time has to elapse?

J. I would say five or ten minutes.

L.S. Do you feel that orgasms are easily experienced, or experienced with difficulty? This is a very subjective question.

J. Assuming that I am with someone I like, they're easy, there's no problem.

L.S. Do you experience orgasm most of the time when you have sex?

J. Yes, most of the time. They vary in intensity. The time I would be least likely to have one would be when I have woken up in the morning. And I think it's always been that way. First I have to go to the bathroom and I have to move around to get my circulation going. I have to be awake.

L.S. Do you feel that the sex act would be enjoyable to you with or without orgasm?

J. If I am ambivalent about someone, no. If I am really close to someone, yes it would be enjoyable.

L.S. Then you are saying that if you are conflicted about a relationship, you insist on sexual satisfaction, and that if you are not conflicted, it is not so important?

J. Yes.

L.S. In general, what do you prefer to do after you have had sex—sleep, talk, think?

J. Probably think, sometimes talk because I like to feel close to the person after it. I don't go to sleep right away. In fact, I'd rather stay up a bit.

L.S. That seems to be more true for women than men. Men usually like to go to sleep . . .Do you feel equally stimulated by seeing photographs of nude females and nude males?

J. I would say that I could be stimulated by them in different ways. If I saw a female, I would feel an identification. If I saw a male, I would fantasy what it would be like. If I saw both, I would think about a past situation that was enjoyable.

L.S. In reading passages in literature, have any books seemed to you particularly stimulating?

J. Well, I can't think of an example now, but I am sure reading a good book about people making love could be stimulating.

L.S. Do you have any particular feelings about talking during sex?

J. I don't usually. If I am feeling very intensely about sex, I won't talk, usually. If we have just fallen into it, and are having a very relaxed time, I might talk quite a lot during the beginning and then would get very involved and not talk.

L.S. Do you think that any words for genitals or the sex act or whatever are very stimulating to you?

J. No.

L.S. Do you have any feelings, one way or the other, about nudity?

J. I am not a great one for walking around nude, but if I feel very comfortable with someone I might traipse around nude.

L.S. How do you feel about being nude with women?

J. That doesn't bother me because my mother and grandmother used to traipse around nude.

L.S. Do you consider yourself a very affectionate person?

J. If I am with someone I like, yes.

L.S. Have the men that you have known tended to be affectionate with you?

J. Until he turned off, Chris was affectionate, which I enjoyed. Fred was not affectionate, and that was upsetting. With him, affection and sexuality are not related. For me, I like affection and sexuality.

L.S. What do you consider to be the most satisfying sexual experience you ever had?

J. I think it was in the last two years when Chris was at L. University. We had gone through a big crisis about a boy, and it was over. Chris was very happy about what he was doing. Our sex life was very good and tuned in.

L.S. Do you consider that to be a more satisfying sexual time in your life than, say, your experience with Fred?

J. There were times with Fred that were very good, but they

were very individual. This was the kind of situation—I remember one three-week rest cure with Chris when he and I spent the whole time in bed, just affectionately, so that it made a total pattern of life being very close to somebody.

L.S. Do you think that generally your sexual responses are like other women, more than other women, less than . . . ?

J. The situation on which I base my feelings is group therapy, and I would say that I am more responsive, because when other people in the group talk about their problems, etc., I am sometimes amazed.

L.S. Do you think you like sex?

J. Yes, but I also think I am selective about it. For a while I thought maybe I really didn't like it because, if I did, I would be doing it all the time. And I thought about it and realized that it was *because* I liked it so much that I could afford to be selective.

L.S. What do you think is your deepest sexual fear?

J. That's an interesting question. How have other women answered it?

L.S. Well, a lot of women are afraid that at some point in their life, they will lose their sexual feeling. This is related to a fear of dying.

J. What comes to my mind first is that I am not beautiful enough, or belly-dancerish enough, not that I'm not responsive enough.

L.S. What if you weren't enough of whatever it is—what would that fear mean?

J. Oh, that I would meet someone truly attractive, very experienced, with more experience than I've had, and that I'd like him, and look attractive, but when I shed my clothes, he'd see that I am pasty white, and my thighs are bigger than they look.

L.S. Your fear is that someplace you might not be enough to please this person whom you want most to please.

Do you feel that men have more urgent sexual needs than women?

J. I think they do. I think that men get stimulated more easily, or perhaps with less emotional attachment. Now, whether that's a cultural thing, I don't know.

L.S. What characteristics about men in general do you find most attractive, and which do you find most unattractive?

J. I don't like men who are wishy-washy. I like men who are strong. I like good-looking men, men of a thin build, with hair, not bald; kind of definite way of moving, control over their bodies. Fat men turn me off. Or a man who looks like a slob. I don't care how they dress. A man who looks self-respecting, healthy, in control of himself. I prefer someone to be a little bit taller, a little bit bigger.

L.S. What kinds of personality traits do you find attractive or repellent?

J. I don't like men who do a lot of bragging, and I love a good sense of humor—that's important, a sense of humor. I like people who are cerebral, and I like men who are capable, know how to fix machines when they go wrong. And when I am blithering around having trouble making small decisions, I like to know that he is there and can help. You know that ad, "A man whom you can lean on." And sensitive.

L.S. Generally speaking, do you think that men find you attractive?

J. Yes.

L.S. What do you think that men find most attractive about you and what do they find least attractive about you?

J. Least attractive, I would think that, if I am in one of my inferior moods, I am not funny enough, I am not sparkly enough, I have to brush my hair, not fashion-platey enough, not enough like my mother, big earrings. And not a swinging enough chick. Most attractive: practically schizophrenic, good sense of humor, my sense of style, my intelligence, and that I am fun to be with, as well as reliable, virtuous, and all those things. And fairly unpredictable.

L.S. Do you think that men ever see you as aggressive?

J. I didn't used to think so, but in my last two relationships I was, to a certain extent. Maybe aggressive is the wrong word, but perfectly definite about my rights, about what I liked. But that old image of myself, the person with the down moods, doesn't recur very often. I mean, about three days out of the year, I wish my hair would stay in place. But I don't really care.

L.S. Which of your parents do you think you resemble, physically or personality-wise?

J. I think I am pretty much of a mixture.

L.S. What is who?

J. My way of speaking and moving is like my mother, except in certain ways I am more definite, which is like my father. I have more energy than my mother had. My eyes are very much like my mother's, but my bone structure is heavier, and that comes from my father's side of the family. A lot of my perceptiveness and intuition probably come from my mother, and my practicality and resilience, that comes from my father. I used to think I was like my mother and the ugly side of my father's family.

L.S. What trait about yourself do you like the most?

J. Somehow it's my wisdom, but that means a lot of things: I've been through so many experiences, etc., that there is a kind of constancy about me and understanding, and an agelessness.

L.S. Do you think that your attitudes about premarital sex changed with time, or that specific thinking or experiencing helped to change then?

J. Well, for one thing, doing it myself changed my feelings. When I did it, I had mixed feelings, but I was glad I did it.

L.S. Do you have any general ideas about sex education for children? Try to think about this in terms of your own children if you had some. You who would be the major influence on that aspect of your children's education.

J. I would want my daughter to feel very good about herself as a female, and my son to feel very good about himself as a male. As for the mechanics, I think I would treat it as very much a part of life. I presume that I would have animals in my house, and as the children grew up and asked questions, I would just answer them. From observing parents, and what they have told children these days, it seems to me that parents sort of overload their children with information, because what is really important is how the parents relate to each other—that the children see adults being affectionate and loving.

L.S. When you came to me, was that your first contact with psychotherapy?

J. Yes.

L.S. And we have been together about three or four years.

J. About four years.

L.S. Do you feel that psychotherapy has altered your sex responses, feelings, the expression of your sexuality, or do you think sex has not changed, but your personality has?

J. I feel that everything has changed but on another level. I feel the best part of me hasn't changed—it's just emerged. So it's like an uncovering. So I feel that what was there has been uncovered, and that's a marvelous feeling. Like a whole straitjacket was removed. So it is like a rebirth, a second chance at life.

L.S. What do you think made you want to participate in this interview?

J. I think that I felt positive enough about myself as a female to examine how I used to feel about myself. I felt I had the guts to look at things that might be wrong about me.

L.S. If we had done this interview two years ago would you have approached it with more misgivings?

J. Yes, I think that I would have. I think that my last two

relationships really changed me. The fact that I could say no, and be turned off and be angry sexually, as well as generally, that I am a person aware of my own dignity, my own worth, my own self.

L.S. Have you had any particular feelings about me during the interview? Have your feelings about me changed any?

J. Yes, they did. I had such a rush of feelings about you just before, feelings that you weren't magic, and that I could compete with you, and then during the interview I felt very, very close to you—it's been wonderful. Having been the outsider all my life, it's very good to know there is someone I feel so connected to, and who feels the way I do about things.

L.S. It was terrific that we did the interview not long after you realized you could compete with me. Is there anything else you want to add? In general, how would you sum up this whole experience?

J. I just feel very together. I feel such knowledge about myself and confidence in myself. I think that I feel that the major work in analysis has been accomplished.

L.S. It's been quite an experience for me, too, and I'll be thinking about all we've talked about for a long, long time ... Thank you so very much for sharing your time—and your life—with me.

CHAPTER NINE

CONCLUSIONS

We have no common sense about sex.
—A.C. Kinsey

Sex must be a very powerful force—because in spite of all the "don't"s we get in childhood, we still end up doing it.
—Della

I feel that most therapists and writers approach sex rather viciously and wrong-headedly. . . . They start off with an idea of what sex *should* be instead of exploring what it *can* be.
—Edward Field, in a letter, 1971.

THIS BOOK has dealt with the sex lives of 30 women from birth to the time of the interviews. It has reviewed, specifically, the sexual feelings and, generally, the human relationships of these women. It has examined the intricate tracery of human sexual history—from the woman's remembered past to a time in her adult life when she sought to voice all the feelings, attitudes, joy, and anguish that made up her history.

My main purpose in writing this book was to try to break the silence surrounding women and sex. This was also the primary reason that each of the thirty women gave over twelve hours of her time, as well as immeasurable amounts of courage, hope, and pain, to participate in the study.

A woman confiding trustfully and as honestly as possible in another woman, who listens with sympathy, empathy, and specialized understanding, who thoughtfully explores in an ordered fashion all the nuances of feeling, memory, and behavior conveyed to her, is probably the best measure anyone has of the perceived effects—satisfaction, sorrows, ecstasies, revulsion—of each woman's sexual experiences.

HIGHLIGHTS OF FINDINGS

An analysis of the specific data derived from the interviews is presented in Appendix B. Some of the major findings are itemized here:

1. The first memories with sexual connotation reported by the women varied greatly in nature and the age at which they occurred, but were finally separated into seven mutually exclusive categories. This indicates a great variety of experiences

for a memory with such specific content.

Very few of the initial memories were guilt-free, with the single exception of several reported memories that involved sexual feelings at the preverbal level. A feeling of guilt and/or revulsion surrounded nearly every other type of early sexual memory, initial as well as subsequent. With such early negative conditioning, it seems almost miraculous that any women in this study could have learned to enjoy sex, let alone experience orgasm.

2. Despite cultural pressure toward increased sexual activity and freedom, there seems to have been little, if any, relaxation of the anxiety and guilt attached to female masturbation. Most of the women in this study expressed intense disapproval of and anxiety about masturbation, whether or not they had done it or done it frequently. When asked which area of the study had aroused the most anxiety, almost all of them answered masturbation.

3. The motivations and feelings surrounding virginity revealed that current cultural pressures differ from those of past eras. In the past, women were ashamed if they lost their virginity before marriage and were reluctant to reveal sexual feelings or needs at any time. Now they seem to be ashamed if they are still virgins at marriage or as young adults, or if they do not experience orgasm.

4. It was easier to nullify early negative teachings that sexual intercourse is painful than early teachings that it is disgusting or "dirty." Pain is an objective phenomenon, which can be tested on reality, whereas disgust is subjective, a value judgment.

5. Not all women with social-emotional problems had accompanying sexual response problems, nor did all women with sexual response problems have social relationship problems. This fact and the unanimity of orgasmic response suggest that sexual responsiveness and emotional stability are *not* necessarily mutually dependent.

6. A particularly striking finding was the unanimous nega-

tive reaction to parental intercourse, seen, overheard, or fantasied. For many women, the feeling of revulsion or disbelief was as intense in adulthood as it had been during childhood. It is quite likely that this reaction stems from the guilt caused by negative parental responses to children's early sexual experiences, and from the realization that the parents themselves were involved in the very act they labeled most taboo: the zenith of "The Big Lie."

7. Orgasm in the human female seems to be a learned, rather than an automatic, response. Rarely did the women in this study experience orgasm spontaneously, without prior knowledge or practice.

Each woman experiences orgasm in a number of ways, depending on the emotional climate at the time and how the experience is induced. Several of the women in this study did not identify the orgasm experienced by other methods (e.g., masturbation) as the same experience that could take place as a conclusion to intercourse. That is, they thought these were entirely different phenomena, until they had sufficient experience to recognize the similarities of their physical feelings in the different contexts.

Many women reported that they felt compelled to reject or deny what gave them sexual release; instead they tried to mold their experiences to what textbooks said they "should" feel. When freed from such imprisoning "theories," they often realized that they had significant experiences that did not fit into conventional theories about female sexuality.

8. The experience of orgasm, in and of itself, is *not* always an integral part of sexual contentment. Many women reported experiencing sexual gratification without sexual climax: gratification in feelings of physical and spiritual closeness, in giving pleasure to a loved one, in "being in control" over oneself or the other person or the situation in general. Other women did not *allow* themselves to become too involved or stimulated sexually. Hence, they did not have much expectation of sexual release from intercourse and suffered little or no

disappointment when the act did not conclude in orgasm.

9. The women reported receiving little accurate sex instruction. No single source provided adequate information for any woman at any one developmental stage. Parents were a very poor source of information and rarely if ever provided emotional support for the child or understanding of her sexual feelings.

SOME SUGGESTIONS ABOUT SEX EDUCATION

The findings of this study suggest some radically different approaches to sex education—for children, for parents, for educators.

It is commonly accepted that parents of the past conveyed to their children the ignorance and repressiveness of their particular eras and cultures. But are contemporary parents likely to do any better with their childrens' sex education? Would the women who participated in this study—all of whom had intelligence, better than average educations, at least some psychological insight, and broad life experiences— be any more enlightened and effective with their own children?

I tend to think *not*. Sexual anxiety, which is of course primarily focussed in the family, so often has a way of surviving education, experience, and even psychotherapy. Many of these women were excellent teachers of other people's children, yet proved to be very poor educators and models for their own children. One woman, who described her own early adult life as "quite promiscuous," recounted

> feeling reluctant to think of my own daughter having premarital relations. All my friends seemed to be aware of this possibility and accepted it casually. *I* was simply shocked when my daughter told me of her relations with a young man: "But, Mother, what did you think we were doing all this time!" I don't know *what* I thought they were doing, to tell you the truth!

Another woman, aged thirty, felt incapable of informing her ten-year-old daughter about "sex." She said that she wanted to convey to her that "sex is something great," but feared that this would encourage her daughter to be "promiscuous." In considering whether her daughter knew about masturbation, she said:

> You know, I've been wondering about this lately. It's so hard for me to look at this lovely little creature who—you would think—is so pure, and to think of her doing things like that . . . Yes, I guess I do mean *dirty* things like that, even though I hate to admit that I'm still thinking in those ways.

The woman herself has been masturbating to orgasm since the age of twelve.

Children's sexuality is apparently frightening and often unacceptable to their parents, even though these adults may be aware of their own childhood sexual feelings and experiences. They seem to forget or ignore the fact that children are constantly experiencing sexuality, that sex education takes place through all the details of family life—physical closeness or distance, attitudes toward toilet functions, nakedness and privacy, bedroom divisions, demonstrations of affection or hostility, parents' senses of their own sexual identities—and not through a single explanation or "little talk."

Anxiety about sexuality in parent-child relationship is ever present in this society, and is communicated with or without any factual information about sex. (*Every* woman in this study said she would rather have talked about sex with an older relative or family friend than with her parents.)

Would schoolteachers be better equipped for factual discussions with children about sex? Not at present, since the adults who become teachers are subject to the same prejudices and conflicts about sex as the adults who become parents. And specialists in related areas—physicians, nurses, counselors, social workers—all too often believe they have fulfilled their obligations by explaining reproduction and/or warning youngsters about the dangers and evil of sex.

A major step toward improved sex education would be to train specialists—informing them both what to teach and how to teach a subject that is so complex and until recently has been taboo. These new specialists could come from related professions or become "sex educators" independently. What is important is that they have a strong interest in and affection for their work.

> The main thing [about sex education] . . . is that it should not be taught by frigid people, with some dried-out members of the school board looking over their shoulders like kippered herring at a wake. In this situation, sex is like humor. Courses in humor, if they are given at all, should be given only by people who have laughed at least once in their lives—and enjoyed it.[1]

A most important requirement in an effective sex education program would be a variety of experiences with psychotherapy. The fundamental confusion in present attempts at sex education is the inability to recognize, understand, and convey the idea that sex is essentially a way of relating to another human being. What is actually said to children is far less important in sex education than the kind of people the educators (parents, teachers, or others) are and the feelings and attitudes they project about themselves and one another. There is no better method known for developing self-awareness and personal honesty than psychotherapy, which would teach prospective teachers about themselves while demonstrating a way to teach others about themselves.

Another excellent tool for enhancing communication about sex would be a modified therapy group, in which young adolescents could exchange their personal thoughts and feelings on this subject: their fears and anxieties, their expectations, desires, attitudes, needs, doubts, and incapacities. If

[1]Eric Berne, *Sex in Human Loving,* p. 38.

young people had such an opportunity to air their concerns and questions about sex before too many misconceptions were permanently imbedded in their personalities, one major problem area in human sexual relationships might be alleviated.

Of course sex discussion groups are valuable for peers of *any* age. In the open environment of the discussion group, perhaps under the guidance of a trained group leader, a woman soon learns that she need not depend upon some "expert" to tell her what is "right or wrong" about sexual feelings and responses. Once she has the opportunity to express herself, she finds that she is the best "expert."

A further possibility is the establishment of classes for adults on parenthood. Like sexual response, parenthood is neither instinctual nor automatic, but the result of a complex and subtle learning process. Just as the first experience of sexual intercourse does not erase naïve or repressive sexual attitudes, so the act of giving birth does not automatically create total understanding of the complexities of parenthood. The parenthood classes could help adults to prepare themselves for the unique responsibilities of being parents and might use psychotherapeutic methods to encourage self-awareness. Courses on parenthood should be no more unusual than driver education courses—and are no less necessary, for the power of parents who raise children is infinitely more lethal than the power of the driver of an automobile.

Since infants and children respond more to attitudes and feelings than to words, *some form of sex education is taking place at all times.* Sex education is inevitable—it behooves us to know who is teaching what, to whom, and how.

GENERAL CONCLUSIONS ABOUT FEMALES AND SEXUALITY

The fact that every woman in the study had experienced orgasm through sexual intercourse was very interesting, since orgasm capacity was not a requirement for participation, nor even a major area of concern. Self-selection may have been an important factor. Two of the women, who had not been able to experience orgasm through intercourse until many years after their first sexual encounters, said that if they had not learned to have a "socially acceptable, mature orgasm," they would not have participated in the study. In other words, woman who considered themselves "sexually inadequate"— for whatever reason and by whatever standard—did not volunteer for this study.

An interesting generalization that can be made about the life patterns of these 30 women perhaps correlates with the finding of 100 percent orgasm capacity. Every woman showed a great deal of life energy—in her striving to achieve happiness and success, and in her constant struggle to defy and defeat many of the negative forces of her past. Some evidence of these struggles can be seen in their careers (8 of the women had changed professions), marriages (5 women were in their third marriages, and 8 in their second), and psychological and emotional changes (all had sought some form of psychotherapeutic or psychoanalytic treatment). Since orgasm through intercourse is the standard measure of female sexual "adequacy," it is not surprising that these energetic, successful women managed to experience it.

For women the means of sexual gratification is apparently not innate, but rather learned. That is, sex is a natural function, but one learns how to experience or express this natural function. The learning experience can develop in either direction—for or against pleasure. Many women have learned, somehow, to inhibit desire, arousal, and gratification. That is, they perceive gratification in terms of *not* having pleasure. A young woman who has been raised to believe that the expression of her sexuality must be denied, and who has received many rewards (in the form of parental approval) for this kind of denial, might find it distressing later in life to have to learn responses that she associates with the psychological threat of punishment from authority symbols. This woman, then, is more comfortable and more able to maintain a state of homeostasis when she is *not* stimulated sexually, when she does *not* permit herself to be aroused, and, interestingly, when she does *not* require for herself the experience of orgasm.

From the findings of this study, it would seem that for civilized humans sex is a drive with a potential for pleasure, which may be fulfilled to a lesser or greater extent. This sexual drive is not necessarily expressed through sensual or procreative functioning; some of it is largely sublimated and expressed in ways not overtly sexual. Some women seem to have strong sexual drives, some deny their sexuality and apparently can "live without it," and some women, perhaps, just do not have very much sexual drive. Kinsey suggests that "the capacity to be aroused psychosexually evidentally depends on something more innate than the culture . . . there appears to be a limit beyond which psychosexual capacities cannot be developed within an individual's lifetime."[2]

Let me draw a comparison, for purposes of clarification, between sexual potential and intellectual potential. Each human female is born with an intellectual potential, which may or may not be fulfilled, depending on her environment and what happens during her lifetime (particularly during the early years), on her object identifications, the values she learns, the motivations she acquires, etc. Some women struggle to find the means to fulfill this capacity, and when they do so, experience a strong sense of fulfillment. Some *never* fulfill their potential, and consequently have strong feelings of frustration. But they don't know how to break through the psychic barriers that may be deterring them. Other women, however, who *never* fulfill their potential feel indifferent to it and find other kinds of gratifications more fulfilling.

The varieties of human satisfaction are infinite, the possibilities are infinite, and the variables affecting satisfaction are infinite. A way of life that will make one person psychotic

[2] A. C. Kinsey *et al.*, *Sexual Behavior in the Human Female,* p. 203.

merely serves to strengthen the resources of another. So, too, in human sexual satisfaction. What one person requires for happiness may be of minimal consequence to another.

Whether sexual fulfillment is necessary for the fulfillment of a human being (and, therefore, necessary for the contribution that a fulfilled human being can make human progress) would be a valuable question for investigation by future researchers. If sexual or orgasmic fulfillment is not essential to a person's pleasure or satisfaction, then society should cease to establish unreal and often meaningless standards for "mature" sexuality. That is, if gratification is an individual matter, then it should be an individual's choice, limited only by concern for the safety and wellbeing of others. If, on the other hand, certain degrees of sexual and/or orgasmic responses *are* necessary for the betterment of human life, then whatever affects that fulfillment must be identified.

While love seems to make the world go round, sex often makes it go askew.

This study was done in the hope of contributing toward humanizing attitudes about sex in our world and perhaps opening the way for human beings to find their own kinds of peace and satisfaction. Ultimately, the aim is to develop better citizens in the world—freer citizens capable of making more and more loving relationships.

Margaret Mead has written, "Where one sex suffers, the other sex suffers also."[3] The converse should also be true. Therefore, it is my hope that this journey into the thoughts and feelings of thirty women, and myself, will increase human understanding and somehow help make life *sweeter* for both sexes.

On that journey, I was very grateful for the companionship of those women, and for the unique, courageous, and poignant contributions of those thirty very human beings.

[3]Margaret Mead, *Male and Female,* p. 300.

APPENDIXES

APPENDIX A

PRELIMINARY QUESTIONNAIRE

1. Name _____
2. Date of Birth _____
3. Place of Birth _____
4. Marital Status (circle one)
     Married   Widowed   Divorced   Separated
5. Your highest level of Education (circle one)
     High School Grad.   College Grad.   Some College   Graduate
     Work
6. Your occupation (if presently housewife, your occupation before marriage) _____
7. Your husband's age _____
8. Husband's Occupation _____
9. Husband's highest level of Education (circle one)
     High School Grad.   College Grad.   Some College   Graduate
     Work
10. How long married _____
11. Previously Married: How Often _____
12. Duration of each marriage _____
13. List your children, giving age and sex _____
     _____
14. Family income (circle one):
     Under $5,000 $5,000–$10,000 $10,000–$20,000   Over $20,000
15. List your brothers and sisters, giving age and sex _____
     _____
16. Your father's age (if living) _____
     His birthplace _____
     If dead, his age at death _____
     Your age at his death _____

17. Your father's highest level of education (circle):
    Elem. School: 1 2 3 4 5 6 7 8
    High School: 1 2 3 4
    College: 1 2 3 4
    Graduate Work:
18. Your father's occupation_____
19. Your mother's age (if living) _____
    Her birthplace _____
    If dead, her age at death_____
    Your age at her death _____
20. Your mother's highest level of education (circle)
    Elem. School: 1 2 3 4 5 6 7 8
    High School: 1 2 3 4
    College: 1 2 3 4
    Graduate Work:
21. Your mother's occupation now and/or before marriage_____
    _____

22. How would *you* classify parents' marriage? (circle one)
    Completely happy   More happy than unhappy
    Equally happy and unhappy   More unhappy than happy
    Completely unhappy
23. To what did you attribute their happiness, if any? _____
    _____

24. Whom do you think *you* tended to credit for any happiness?
    (choose one) Mother_____ Father _____
                  Equally mother and father _____
    To what did you attribute their happiness, if any? _____
    _____

25. Whom do you think *you* tended to blame more for any unhappiness?
    (choose one) Mother_____ Father _____
                  Equally mother and father _____
    To what did you attribute their *un*happiness, if any?_____
    _____

26. If parents still alive, are they living together? _____
    If not together, are they divorced? Yes_____ No_____
27. Your age when separation occurred _____

INTERVIEW GUIDE

The questions for this study are divided into age categories, beginning with Early Childhood and Prepuberty. The first questions will concern any experiences or feelings you may have had, from as early as you can remember up to age 12.

I. Early Childhood and Prepuberty

1. To the best of your knowledge, what seems to you to be the very, very earliest recollection of any kind of any sexual connotation whatsoever? (It can be an actual experience, something you oversaw, overheard, a fantasy, a dream, a daydream—of any nature whatsoever—that seems to you to have some kind of sexual connotations, significance, or overtones.)

2. Do you feel there were any other strongly influential experiences of this nature in your childhood?

3. Do you recall your experiences with toilet training as a child? Please describe as much of this as possible.
   Do you recall whether or not, as a child, you were fond of prolonging the act of moving your bowels—for the sake of any kind of pleasure or other gains? Did voiding urine give you any similar feelings?

4. Do you recall your reactions, during childhood, to hearing so-called obscene words or phrases which you heard or saw written or even uttered to yourself?

5. Many children, before puberty, have some masturbatory experience. Did you ever have such experience? (For the purposes of this study, masturbation is defined as *any form* of genital sexual excitation which may or may not conclude in orgasm.)

6. *(if yes)* What was your earliest remembered experience with masturbating?
   What was the nature of the experience? That is, how did you masturbate; were you alone or in the presence of anyone else? What motivated you to do this? Do you associate any other person or persons with this activity or experience?
   How frequently did you masturbate?
   How often would it conclude in orgasm?
   How would you bring orgasm about, what method?

What were your first feelings about this orgasm? What did you think it was?

7. When, if ever, did you begin to have daydreams or fantasies as a part of the pleasure of masturbation?
   (if yes) Were daydreams of yourself in a sexual situation with another person always an essential part of your pleasure in masturbating? Was the other person a boy, girl, man, woman? Can you describe this fantasy or fantasies in as much detail as possible? Were they always the same?
   How did you feel about having this or these fantasies?

8. In general, what were your feelings about masturbating?

9. Were you ever punished or threatened with punishment or warned of what would happen to you if you masturbated?

10. *(if practice discontinued)* Did you discontinue for reasons of guilt, discovery, or lack of satisfaction, or other reasons?

11. *(if no)* Were you aware of *not* masturbating? That is, that perhaps other children did this, but that you did not? If you were aware of not doing this, *why* didn't you? Any specific reasons? Any specific person or persons?

12. *(either yes or no)* What advantages or disadvantages do you feel you experienced as a result of your experience in this area?

13. Were your parents very affectionate with each other? Were they very affectionate with you? How did they express their affection?
    Did they seem to be equally affectionate with all siblings?

14. At what age did you first learn *how* babies were born? From whom did you receive this information?
    (if no recall) Was there ever anyone among your family or friends who was pregnant, during your childhood, who might have aroused your curiosity?
    How did you react to this knowledge?
    How did you feel about the thought that your parents participated in such an act?

15. In your childhood, did you connect the sexual act and having babies and love? Describe your experiences around making these connections.

16. Was it clear to you, or unclear, as to just *what* the act of intercourse was?

17. As a child, did you ever oversee or overhear, in actuality or in fantasy,

your parents involved in sexual activity? Any other adults? Who? Describe as fully as you can your reactions to these experiences.

18. What outlets did you use for your sexual feelings during childhood? For example, was it through reading, movies, fantasy-play with others, and so forth?

19. Do you recall having sexual daydreams in childhood?
Have any of those continued into adulthood?

20. Do you recall any sexual sleeping dreams in your childhood?
Have any of those continued into adulthood?

21. Did you have brothers and/or sisters? Were you aware of any special feelings or thoughts or fantasies about any or all of them?
What was the nature of those feelings?
What were your feelings about having those feelings?
How did you handle those feelings?

22. Can you describe your experiences and feelings, if any, with curiosity about *looking* at the sexual organs of others (other children, other adults, male or female, parents); of yourself?
How would you characterize the experiences? For example, were they thrilling, delightful, disgusting, frightening, or otherwise?

23. Do you recall any wishes to be a boy? What do you think this meant to you?
Do you think you literally wanted to have a penis or did you feel that there were advantages to be gained from the change of identity, such as parental approval, greater freedom, and so forth?

II. Puberty and Early Adolescence

24. At what age did you first menstruate?

25. How did you first learn about menstruation? What did you expect the experience to be like?
Did the information you received about menstruation prove to be valid or invalid? If the latter, what effect did this have on you?

26. Can you recall your first experience with regard to menstruation?
Did the onset of menstruation affect your sexual attitudes or responses?

27. Did you connect the phenomenon of menstruation with pregnancy?

28. What was the general attitude in your family about menstruation?
Was it treated openly, secretively, matter-of-factly, or how?

29. Did you, during puberty or early adolescence, experience intense emotional relations with any other girl or woman?
    (if yes) Exactly when did you begin this? How did it come about?

30. Did you learn at this time in your life about homosexuality?
    (if yes) From whom did you learn about it?
    What were your feelings about it? (If you had later experiences of this sort, you may talk about them now or you may wait until I ask this question in the next age period.)

31. During this period of your life, did you discuss your sexual feelings or experiences with anyone?
    (if yes) Do you think those opportunities had an effect on your achieving actual satisfaction as an adolescent or as an adult? How?
    (if no) Would you have liked to have such opportunities? With whom? What do you think it would have done for you? How might it have altered the sexual pattern of your adolescence or your adult life?

32. Describe your first experience of kissing a boy.

33. On dates, what was the nature of the sexual interaction? Did you kiss, neck, pet?
    Did you ever experience orgasm during any of this activity?
    Did you feel popular with your peers, especially boys, in grade or high school?

34. What were your outstanding sex problems during childhood and/or adolescence? For example, popularity, strong necessity to control sexual feelings, anxieties about virginity and premarital pregnancy? How did you handle these problems?
    What were your feelings about your methods of handling your problems?

III. Late Adolescence and Premarital

35. Did you have any relationships which you might consider to have been of a homosexual nature? That is, some kind of degree of expression of feelings between yourself and another female? These are feelings which are often experienced during this period of life and they can take the form of intimate feelings for a girl friend of your own age, of idolizing a female teacher or some other older female.

36. *(if yes)* Were those feelings expressed in any kind of sexual way, such as touching, kissing, intimate fondling, and so forth?

37. *(if yes)* How often did such expressions of affection occur? With whom?

Was the experience associated with sex in your own mind at any time? At all times?

What form did such expressions of affection take?

Did you or the person or both of you reach a climax? (That is, a physical feeling of relief.)

Were the experiences satisfying?

What were your special reasons for engaging in this activity?

38. Were there any particular persons or events that influenced you toward this activity?

What were your feelings about these experiences?

(if negative) Why did you continue them?

Do you feel that these experiences helped or hindered your sexual attitudes and responses in your present life? In what way?

39. *(if no)* Would it make you uncomfortable to have a girl or woman put her arm around you or make other physical demonstrations of friendliness or affection? Did you go out of you way to avoid such feelings or experiences?

(if yes) Why do you think this was so?

40. Have you ever had any fantasies of intimate situations with a female in which something was being done to produce sexual satisfaction? How do you feel about having such feelings or fantasies?

41. At what age did you become aware of homosexuality as a phenomenon?

What were your feelings about it when you learned of it? For instance, did the idea frighten you, thrill you, appall you?

42. During your adolescence, in what way do you feel you expressed your romantic or your sexual feelings? Did you express them in dating, identification through fantasies, through movies or other direct ways?

Do you feel that you expressed them in some indirect way, such as studying, listening to music, participating in sports, reading?

43. Do you think *crying* was an indirect outlet for these feelings?

44. What were your dating experiences? That is, in general, what were your sexual activities before age 18? Did you kiss, pet, neck?

Did you ever experience a climax during any of those activities?

(if yes) Did you know what it was?

(if no) What did you think it was?

Did you have any specific knowledge or perhaps some feeling that some kind of feeling of release *could* occur from such stimulation?

45. In general, what kind of physical feelings did you have during such stimulation? Or emotional feelings?

46. During this period of your life, did you *ever* experience climax?
    (if yes) Was this the first time you ever experienced it?
    In what manner was your first climax reached?
    Were there other times that you experienced climax?
    What were the methods by which you attained it?
    How did you *know* that you had experienced climax?
    What did it feel like?

47. *(if had heterosexual relations)* Have you ever had difficulty in achieving orgasm through heterosexual relations, or has it seemed to you to be relatively easy for you to do so?

48. *(if difficulties)* Why do you think you had these difficulties? What are your feelings about them?

49. What were your earliest ideas about what sexual intercourse was or would be like?
    From what source did you get these ideas?

50. Describe the first experience you had with sexual intercourse? Was it pleasurable, painful, anxious?
    Was it in any way like you had expected it to be? What *had* you expected it to be like? If the experience was different from what you expected, how was it different?
    What were your feelings about all of this?

51. What do you think motivated you to have sexual intercourse before marriage?

52. Did you have any regrets over the decision to experience premarital relations?
    (if yes) What were those regrets?

53. Was the factor of future marriage an important or unimportant factor in your decision to have or not have premarital sexual relations with any particular man/men in your sexual experience?

54. Regarding your premarital sexual experiences, or lack of them, do you think you have helped or hindered the sexual satisfactions you may, or may not, have with your husband?

55. Were you ever pregnant before marriage?
    (if yes) What were your feelings about this? What were your fears? What were your experiences in this regard?

(if no) What were your feelings about premarital pregnancy? What were your fears?

56. Can you think of any additional important events or feelings that influenced your life in any significant way which took place during your adolescence up to age 18?

IV. Marital and Adult

57. How did you meet your husband?
    How long did you go together before you married? What was the courtship like?
    And your later married life?
    What would you say was the main source of trouble, if any, between you and your husband?

58. *(if more than one marriage)* What was the source of trouble with your first (second) husband?

59. Did you and your husband have intercourse with each other before your marriage?
    (if yes) Was your decision to have intercourse based on an expectation of marriage?

60. Did you both feel that the sexual relations were successful? Unsuccessful? How?

61. Did the nature of your sexual relationship change *after* you were married?

62. Did you feel any regrets about not being a virgin when you married?
    (if no) Did you expect to have intercourse on your wedding night?

63. In what way did you learn that this was to happen?
    What did you feel the first time you had intercourse? Pain? Pleasure? Surprise? Disgust?

64. About how long was it before you began to experience orgasm during intercourse?

65. If the sex act has ever been distasteful to you, why was it so?

66. Was your husband a virgin when you married him? How did you feel about this?

67. Is your husband sexually attractive to you?
    (if yes) Has he always been?
    (if no) Has he ever been?
    Has this feeling about him changed since your marriage? How do you account for this?

68. About how often do you and your husband have intercourse?
Do you both agree on how often?
(if no) How do you adjust to this difference? What do you feel about making this adjustment? What does your husband feel about making this adjustment?

69. Has the frequency changed since you were first married?
(if yes) How do you feel about the changes? What has seemed to be the reason for the changes?

70. When you have difficulties achieving pleasure from intercourse, how do you feel about it?

71. Are there times when you don't experience orgasm, but feel pleasure anyway?
What is this pleasure like?

72. Have you ever felt that it was necessary to "pretend" or "fake" orgasm?
(if yes) For what reasons?
How did you feel about doing it?
Do you think your husband *knows* when you have an orgasm?
How do *you* know when you have an orgasm during, or as a result of, sexual relations?
Can you describe the feeling? Can you describe where and how it seems to take place?

73. Do you prefer that your partner be the more sexually aggressive one, or that you be the more sexually aggressive? That it vary from time to time?

74. What, if anything, does your husband do, either before or during intercourse, to increase your pleasure? What do you feel that *your* pleasure and satisfaction means to him?
What does the fulfillment of his enjoyment mean to *you?*

75. What conditions seem to increase your likelihood of having orgasm in relations with your husband?
What, if anything, do you do to make it possible for your husband to have orgasm?
What does he do to make it possible for you?

76. What, if anything, do you do to increase your own pleasure either before or during or after intercourse with your husband?

77. Are you able to tell your husband, in one way or another, what actions are most satisfying or stimulating to you?
Are you aware of what is most stimulating to you?

78. About how frequently, if at all, have you masturbated since your marriage?

    What are your feelings about this?

    (if at all) What are the circumstances that lead up to your masturbating?

79. What method of contraception, if any, do you and your mate use? Do you feel that this method affects your sexual responses in any way? Your husband's?

    Have you always used this method of contraception during your married life?

    (if no) Why did you make a change?

    Did you notice any differences in your sexual responses after changing?

80. Would you say that your married life is a happy one?

    (if no) Why not?

81. Do you feel that satisfactory sexual relations can "make or break" a marriage? That is, how great a part do you think sexual satisfaction plays in marital happiness?

    (if not happily married and believes sexual satisfaction important) Do you think unsatisfactory sexual relations with your husband are a sufficient cause to consider separation or divorce?

    (if no) What have you done to make the situation better? How do you feel about your solution(s)?

82. How do you think your marriage compares with your parents' marriage?

    How do you think your sexual satisfactions compare with those of your parents?

83. *(if subject has children)* How did your pregnancy affect your sexual relations with your husband? Did you continue sexual relations during the entire pregnancy? How often would you have intercourse? How did this compare with your sexual relations before the pregnancy? After the pregnancy?

    Did you have any substitutions for sexual relations during pregnancy? How did you feel about this?

    What are your general feelings and opinions about intercourse during pregnancy?

84. After you were married, what were your experiences with sexual relations outside marriage?

    (if had) Are there differences in the feelings, the amount of pleasure or displeasure in this (those) relationships?

(if yes) What do you feel made the difference? Technique? Experience? Circumstances? An illicit feeling?

85. Have you ever found that intercourse with a man you did *not* love was physically satisfying?

    Can you "let yourself go" sexually more easily with a man that you love or with one that you do *not* love?

86. Aside from having sexual relations with a man outside the marriage, have you ever found yourself attracted to men other than your husband?

    (if yes) How often?

    How do you feel about having these attractions?

    What do you do about them?

87. Has there been any notable difference in your ability to experience orgasm during intercourse during your marriage?

    Any difference between your ability maritally and premaritally?

    Any difference between your ability maritally and extramaritally?

V. Conclusions and Reactions (including Opinions and Attitudes)

88. How do stimulants affect you sexually? Do you feel that they increase or decrease your pleasure?

    Do you feel that you need to have them to enjoy sex?

    (if yes) Why?

89. Are there things you consider sexually perverted? Have you ever done any of those things that you feel are perverted?

    (if yes) What? *(if no)* Why not?

    Did you used to feel that some things were perverted, but later changed your opinion?

    What do you feel caused you to change your opinion?

90. Do you feel, in general, that you enjoy sex?

91. How would you characterize your ability to have an orgasm? Is it easier or difficult for you? Why?

    Is it easier or more pleasurable for you to have an orgasm from clitoral stimulation alone; that is, without penetration?

    (if mentions vaginal vs. clitoral orgasms) How do you feel about this?

    What are your thoughts on the differences?

    What is your preferred method of achieving orgasm?

92. Have you ever experienced multiple orgasm? That is, have you ever had more than one orgasm during any kind of sexual stimulation?

93. How do you feel during the sexual act? After the sexual act?

94. What experiences have you ever had seeing photographs of nude men or women?
    (if had) What were your feelings when you saw nude men? Women? Both together?

95. Do you ever become sexually aroused by reading erotic passages in literature?
    (if yes) Could you describe those experiences? What were the passages about specifically?

96. How do you feel about seeing your husband or lover or any other man nude? Pleasurable, distressing, thrilling?
    Do you usually have intercourse with the lights on or off? Why?
    Do you find it pleasurable, distressing, thrilling or otherwise to have your husband or lover see *you* nude? Do you feel that you are more or less modest than most women about exposing your body to your husband or other men?
    What are your feelings about nudity in your home, in general?
    Have your feelings about it, in the sexual act or around the house, changed since your marriage?
    How do you feel about the attitudes you have?

97. What are your feelings about bathroom privacy?
    If you and your husband have different feelings about nudity and/or privacy, how do you, or have you, solved them?

98. What feelings do you have about intercourse during your menstrual period?
    Do you feel any difference in your sexual drive around the time of your period? When?
    What do you do about it?
    How do you think your husband feels about having intercourse during your period?
    How have other men seemed to react to you during this time?

99. What are your feelings about *talking* during intercourse? Do you find the use of certain words or phrases stimulating? Stultifying? Disgusting?

100. Do you feel that men, in general have more urgent or stronger sexual needs than women?
    On what do you base your feeling?

101. Do you think or feel that you are different from other women you know in your sexual responses? (About the same? Like some and not like others?)

102. Do you consider yourself a very affectionate person?
    (if yes) How do you show your affections?
    (if no) Would you like to be more openly affectionate?
    What prevents you from showing your affectionate feelings?

103. Were your parents affectionate toward you? Toward each other?

104. How do you feel about men being affectionate toward you? Your husband or men you may have been involved with sexually?

105. Were you taught to be afraid of men? Explain. Before you ever had any physical, sexual contact with men, what were your feelings and fantasies about what it would be like?
    (if taught to be afraid) Do you think your feelings have *changed* significantly? Or do you feel that you have made forced "adjustments"? That is, adjustments in order to live more comfortably, without having changed your basic *attitudes* about men.

106. If there have been times when you felt you received no satisfaction of *any* kind from sexual relations, why do you feel that you continued to have those relations?

107. Which parent do you think you most resemble in personality? How? What characteristics?
    Which parent do you feel had most to do with your becoming the kind of person you now are?

108. Do (did) you perceive your mother as a very feminine person? Average feminine? Less than average?
    Do you see yourself as being like your mother in this regard?

109. Tell me something about how you perceived your parents' sexual life together? Active? Abusive? Loving? Demanding? Repressed?

110. What are or were some of your mother's expressed attitudes towards sex? Your father's?
    How do you think your parents' attitudes in this area affected your own feelings and activities?

111. What factual knowledge did your parents give you about sex?
    What sort of attitudes did they seem to have when they were talking to you about sex?
    What sort of attitudes did they seem to express by the way they lived?
    What were your parents' attitudes about premarital sex of any type?

112. What characteristics in men do you find most attractive? What traits? Why physical types?

113. What are your feelings about the size of a man's penis? (Length, width)

114. What characteristics, emotional and physical, do you find most repellent in men?
     How does your husband fit into this picture?

115. What characteristics in *you* do you think men find most attractive? Most unattractive?

116. What is your deepest sexual fear today?

117. What kind of sex education do you plan, or are you already giving, for your children?
     Do you plan a different kind of education for your son(s) than for your daughter(s)?

118. How do you feel about the possibility of your child or children having premarital sexual relations?
     Are your feelings influenced by whether you did or did not have such relations yourself?
     Do you have different feelings about such relations for a son than for a daughter?

119. Have your experiences in psychotherapy altered in any way your sexual experiences or feelings?
     (if yes) How?

120. What made you wish to participate as a subject in this research project?

121. How did you feel during our interviews?
     Have you gained any new insights into your sexual response as a result of this/these interviews?

122. What questions did you think I might ask?
     What questions were you most *afraid* I would ask?
     What questions that I *did* ask troubled you the most? Why?

123. If you could, would you change any of your sexual behavior at any time in your life?
     (if yes) At what particular time or times? Why?

APPENDIX B

TABLE 1

NUMBER AND PERCENT OF RESPONDENTS REPORTING
SPECIFIC EXPERIENCES RE: EARLY SEX MEMORIES (TO 12
YEARS)
(N=30)

	No.	Percent Total Group
Initial memory (age range: less than 1 year to over 8 years)		
Types of Memories		
Sensual feelings	12	40.0
Mutual exploration	5	16.7
Requests for or about sexual activity	4	13.3
Mutual exposure	3	10.0
Traumatic experience	3	10.0
Physical attraction	2	6.7
Self-exposure	1	3.3
Feelings surrounding Initial Memory		
Primarily distress	19	63.3
Primarily pleasure	11	36.7
Total Memories		
No awareness of genital sameness of difference between self and others	22	73.3
Such an awareness	8	26.7
No wish to have a penis or be a boy	20	66.7
Such a wish	10	33.3
No felt or expressed need for inner controls	23	76.7
Such a need	7	23.3

TABLE 2

NUMBER AND PERCENT OF RESPONDENTS REPORTING
SPECIFIC EXPERIENCES RE: MENSTRUATION
(N=30)

Conditions Surrounding Phenomenon	No.	Percent Total Group
Menarche		
Prior knowledge of phenomenon	26	86.7
No prior knowledge	4	13.3
Emotional Response at onset vs. prior knowledge		
Positive, previous	13	43.3
Negative, previous	7	23.3
Negative, no previous	4	13.3
Neutral, previous	6	20.0
Emotional response at onset		
Primarily pleasure	13	43.3
Primarily displeasure	11	36.7
Neutral	6	20
Source of initial knowledge of phenomenon		
Mother or stepmother	13	43.3
Girl friends	7	23.3
Other female family	4	13.3
Other adults	2	6.7
Books, pamphlets	3	10.0
Mother's reaction to subject's onset		
Neutral	18	60.0
Primarily displeasure	9	30.0
Primarily pleasure	3	10.0
Subject's response to mother's reaction		
Primarily accepting	21	70.0
Primarily anger or disappointment	9	30.0
Father's reaction to subject's onset		
Noncommunicative	23	76.7
Absent from home	5	16.7
Primarily pleasure	2	6.7

TABLE 2—*Continued*

Conditions Surrounding Phenomenon	No.	Percent Total Group
Post-Menarche		
Preferences for coitus during menstruation		
Neutral	12	40.0
Likes	11	36.7
Dislikes	6	20.0
No experience	1	3.3

TABLE 3

NUMBER AND PERCENT OF RESPONDENTS REPORTING
SPECIFIC EXPERIENCES RE: INITIAL INTERCOURSE
(N=30)

Related Conditions	No.	Percent Total Group
Age at initial intercourse		
14–15	4	13.3
16–17	5	16.7
18–19	13	43.3
20–21	3	10.0
22–23	3	10.0
24–25	2	6.7
Petting experior prior to initial intercourse		
Yes	27	90.0
No	3	10.0
First Climax		
Prior to initial intercourse	18	60.0
At some later time	10	33.3
During initial intercourse	2	6.7
Source of prior orgasm		
None experienced	12	40.0
Masturbation	10	33.3
Petting	5	16.7
Dreams	2	6.7
Oral stimulation	1	3.3
Marital expectations with initial partner		
No	14	46.7
Yes	9	30.0
Already married	7	23.3
Expectations realized		
Not expected	14	46.7
Already married	7	23.3
No	6	20.0
Yes	3	10.0
Expectations vs. experiences		
Orgasm:		
Not expected	17	56.7
Not experienced	27	90.0
Expected	13	43.3
Experienced	3	10.0
Pleasure:		
Not expected	15	50.0
Not experienced	26	86.7
Expected	15	50.0
Experienced	4	13.3

TABLE 3—*Continued*

Related Conditions	No.	Percent Total Group
Pain:		
Not expected	14	46.7
Not experienced	13	43.3
Expected	16	53.3
Experienced	17	56.7
Regret felt at having retained virginity until marriage		
Premarital intercourse	23	76.7
No regret	4	13.3
Regret	3	10.0
Feelings of shame about intercourse in general		
Yes	17	56.7
No	13	43.3
Feelings of shame vs. pain		
Yes; expected	12	40.0
Yes; experienced	9	30.0
Yes; did not expect	5	16.7
Yes; did not experience	8	26.7
No; did not expect	9	30.0
No; did not experience	5	16.7
No; expected	4	13.3
No; experienced	8	26.7

TABLE 4

NUMBER AND PERCENT OF RESONDENTS REPORTING SPECIFIC EXPERIENCES RE: CLIMAX
(N=30)

Related Conditions	No.	Percent Total Group
Sources of first orgasm in initial intercourse or after		
Prior to initial	18	60.0
Premarital coitus	5	16.7
Marital coitus	3	10.0
Extramarital coitus	1	3.3
Premarital petting	3	10.0
Pretense (simulated orgasm)		
At some time	17	56.7
Never	12	40.0
Pretense of not having orgasm	1	3.3
Necessity of orgasm for experiencing pleasure		
Yes	15	50.0
No	15	50.0
Evaluation of marital vs. pre- or extra-marital intercourse		
Marital better	18	60.0
Extramarital better	7	23.3
Premarital better	5	16.7
Fantasy to orgasm (no masturbation)		
Never	29	96.7
At times	1	3.3
Perceived perversions		
None perceived	20	66.7
Some perceived	10	33.3
Types of perceived perversions		
Sado-masochism	5	
Homosexuality	4	
Anal intercourse	2	
Bestiality	2	
Child-parent incest	1	
Masturbation	1	
Coitus without orgasm	1	
Masturbation history		
Began in childhood	13	43.4
To orgasm	7	23.3
Began in adolescence, premaritally	7	23.3
To orgasm	5	16.7
Began as adult or after marriage	9	30.0
To orgasm	9	30.0
Never began	1	3.3
Never to orgasm	1	3.3

BIBLIOGRAPHY

Books

Anthony, Rey. *The Housewife's Handbook of Selective Promiscuity: A Psychosexual Document.* Tucson: Seymour Press, 1960.

Baber, Ray E. *Marriage and the Family.* New York: McGraw-Hill Book Co., 1953.

Baruch, Dorothy W. *New Ways in Sex Education.* New York: McGraw-Hill Book Co., 1959

Benedek, Therese. *Studies in Psychosomatic Medicine: Psychosexual Functions in Women.* New York: Ronald Press, 1952.

Bergler, Edmund, and W. S. Kroger. *Kinsey's Myth of Female Sexuality.* New York: Grune & Stratton, 1954.

Berne, Eric. *Sex in Human Loving.* New York: Simon & Schuster, 1970.

Bettelheim, Bruno. *Symbolic Wounds.* New York: Crowell Collier & Macmillan, 1962.

Bonaparte, Marie. *Female Sexuality.* New York: International Universities Press, 1953.

Calderone, Mary Steichen. *Release from Sexual Tensions.* New York: Random House, 1960.

Chesser, Eustace. *The Sexual, Marital and Family Relationships of the English Woman.* New York: Roy Publishers, 1957.

――――. *Women.* London: Jarrolds Publishers, 1958.

Clark, LeMon. *The Enjoyment of Love in Marriage.* New York: Bobbs-Merrill Co., 1949.

――――. *150 Sex Questions and Answers.* New York: Health Publications, 1960.

Dalton, Katharina. *The Menstrual Cycle.* New York: Pantheon Books, 1969.

Davis, Katherine B. *Factors in the Sex Life of Twenty-Two Hundred Women.* New York: Harper & Bros., 1929.

Davis, Maxine. *The Sexual Responsibility of Women.* New York: Dial Press, 1956.

Dearborn, Lester. "Masturbation." In *Sexual Behavior and Personality Characteristics,* edited by Manfred F. DeMartino, New York: Citadel Press, 1963.

de Beauvoir, Simone. *The Second Sex.* New York: Alfred A. Knopf, 1952.

DeMartino, Manfred F. *Sexual Behavior and Personality Characteristics.* New York: Citadel Press, 1963.

Dengrove, Edward. *The X Report.* New York: Belmont Books, 1962.

Deutsch, Helene. *The Psychology of Women.* Vols. 1 and 2. New York: Grune & Stratton, 1944–45.

Dickinson, R. L. and Laura Beam. *A Thousand Marriages.* Baltimore: Williams & Wilkins Co., 1932.

Duvall, Evelyn Mills. *Love and the Facts of Life.* New York: Associated Press, 1963.

Eisenstein, V. W., ed. *Neurotic Interaction in Marriage.* New York: Basic Books, 1956.

Ellis, Albert. *The American Sexual Tragedy.* New York: Lyle Stuart, 1954.

————. *Sex Without Guilt.* New York: Lyle Stuart, 1958.

————. *The Folklore of Sex.* New York: Grove Press, 1951 and 1961.

————. "Is the Vaginal Orgasm a Myth?" In *Sexual Behavior and Personality Characteristics,* edited by Manfred F. DeMartino. New York: Citadel Press, 1963.

————, and Albert Arbarbanel, *The Encyclopedia of Sexual Behavior.* Vols. 1 and 2. New York: Hawthorne Books, 1961.

Ellis, Havelock. *Studies in the Psychology of Sex.* Vols 1 and 2. New York: Random House, 1939.

Faberow, Norman, ed. *Taboo Topics.* Englewood Cliffs, N.J.: Prentice Hall, 1963.

Ford, Clellan S., and Frank A. Beach, *Patterns of Sexual Behavior.* New York: Harper & Bros., 1951.

————. "Self-Stimulation." In *Sexual Behavior and Personality Characteristics,* edited by Manfred F. DeMartino. New York: Citadel Press, 1963.

The French Institute of Public Opinion. *Patterns of Sex and Love: A Study of the French Woman and Her Morals.* New York: Crown Publishers, 1961.

Freud, Sigmund. *New Introductory Lectures on Psychoanalysis.* New York: W. W. Norton & Co., 1933.

————. *Three Essays on the Theory of Sexuality.* London: Imago Publishing Co., 1949.

————. *Collected Papers.* Vol. 5. Edited by James Strachey. New York: Basic Books, 1959.

Friedan, Betty. *The Feminine Mystique.* New York: W. W. Norton & Co., 1963.

Friedman, Leonard J. *Virgin Wives: A Study of Unconsummated Marriages.* Springfield, Ill.: Charles C. Thomas, 1962.

Guttmacher, Alan F., M.D. *The Complete Book of Birth Control.* New York: Ballantine Books, 1961.

Hamilton, G. V. *A Research in Marriage.* New York: Albert and Charles Boni, 1929.

Hardenbergh, W. E. "Sex, Society and the Individual." In *The Psychology of Feminine Sex Experience,* edited by A. P. Pillay and Albert Ellis. Bombay: International Journal of Sexology, 1953.

Harding, Esther. *The Way of All Women.* New York: Longmans, Green & Co., 1933.

Hastings, D. W. *Impotence and Frigidity.* Boston: Little, Brown & Co., 1963.

Hegeler, Inge and Sten Hegeler. *An Adult View of Love and Sex.* Los Angeles: Holloway House Publishing Co., 1963.

Himelhoch, Jerome and Sylvia Fava, eds. *Sexual Behavior in American Society.* New York: W. W. Norton & Co., 1955.

Hirsch, A. M. *The Love Elite.* New York: Julian Press, 1963.

Horney, Karen, *The Collected Works of Karen Horney.* Vol. 1. New York: W. W. Norton & Co., 1937–45.

Jahoda, Marie, Norton Deutsch, and Stuart W. Cook. *Research Methods in Social Relations.* Part 1. New York: Dryden Press, 1951.

Jersild, Arthur T., and Eva Allina Lazar, with Adele M. Brodkin. *The Meaning of Psychotherapy in the Teacher's Life and Work.* New York: Bureau of Publications, Teachers College, Columbia University, 1962.

Jersild, Arthur T. *Psychology of Adolescence.* New York: Macmillan Co., 1957.

Kaufman, Joseph J., and Griffith Borgenson. *Man and Sex.* New York: Simon & Schuster, 1961.

Kelly, G. Lombard. *Sexual Feeling in Married Men and Women.* New York: Pocket Books, 1961.

Kinsey, A. C., *et al., Sexual Behavior in the Human Female.* Philadelphia: W. B. Saunders Publishing Co., 1953.

————. *Sexual Behavior in the Human Male* Philadelphia: W. B. Saunders Publishing Co., 1948.

Klein, Melanie. *The Pschoanalysis of Children.* London: Hogarth Press, 1954.

Klein, Viola. *Feminine Character.* London: Kegan Paul, Tron, Trubner & Co., 1946.

Koedt, Ann. "The Myth of the Vaginal Orgasm." In *Voices from Women's Liberation,* edited by Leslie B. Tanner. New York: Signet Books, 1970.

Komarovsky, Mirra. *Women in the Modern World.* Boston: Little, Brown & Co., 1953.

Krich, A. M., ed. *The Anatomy of Love.* New York: Dell Publishing Co., 1960.

_____, and Margaret Mead, eds. *Women: The Variety and Meaning of Their Sexual Experiences.* New York: Dell Publishing Co., 1953.

Landis, C., *et al. Sex in Development.* London: Paul B. Hoeber, 1940.

Lastrucci, C. L., "The Dynamics of Sexual Motivation." In *Sex, Society and the Individual,* edited by A. P. Pillay and Albert Ellis. Bombay: International Journal of Sexology, 1953.

Lundberg, F., and Marynia F. Farnham. *Modern Woman: The Lost Sex.* New York: Harper & Bros., 1947.

Masters, W.M., and Virginia Johnson. *Human Sexual Response.* Boston: Little, Brown & Co., 1966.

_____. "Orgasm, Anatomy of the Female." In *The Encyclopedia of Sexual Behavior,* vol. 1, edited by Albert Ellis and Albert Arbarbanel. New York: Hawthorn Books, 1961.

McCarthy, Mary. *On the Contrary.* New York: Noonday Press, 1951.

Mead, Margaret. *Male and Female.* New York: William Morrow & Co., 1949.

Pillay, A. I. and Albert Ellis, eds. *Sex, Society and the Individual.* Bombay: International Journal of Sexology, 1953.

Pomeroy, Wardell. "Human Sexual Behavior." In *Taboo Topics,* edited by Normal Farbarow. Englewood Cliffs, N. J.: Prentice-Hall, 1963.

Rainer, Jerome, and Julia Rainer. *Sexual Pleasure in Marriage.* New York: Julian Hessner, 1959.

Reich, Wilhelm. *The Function of the Orgasm.* New York: Orgone Institute Press, 1942.

Reik, Theodore. *Psychology of Sex Relations.* New York: Rinehardt & Co., 1945.

Reisman, David. *Individualism Reconsidered.* Glencoe, Ill.: Free Press, 1954.

Robinson, Marie N., M. D. *The Power of Sexual Surrender.* New York: Doubleday & Co., 1959.

Robinson, Victor, M. D., ed. *Encyclopaedia Sexualis.* New York: Dingwall-Rock, 1936.

Scheinfeld, Amram, *Women and Men.* New York: Harcourt, Brace & Co., 1943.

Seward, Georgene H. *Sex and the Social Order.* New York: McGraw-Hill Book Co., 1946.

Stekel, Wilhelm. *Frigidity in Women.* Vols. 1 and 2. New York: Boni and Liveright, 1926.
Street, Robert. *Modern Sex Techniques.* New York: Archer House, 1959.
_____ and Louis Berg, M. D. *Sex: Methods and Manners.* New York: McBride Co., 1953.
Taylor, G. Rattray. *Sex in History.* New York: Ballantine Books, 1954.
Thompson, Clara. *Psychoanalysis: Evolution and Development.* New York: Heritage House, 1950.
Van De Velde, T. H. *Ideal Marriage.* New York: Random House, 1930.
Webster's New World Dictionary of the American Language. College ed. Springfield, Mass.: G. & C. Merriam Co., 1960.
The X Report from Sexology Magazine. New York: Belmont Books, 1962.

Periodicals

Abel, Theodora. "Cultural Backgrounds of Female Puberty." *American Journal of Psychotherapy,* vol. 4, no. 1 (1950), 90–113.
Brierly, Margaret. "Some Problems of Integration in Women." *International Journal of Psychoanalysis,* vol. 8 (1932), 433–48.
Duffy, J. "Masturbation and Clitoridectomy." *Journal of the American Medical Association,* vol. 19 (1963), 246–48.
Ehrmann, W. "Some Knowns and Unknowns in Research into Human Sex Behavior." *Marriage and Family Living,* vol. 19, no. 1 (1957), 16–24.
Elkan, E. "Evolution of Female Orgastic Ability: A Biological Survey." *International Journal of Sexology,* vol. 2. (1948), 1–13, 84–93.
_____. "Orgasm Inability in Women," *International Journal of Sexology,* vol. 4 (November, 1951), 243.
El Senoussi, Ahmed, Andrea L. Conroy, and Richard D. Coleman. "Factors in Marital Discord." *Journal of Psychology,* vol. 44 (1957), 193–222.
Glassberg, B. Y. "Educators Fear Sexuality—Not Sex." *Marriage and Family Living,* vol. 21, no. 3 (1959), 233–34.
Harper, Robert A., and Frances R. Harper. "Are Educators Afraid of Sex?" *Marriage and Family Living,* vol. 19, no. 3 (1957), 240–44.
Heiman, N. "Sexual Response in Women." *Journal of the American Psychoanalytic Association,* vol. 9 (April, 1963), 360–85.
Kestenberg, Judith S. "Vicissitudes of Female Sexuality." *Journal of the American Psychoanalytic Association,* vol. 4, no. 3 (1956), 453–76.
Marmor, Judson. "Some Considerations Concerning Orgasm in the Female." *Psychosomatic Medicine,* vol. 16 (1954), 240–45.
Masters, W. H., and Virginia Johnson. "The Sexual Response Cycle of the

Human Female. I. Gross Anatomic Considerations." *Western Journal of Surgery, Obstetrics and Gynecology,* vol. 68 (January–February, 1960), 57–72.

———. "The Sexual Response Cycle of the Human Female. III. The Clitoris: Anatomic and Clinical Considerations." *Western Journal of Surgery, Obstetrics and Gynecology,* vol. 70 (1962), 248–57.

Mudd, Emily H., N. Stein, and N. E. Mitchell. "Paired Reports of Sexual Behavior of Husbands and Wives in Conflicted Marriages." *Comprehensive Psychiatry,* vol. 2, no. 3 (June, 1961), 149–56.

O'Hare, Hilda. "Letter to the Editor." *International Journal of Sexology,* vol. 4 (May, 1950), 117–18.

———. "Letter to the Editor." *International Journal of Sexology,* vol. 4 (November, 1951), 243–44.

Rado, Sandor. "Sexual Anesthesia in the Female." *Quarterly Review of Surgery, Obstetrics and Gynecology,* vol. 16 (1959), 249–53.

Terman, L. M. "Correlates of Orgasm Adequacy in a Group of 556 Wives." *Journal of Psychology,* vol. 32 (1951), 115–72.

Thompson, Clara. "Cultural Pressures in the Psychology of Women." *Psychiatry,* vol. 5, no. 3 (August, 1942), 331–39.

———. "Penis Envy in Women." *Psychiatry,* vol. 6, no. 2 (May, 1943), 123–25.

Wallin, Paul. "A Study of Orgasm as a Condition of Women's Enjoyment of Intercourse." *Journal of Social Psychology,* vol. 51 (February, 1960), 191–98.

———, and Alexander Clark. "Marital Satisfaction and Husbands' and Wives' Perception of Similarity of their Preferred Frequency of Coitus." *Journal of Abnormal Social Psychology,* vol. 57, no. 3 (1958), 370–73.

Woodside, Moya. "Orgasm Capacity Among 200 English Working Class Wives." *International Journal of Sexology,* vol. 1 (February, 1948), 103–109.

Wright, Helena. "A Contribution to the Orgasm Problem in Women." *International Journal of Sexology,* vol. 3 (August, 1949), 97–102.

Pamphlets

Mead, Margaret. "Cultural Contexts of Puberty and Adolescence." Freud Memorial Lecture presented to the Philadelphia Association of Psychoanalysis, May 1, 1959.

———. "Cultural Determinants of Sexual Behavior." Monograph reprint from *Sex and Internal Secretions,* 3d ed., edited by William C. Young. Baltimore: Williams & Wilkins Co., 1961.

Newspaper

Whitehorn, Katherine. Column in *London Observer,* August 16, 1963.

Unpublished Material

Brown, Daniel. "Survey of Literature on Female Orgasm." Paper presented at the Conference of the American Association of Marriage Counselors, Chicago, Ill., February 7–8, 1964.

Greenwald, Harold. "A Study of Deviant Sexual Occupational Choice in a Group of 20 New York Women." Unpublished Ph.D. dissertation, Teachers College, Columbia University, New York, 1956.

Vahanian, Tilla. "How Women Feel about Being Women." Unpublished Ph.D. dissertation, Teachers College, Columbia University, New York, 1954.